THE ROUGH GUIDE TO
The Royals

ROUGH
GUIDES

www.roughguides.com

Credits

The Rough Guide to the Royals

Editing and typesetting: Matt Milton
Additional contributions and picture research: Rough Guides
Family trees: Katie Lloyd-Jones
Production: Rebecca Short

Rough Guides Reference

Editors: Kate Berens, Tom Cabot, Tracy Hopkins, Matthew Milton, Joe Staines
Director: Andrew Lockett

Publishing Information

Published April 2012 by
Rough Guides Ltd, 80 Strand, London WC2R 0RL
Email: mail@roughguides.com

Penguin Group (USA), 375 Hudson Street, NY 10014, USA
Penguin Group (India), 11, Community Centre, Panchsheel Park, New Delhi 110017, India
Penguin Group (Australia), 250 Camberwell Road, Camberwell, Victoria 3124, Australia
Penguin Group (New Zealand), 67 Apollo Drive, Rosedale, Auckland 0632, New Zealand

Rough Guides is represented in Canada by Tourmaline Editions Inc.,
662 King Street West, Suite 304, Toronto, Ontario, M5V 1M7

Printed in Singapore by Toppan Security Printing Pte. Ltd.

280 pages; includes index

A catalogue record for this book is available from the British Library

ISBN: 978-1-40539-004-0

1 3 5 7 9 8 6 4 2

THE ROUGH GUIDE TO

The Royals

by

Alice Hunt, James McConnachie, Samantha Cook

Rob Humphreys and Rupert Matthews

ROUGH
GUIDES

www.roughguides.com

Contents

Introduction

Britain's national anthem, "God Save the Queen", has as its penultimate line the words "Long to reign over us" – something that the current monarch, Queen Elizabeth II, has certainly managed to achieve. The year of her diamond jubilee, marking the sixtieth anniversary of her accession, seems an appropriate occasion to cast an amused and quizzical eye over British royal families of the present, past and future.

One hundred years ago almost every country in Europe was a monarchy. Now there are only twelve, with Britain having the most visible and heavily scrutinized royal family of them all. The famously acerbic Prince Philip, the Queen's consort, is credited with dubbing the British royals "the firm", suggesting the idea of a family business – with its connotations of duty, obligation and inescapability. So we begin *The Rough Guide to the Royals* with a run-through of the current royal family, listing the key members and finding out precisely what they are called on to do.

Elizabeth II has a familial connection to all 55 of her predecessors (listed on the inside back cover). But just how British is the family that for many represents the purest embodiment of patriotic values? In Chapter 2 the foreign ancestry of the House of Windsor is looked at in detail. In case this sounds too serious, Chapter 3 presents a highly selective round-up of British kings and queens through the ages, concentrating on the most memorable monarchs – whether for good or bad. All the old favourites are here, from the indomitable Elizabeth I to the dissolute George IV, whose scandalous behaviour, as the early nineteenth-century Prince Regent, brought the monarchy's status to its lowest ebbs.

It survived, of course, although since the eighteenth century the monarch's political power has been largely symbolic. Yet, despite an absence of any real power, an aura still surrounds the royals which gives them a degree of influence that is, arguably, disproportionate to any expertise they may have. Chapter 4 explains one of the reasons why: scrutinizing the ceremonies, heritage and pageantry that mark out royalty as something special.

Chapter 5 investigates the royal controversies, misdemeanours and human foibles that have endeared, enraged and entertained the monarch's subjects throughout history. In modern times, these have become the stuff of soap opera and an endless source of fascination for millions worldwide – one reason, perhaps, why British royalty has survived into the celebrity obsessed twenty-first century.

Of course, all of this is seen as irrelevant by republicans, who argue that achieving high office by virtue of the family you were born into is irreconcilable with the notion of a modern democracy, and that an unelected head of state preserves moribund notions of privilege and deference. The arguments both for and against the monarchy are rehearsed in detail in Chapter 6. It also shines a light on some of the more murky aspects of the institution, such as how much the monarch is paid for the "job" and what the sources are of the Queen's very considerable income and wealth.

Royal supporters would argue that, notwithstanding its privileges, the monarchy has been getting closer to the people over the sixty years of Elizabeth II's reign. It has modernized and remade itself, abandoning the more stuffy conventions and rituals. In the wake of the huge interest in Prince William and his wife, it remains to be seen whether the couple can continue to project a more contemporary image, finding a balance between distance and familiarity. Accordingly, Chapter 7 examines representations of the royals both official (such as portraits and statues) and unofficial (films, TV programmes and satire), which have shaped the way we see this historic family and institution.

Finally, the book concludes with 101 of the more extraordinary royal facts of the last thousand years. Here you'll find out all about Queen Victoria's stalker, Princess Diana dancing at the Royal Opera House, and some of the Queen's more unexpected hobbies.

"Above all things our royalty is to be reverenced," wrote Walter Bagehot in *The English Constitution* (1867), "and if you begin to poke about it you cannot reverence it ... Its mystery is its life." *The Rough Guide to the Royals* does its fair share of poking about, but finds there's still enough mystery in "the firm" to ensure its continued existence for a good while yet.

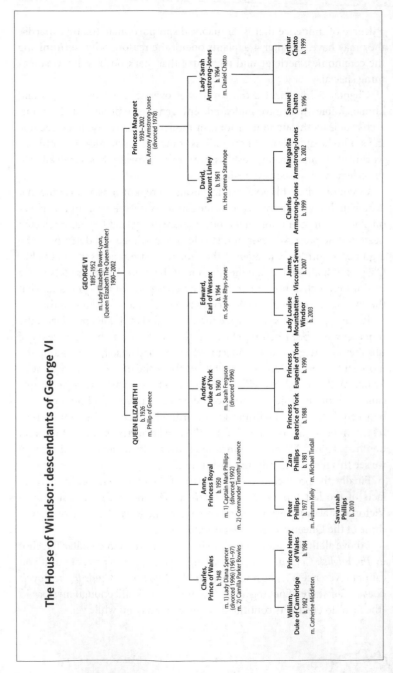

The House of Windsor: descendants of George VI

GEORGE VI
1895–1952
m. Lady Elizabeth Bowes-Lyon,
(Queen Elizabeth The Queen Mother)
1900–2002

QUEEN ELIZABETH II
b. 1926
m. Philip of Greece

Princess Margaret
1930–2002
m. Antony Armstrong-Jones
(divorced 1978)

**Charles,
Prince of Wales**
b. 1948
m. 1) Lady Diana Spencer
(divorced 1996) (1961–97)
m. 2) Camilla Parker Bowles

**Anne,
Princess Royal**
b. 1950
m. 1) Captain Mark Phillips
(divorced 1992)
m. 2) Commander Timothy Laurence

**Andrew,
Duke of York**
b. 1960
m. Sarah Ferguson
(divorced 1996)

**Edward,
Earl of Wessex**
b. 1964
m. Sophie Rhys-Jones

**David,
Viscount Linley**
b. 1961
m. Hon Serena Stanhope

**Lady Sarah
Armstrong-Jones**
b. 1964
m. Daniel Chatto

**William,
Duke of Cambridge**
b. 1982
m. Catherine Middleton

**Prince Henry
of Wales**
b. 1984

**Peter
Phillips**
b. 1977
m. Autumn Kelly

**Zara
Phillips**
b. 1981
m. Michael Tindall

**Princess
Beatrice of York**
b. 1988

**Princess
Eugenie of York**
b. 1990

**Lady Louise
Mountbatten-
Windsor**
b. 2003

**James,
Viscount Severn**
b. 2007

**Charles
Armstrong-Jones**
b. 1999

**Margarita
Armstrong-Jones**
b. 2002

**Samuel
Chatto**
b. 1996

**Arthur
Chatto**
b. 1999

**Savannah
Phillips**
b. 2010

1

House of Windsor

King George V became the first monarch of the House of Windsor in 1917, when the family changed its name in the wake of hostility to all things German (see p.65); the present queen is the fourth. Those living members of her immediate family, their descendants and (in some cases) their spouses are what constitute the current royal family. Precisely who qualifies for this questionable privilege and who doesn't is outlined below, as are their duties and privileges as well as those things they'd rather we didn't know about.

Who's in and who's out

What makes a royal? The obvious answer is whoever is on the throne, plus his or her closest relations. But how close is close and at what point are you too distant to matter? Which family members get the ringside seats at state functions, appear on the Buckingham Palace balcony, or, indeed, get paid for the "job"? As usual with matters royal, the rules and regulations that govern such things are an odd mixture of convention and legislation. As a broad definition, the royal family constitutes the monarch and his or her children and grandchildren and their spouses. However, letters patent (a kind of royal command) of 1917 stipulated that only the monarch's children, and those grandchildren descended through the male line – in other words, the children of the monarch's sons – were to be given princely status and styled His or Her Royal Highness (HRH). These are the key members of the royal family (what Prince Philip refers to as "the firm"), the ones who are expected to carry out royal duties and who receive payment for doing so (see p.203). Of the Queen's generation, these are herself and Prince Philip, and her four first cousins: the Duke of Gloucester, the Duke of Kent, his brother Prince Michael and their sister Princess Alexandra.

The situation has changed significantly in more recent times. So that while the Queen's four children all have princely status, only Prince Charles and Prince Andrew's children do so. In a break with tradition, Prince Edward's son and daughter are not styled prince or princess (but do have other titles), while Princess Anne's two children, Peter Phillips and Zara Tindall, have no titles at all (in accordance with their parents' wish that they lead relatively normal lives). Of the Queen's eight grandchildren, only the princes William and Harry carry out any major official duties. Her nephew and niece, David and Sarah Armstrong-Jones, offspring of her late sister, Princess Margaret (see p.187), have no royal duties. While David has the title Viscount Linley, and will eventually inherit the Earldom of Snowdon, his sister is simply known as Lady Sarah Chatto.

In a sense, a distinction exists between the Queen's family (her close relations) and the royal family (those close relations called on to represent her). This is reflected in the Queen's own website (www.royal.gov. uk), which has just seventeen names under a list headed "The current royal family". These are as follows: the Duke of Edinburgh, the Prince of

THE MONARCHY – WHEN DOES IT START?

King Offa (between 757 and 796), ruler of Mercia (an area roughly equivalent to the Midlands), was the first ruler to call himself "King of the English", although his official title was *Rex Anglorum*, which could be translated as "King of the Angles", a much narrower title. The current royal family don't bother with Offa; instead the official royal website proudly claims that the Queen is 38th in direct line of descent from Egbert (769–839), the Anglo-Saxon King of Wessex. Egbert gets the nod as the first King of England because for a few years he had the upper hand over his main rivals in Mercia and Northumbria, and was referred to in *The Anglo-Saxon Chronicle* as a *bretwalda* or ruler of Britain. Egbert himself only ever used the title "King of the West Saxons", but his grandson, Alfred the Great (848–899), styled himself *Anglorum Saxonum rex* (King of the Anglo-Saxons). However, it was Alfred's grandson, Æthelstan (893–939), who became the first king of a unified England and bore the title *rex totius Britanniae* (King of All Britain), conquering Cornwall, and forcing Constantine II of Scotland to submit to him.

Wales, the Duchess of Cornwall, the Duke and Duchess of Cambridge, Prince Harry, the Duke of York, the Earl and Countess of Wessex, the Princess Royal, the Duke and Duchess of Gloucester, the Duke and Duchess of Kent, Princess Alexandra, Prince and Princess Michael of Kent. Presumably, should anyone else – such as Beatrice and Eugenie, daughters of Prince Andrew – join the ranks of "working royals", then they too would be added to the list.

What they do

It is often reported that certain royals are "hard-working" but even the most ardent monarchists would be hard-pressed to say exactly what they all do all of the time. High-profile ceremonial occasions, such as the State Opening of parliament, Trooping the Colour, and state weddings and funerals, are relatively rare events, as are the highly publicized royal tours such as the Queen and Prince Philip's ten-day visit to Australia in 2011. Many of these activities are, of course, a form of public relations. Tours, for example, are a way of keeping in touch with those other countries where the Queen is still head of state; especially significant in the case of Australia where the debate about republicanism is even more heated than it is in the UK.

As head of state, the Queen carries out many of the same duties that a president would, such as hosting official visits and entertaining leaders of other countries. In 2006, her eightieth year, she undertook 380 engagements in Britain as well as visits to Australia, Singapore and the Baltic states. But as a constitutional monarch within a parliamentary democracy, she has no political power. And although all legislation is signed and often scrutinized by the monarch, it is made and passed by an elected parliament. She is also head of the armed services and "Defender of the Faith and Supreme Governor of the Church of England" but, again, these are largely symbolic roles.

In the eyes of the palace, the Queen is also "Head of Nation", providing, in the words of her website, "a focus for national identity, unity and pride; giving a sense of stability and continuity; recognising success, achievement and excellence; and supporting service to others, particularly through public service and the voluntary sector." Quite how meaningful or valuable this role is for the nation's wellbeing depends on your point of view (see Chapter 6).

As for the other senior royals, most have been content to act as her proxies at those less glamorous events that, apparently, need a royal presence: the opening of a school or a hospital, a visit to an army regiment or a factory. But they also regularly travel abroad in the capacity of unofficial ambassadors, supporting diplomatic efforts and flying the flag for British trade. While the Queen was in Australia in October 2011, Princess Anne and Prince Andrew were undertaking less publicized trips to West Africa and the Far East respectively. Then there is the charity work. As part of the so-called "welfare monarchy", all the royals are involved, to a greater or much lesser extent, in charity work. Several, including Prince Charles and Princess Anne, have set up their own charities supporting causes they care particularly strongly about.

For anyone wishing to know in greater detail what members of the royal family are officially up to, the place to go is the Court Circular, a publication introduced by George III in 1803 to counter false reporting by the press. The circular provides a record of all the events attended by the senior royals on the previous day, and is printed in three newspapers, *The Times*, *The Daily Telegraph* and *The Scotsman*. An archive of previous circulars is available on the royal website.

The succession

On the death of the monarch, his or her successor automatically becomes king or queen (the coronation is simply the religious endorsement of the fact). Eligibility for the position is strict, and the monarch can only be succeeded by a blood relative; spouses do not qualify even when (as with Prince Philip) they are closely related. But the most obvious longstanding "rule" of royal succession in Britain has always been male primogeniture, whereby the deceased monarch is succeeded by his (or her) eldest son. If the monarch has no sons – as in the case of King George VI – then the eldest child inherits the throne. Sons have always taken precedence irrespective of birth date, so that even though Princess Anne is the Queen's second child, her two younger brothers, Prince Andrew and Prince Edward, are ahead of her in the line of succession.

Not only that, but their children take precedence (whether girls or boys, see box opposite), which means that the princesses Beatrice and Eugenie (Prince Andrew's only children) currently stand at five and six in line to the throne, whereas Princess Anne is at number ten. It could be argued that the list is largely hypothetical, and that the likelihood of, say, the top seven candidates all being wiped out in one fell swoop is pretty remote. Nevertheless, if avian flu or a terrorist plot did pull it off, it would result in the necessarily

THE LINE OF SUCCESSION – THE TOP TWENTY

The list below indicates the line as it was in December 2011. It changes at fairly regular intervals as the younger royals procreate, with Savannah Phillips, the latest arrival, entering the list at No.12 following her birth in December 2010. However, in October 2011, the government proposed legislation that would end the tradition of male primogeniture. This means that should the Duke and Duchess of Cambridge produce a baby girl as their firstborn child, she would retain her position in the succession irrespective of whether their next child was a boy or not. This will apply only to the grand-children of the current Prince of Wales and their descendants, and would not be applied retrospectively to anyone else.

Queen Elizabeth II (current Sovereign)

1. The Prince of Wales (eldest son of the Queen)
2. The Duke of Cambridge (eldest son of no.1)
3. Prince Henry of Wales (second son of no.1)
4. The Duke of York (second son of the Queen)
5. Princess Beatrice of York (eldest child of no.4)
6. Princess Eugenie of York (second child of no.4)
7. The Earl of Wessex (third son of the Queen)
8. Viscount Severn (son of no.7)
9. The Lady Louise Mountbatten-Windsor (second child of no.7)
10. The Princess Royal (second child and only daughter of the Queen)
11. Mr Peter Phillips (son of no.10)
12. Miss Savannah Phillips (eldest child of no.11)
13. Miss Zara Phillips (second child of no.10)
14. Viscount Linley (son of Princess Margaret, the Queen's sister)
15. The Hon. Charles Armstrong-Jones (son of no.14)
16. The Hon. Margarita Armstrong-Jones (second child of no.14)
17. The Lady Sarah Chatto (daughter of Princess Margaret, the Queen's sister)
18. Master Samuel Chatto (eldest son of no.17)
19. Master Arthur Chatto (second son of no.17)
20. The Duke of Gloucester (second son of Henry, Duke of Gloucester, the Queen's uncle)

inexperienced Viscount Severn (he's only four years old) succeeding to the throne, in preference to his highly experienced aunt, Princess Anne.

The succession also discriminates on grounds of religion. The Bill of Rights (1689) and the Act of Settlement (1701) excluded Roman Catholics from the throne and forbade the monarch from marrying a Catholic. The Queen's first cousin Prince Michael of Kent was automatically excluded when he married a Catholic, but his son Lord Frederick Windsor kept his place in the succession because he was baptized into the Church of England. The monarch is also obliged by law to maintain the Protestant religion; this appears to discriminate against other faiths though only Roman Catholicism is mentioned by name.

Over the years, many have attacked the discriminatory nature of both male primogeniture and Catholic exclusion, and in October 2011, at the Commonwealth Heads of Government Meeting in Australia, Prime Minister David Cameron announced that the laws of succession were, at last, being changed and updated with the agreement of all fifteen Commonwealth realms where the Queen is head of state. First, the monarch would be allowed to marry a Catholic. Second, the firstborn child of the Duke and Duchess of Cambridge would become heir whether that child was a boy or a girl. "The idea a younger son should become monarch instead of an elder daughter simply because he's a man," Cameron declared, "is at odds with the modern countries we have become".

What Cameron chose not to stress was the fact that the monarch himself (or herself) was still forbidden to be a Catholic, on penalty of forfeiting the throne (see p.153). He also left it to others to point out that it was rather at odds with modernity, and indeed equality, that the child of one particular family should inherit the top job, regardless of merit. The campaigning group Republic duly stepped in. "The monarchy discriminates against every man, woman and child who isn't born into the Windsor family," a spokesman said. "To suggest that this has anything to do with equality is utterly absurd."

The prime minister also failed to mention illegitimacy, another archaic anomaly, which continues to exclude a child of a member of the royal family from the succession. William IV was survived by eight of his ten illegitimate children by his long-standing mistress Dorothea Jordan (see p.158), all of whom were given titles or married into the aristocracy but were barred from the succession. His two legitimate daughters by his wife Princess Adelaide of Saxe-Meiningen both died when a few months old, leaving the way clear for the king's niece Victoria to succeed to the throne. More recently, the first two children of the current Earl of Harewood were both born "out of wedlock", which meant that they were barred from the royal succession, despite later being legitimized and given the title "Honourable". The earl's two subsequent children were both born in wedlock and stand at 45 and 46 in the line of succession.

The succession is not affected if the monarch is divorced or marries a divorced person. In 1936 Edward VIII (see p.160) abdicated on the

BORN TO BE KING?

Is Elizabeth II Britain's rightful monarch? Constitutionally the answer is yes, because she is a direct Protestant descendant of Sophia, Electress of Hanover, as stipulated by the Act of Settlement (1701) – legislation that excluded Catholics from the succession (see p.5). Some believe that there are others who have a more rightful claim to the throne. Among several candidates, there are two whose credentials stand out – but don't hold your breath for a change of dynasty any day soon, since neither is remotely interested in pressing their claim.

Franz Herzog von Bayern, Duke of Bavaria (b. 1933)

Though the last Stuart King, James II, was deposed, he was succeeded by his daughters, Mary II and Queen Anne. Both were Protestants but neither had children who survived so the throne passed to the German Hanoverian dynasty. But James II also had a son, James Edward Stuart, by his second marriage. Brought up a Catholic, he had a strong claim to the throne which he tried and failed to win by force of arms in 1715 (see p.170). When his line ended in 1807, the Stuart claim passed down through James II's sister Henrietta, the wife of the Duke of Orléans. The current inheritor of the claim is Henrietta's descendant, Franz, Duke of Bavaria, an unmarried economics graduate who survived a childhood partly spent in Dachau (his family were anti-Nazi) and now lives in Munich's Nymphenberg Palace. Were the ban on a Catholic monarch ever to be lifted and applied retrospectively, this would make him, arguably, the rightful claimant to the British throne.

Michael Abney-Hastings, 14th Earl of Loudoun (b.1942)

Historian Dr Michael Jones has recently found strong evidence to suggest that King Edward IV (1442–83) was illegitimate, and that the Plantagenet dynasty should have continued through his brother, George, Duke of Clarence. The succeeding Tudor dynasty was so concerned about the Clarence offspring that they executed both his son, Edward Plantagenet, Earl of Warwick, and his daughter, Margaret Pole, Countess of Salisbury (who the Catholic Church consider a martyr). Margaret's direct descendants culminate in Michael Abney-Hastings, who emigrated from England to Australia in 1960 where he worked for Rice Research Australia as a forklift operator. Known to his friends as Mike Hastings, he is a committed republican. About his own aristocratic roots, he has said: "I never used the titles when I got over here [Australia], they'd have eaten me alive, it was bad enough being a Pom."

advice of the prime minister, Stanley Baldwin, but only because it was felt that public opinion was, for the most part, opposed to him marrying the American divorcee Wallis Simpson. However, seventeen years later, when Princess Margaret, the Queen's sister, wished to marry the divorced Group Captain Townsend (see p.186), the Church of England refused to recognize such a potential union unless the princess relinquished her place in the succession – she was third in line at the time. Similarly, parliament refused to sanction the marriage, and the princess duly gave up the man she loved, quoting the Church's teachings (which oppose divorce) and her "duty to the Commonwealth".

Prior to Prince Charles's second marriage to the divorced Camilla Parker Bowles, the argument centred on whether it was even legal for a member of the royal family to be married in a civil ceremony. The then Lord Chancellor, Lord Falconer, decided that it was, citing the 1949 Marriage Act and the 2000 Human Rights Act. Charles and Camilla were duly married at Windsor Guildhall followed by a blessing in St George's Chapel, Windsor Castle. The Queen and the Duke of Edinburgh attended the latter ceremony but not the former.

Precedence

This refers to the hierarchy of rank for the royal family and other state officials – in other words, their order of seniority. It is employed at functions at which members of the royal family, the nobility, senior clergy and members of the Orders of Chivalry are present, determining the order in which individuals arrive and depart, and how they are seated at royal banquets and similar occasions. There are two official tables of precedence – one for men and one for women – with the sovereign at the head of both.

To some extent precedence reflects the order of succession but the two are not identical. Thus the traditional ordering for men begins with the sovereign's sons (in order of birth), followed by the sovereign's grandsons, brothers, uncles, nephews and male first cousins. The table of precedence for women is a little more complicated. The Queen dowager (the widow of a deceased king) traditionally heads the list, followed by the wife of the sovereign's eldest son, the wives of the sovereign's younger sons, the sovereign's daughters, wives of the sovereign's grandsons, the sovereign's granddaughters, wives of the sovereign's brothers, the sovereign's sisters, wives of the sovereign's uncles, the sovereign's aunts, wives of the sovereign's nephews, the sovereign's nieces, wives of the sovereign's cousins and the sovereign's female first cousins. Presumably, the planned reform of the rule of male primogeniture will mean that in future seniority will be established simply by order of birth and with no reference to gender.

Should we be sitting here? Four royals at Prince William's wedding in 2011.

Precedence is based on a combination of law and convention, which means that the order can be changed at the request of the monarch, and often is. Thus, the Duke of Edinburgh is currently the most senior royal after the Queen, having been assigned his position by a warrant of 1952.

Prince Charles comes next, followed by his two brothers, Prince Andrew and Prince Edward, and then by the sovereign's grandsons: the Duke of Cambridge, Prince Harry, Viscount Severn and Peter Phillips. Next come the Queen's three first cousins: the Dukes of Gloucester, Duke of Kent and Prince Michael of Kent.

The current table of precedence for women also departs from tradition by making the Queen's daughter, Princess Anne (the Princess Royal) the most senior female, followed by the Queen's granddaughters – the princesses Beatrice and Eugenie, Lady Louisa Windsor and Zara Phillips – and then the Queen's cousin, Princess Alexandra. Only at this point does the heir apparent's wife, Camilla, Duchess of Cornwall, appear, followed by the Duchess of Cambridge (Prince William's wife) and the Countess of Wessex (Prince Edward's wife). This has been interpreted by some as a slight to Camilla, since court etiquette – still taken very seriously – requires women to curtsey to all those above them at official and unofficial functions. At private family events precedence is observed or not at the Queen's discretion.

When it comes to non-royals, the top four state officials (all technically appointed by the sovereign) are – in order of precedence – the Archbishop of Canterbury, the Lord High Chancellor, the Archbishop of York and the Prime Minister.

Team Royal

Queen Elizabeth (1926–)

The eldest of two siblings, "Lilibet", as she was known as a child, was never expected to become Queen, being third in line after her uncle David (who became Edward VIII) and her father Bertie (later George VI). Yet she acceded to the throne at the age of 26, and has reigned for so long that, for at least three generations of her subjects, it is hard to picture anybody else wearing the crown.

Elizabeth and her younger sister Margaret were educated at home under the supervision of their mother, Queen Elizabeth, and their governess, Marion "Crawfie" Crawford. She received private tuition in constitutional history and learned French from a succession of native-speaking governesses. Her childhood coincided with World War II, and her family spent most of it at Windsor Castle. She was a thoughtful, serious child, and Winston Churchill once commented that she had an "air of authority and reflectiveness astonishing in an infant." Aged fourteen, she made her first ever radio broadcast, addressing her peers on the BBC's *Children's Hour* during the war and reassuring them that "in the end all will be well". Just before her nineteenth birthday, she was permitted to join the Auxiliary Territorial Service, and received six weeks of training at Aldershot that made her an expert driver, map reader and mechanic, teaching her how to strip an engine and repair it. Photographs of the princess in overalls changing tyres became part of wartime propaganda; on VE Day, wearing her ATS uniform, she slipped out of the palace with Margaret and several officers to join in the singing in the streets.

She first met Philip, her future husband, when she was just thirteen, on a tour of the naval college where he was training. He apparently "showed off a good deal", but "the little girls were much impressed" – despite the fact that he teased "plump little Margaret" rather a lot. Philip joined the royal family for tea on their yacht the next day, and Elizabeth was impressed by his appetite – he apparently wolfed down several platefuls of shrimps and a banana split. They corresponded during the war and met again a few years later. According to Crawfie, Elizabeth began to take more care of her appearance, and took to playing the tune "People Will Say We're in Love" from *Oklahoma*.

Elizabeth and Philip on a royal tour of Nigeria in February 1956.

While her parents eventually grew to like Philip, her mother is said to have referred to him in private as "The Hun", and of his surviving German relatives only his mother was invited to his wedding in 1947. The new queen's grandmother, Queen Mary, put her foot down over the surname of her daughter's offspring and enlisted Winston Churchill's help: she was determined that the House of Windsor was not going to morph into Mountbatten – the surname Philip had adopted from his maternal grand-parents. Elizabeth would later offer a sop to her husband once Queen Mary had died, changing the protocol so that male-line descendants would henceforth take the surname Mountbatten-Windsor.

While George VI had always had health problems, his death in 1952 was unexpected and occurred when Elizabeth and Philip were on an official visit to Kenya. His ill health had meant she had already carried out royal visits and appointments and, when she succeeded to the throne, she took her role extremely seriously. Her coronation was watched by millions around the world: the BBC set up their biggest ever outside broadcast to provide live coverage of the event on radio and TV – the first time this had happened. Elizabeth was depicted as a rather glamorous figure by the media, and the start of her reign was greeted as a "new Elizabethan age", an antidote to post-war austerity and rationing.

THE QUEEN MOTHER (1900–2002)

One famous anecdote concerning the Queen Mum tells how, having been inexplicably kept waiting for her evening cocktail, she once phoned down to her Clarence House footmen with the following quip: "I don't know what you two old queens are doing down there, but this old queen is dying of thirst." True or not, it's certainly in keeping with the bluff, non-PC sense of humour that old-school royalty is famous for. She was reportedly bitterly opposed to the idea of royalty paying tax, and kept a large staff (three chauffeurs, five chefs, two pages, three footmen, two dressers and thirty assorted secretaries, maids, treasurers and housekeepers). She bred racehorses as a hobby and ran up a £4m overdraft at Coutts. She enjoyed a triple gin before eating and a glass of champagne with her meal. However, if anything, it is these very old-fashioned excesses that helped make her so popular with the British public.

Born Elizabeth Bowes-Lyon into a wealthy Scottish family, she was seen as a bit of a catch among the Society set. Albert (the future King George VI) had to propose three times before she said yes. (The first time, the painfully shy duke used a go-between.) "I felt it my duty to marry Bertie," she admitted, "and fell in love with him afterwards." After Bertie unexpectedly became King, Elizabeth became the first queen consort to be authorized to sign royal papers as a deputy to the monarch, and her throne at Westminster Abbey was placed level with his. She blamed Edward VIII's abdication for her chain-smoking husband's premature death in 1952, and is thought to have ostracized Edward and his wife, the Duchess of Windsor, after he stepped down. The closest she came to a reconciliation was to send a representative to visit her sister-in-law in Paris every six months when her health began to seriously fail.

While Elizabeth and her husband had supported appeasement of Hitler, it was her pitching in with the war effort that was the public making of her. She put Buckingham Palace on the same rations as the rest of the country, toured air-raid shelters and visited bombed-out industrial cities. Her "national treasure" status was cemented, and she ended up making many more royal trips after her husband's death than when she was queen. This was partly due to the dawn of the jet age, allowing the QM to be "Mambo Kazi" (Big Mother) to Rhodesian chiefs in 1957, a rainmaker to the Masai in Kenya in 1959 and, very briefly, a hula dancer in Honolulu in 1966. In her long life she went from presiding over Edwardian pomp to learning how to do Ali G impressions from her great-grandsons after Christmas dinner in the noughties. Quite a trip.

The initial euphoria did not last long. The age of deference was already beginning to wane and during her long reign the press has gone from being discreet and respectful in their dealings with her family to voracious and ruthless in their search for a scoop. But even in the 1950s criticism was

"DICKIE" – THE POWER BEHIND THE THRONE?

Boundlessly ambitious, a consummate schemer and a brilliant self-publicist, Lord Louis Mountbatten (1900–79) succeeded in inveigling his way to the heart of the royal family, over whom he exerted a powerful influence for many years. Known as "Dickie" to his family, he was the youngest child of a minor German prince, Louis Battenberg, who moved to Britain and married a granddaughter of Queen Victoria. The family were relatively poor, a setback that Mountbatten overcame by marrying an aristocratic heiress, Edwina Ashley, in 1922. Theirs was very much an "open" marriage, and several writers and historians have suggested that both were bisexual and indulged in several affairs throughout their lives.

Like his father, Lord Mountbatten had a distinguished naval career, attaining the position of First Sea Lord – the highest in the navy. However, his service in World War II remains controversial. It reached its apogee in his appointment by Churchill as chief of Combined Operations, co-ordinating the three services, and then as supreme commander in South East Asia. While his energy has never been questioned, his judgement has – notably in the case of the Dieppe Raid, an attack on the French coast by 5000 Canadian troops, two thirds of whom were killed. Historians are equally divided on his success, or otherwise, at overseeing the 1947 independence and partition of India as the country's last viceroy.

Mountbatten's ambition within the royal family was dynastic, and his constant activities as a matchmaker – his private secretary called him the "royal procurer" –

gathering that she and the palace were out of touch with the modern world. One of the most damning critiques – because from an insider – was voiced by Lord Altrincham in a 1957 article in which he lambasted the court as a "tight little enclave … of the 'tweedy' sort" under whose guidance the queen came across as a "priggish schoolgirl". This did indeed reflect a conflict within the palace between modernizers and traditionalists. The Queen herself, essentially conservative, leaned more towards the latter. Some maintain that her aloof, rather detached manner (exemplified by her strangulated vowels and stilted delivery) is the secret of her success: that by avoiding controversy she has remained the immovable and reliable figurehead of a family that has played out several soap-operas' worth of scandal and loss.

One of the Queen's regular tasks is to read through, and if necessary sign, the government documents which are delivered to her each day in "red boxes". She also has a weekly audience with the prime minister, whenever she is in residence in London, at which they discuss the state of the nation. Given her limited constitutional powers, such attention to detail is not strictly necessary, but it certainly reflects her overwhelming sense of duty as head of state. This devotion to the job inevitably lim-

had their greatest success when his nephew Prince Philip (who had adopted his surname) became engaged to the heir to the throne. Some have even suggested that Mountbatten's plan was for Philip to be King Consort; certainly he was keen that Elizabeth should take her husband's name and become the first ruler in the House of Mountbatten. He was no less attentive to her son and heir, Charles, acting as his honorary grandfather and mentor figure.

This was despite being instrumental with Prince Philip in sending the sensitive Charles to a school, Gordonstoun, which he hated. Later Mountbatten encouraged Charles to "have as many affairs as he can before settling down" and facilitated this by making his own home, Broadlands in Hampshire, available for various princely trysts. Mountbatten's game plan was that Charles would eventually marry his young granddaughter, Amanda Knatchbull, a scheme she kiboshed by turning the prince down.

Intrigue and self-promotion continued into his old age. There was his connection to individuals considering a coup to topple the Labour government in 1968, discussed at the time he was working on a 12-part TV series, *The Life and Times of Lord Louis Mountbatten*, in which he rewrote history to his own advantage. His end was as dramatic as his life: in the summer of 1979, while on holiday in Ireland, he was one of a party out fishing at sea when his boat exploded, killing him, his grandson and a local boy. A bomb had been secreted on board by the IRA. Prince Charles, in particular, was utterly devastated; many politicians rather less so.

ited her role as a parent. Even taking into account the hands-off style of parenting that was still the norm among the upper classes in the 1950s, the Queen was remarkably uninvolved in the everyday life of her young children – Charles and Anne in particular – who were largely taken care of by nannies. The five-year-old Charles was especially upset when, shortly after the coronation, his parents disappeared for a six-month tour of Commonwealth countries. But even when her children were adults, it has not always been easy to gain access to their mother, and communication between them has remained a challenge.

The Queen's sang-froid has stood her in good stead on at least two occasions. During the 1981 Trooping the Colour ceremony, shortly before Charles and Diana's wedding, six shots were fired at the Queen from close range as she rode down the Mall on horseback. Although the shots were blanks, the seventeen-year-old assailant, Marcus Sarjeant, was sentenced to five years in prison and released after three. The following year, the Queen awoke in her bedroom at Buckingham Palace to find an intruder, a troubled young man named Michael Fagan, in the room with her. She kept calm, made two calls to the palace police switchboard, and spoke to Fagan while he sat at the foot of her bed until assistance arrived seven minutes later. The incident revealed not just the lax security, but also that she and Prince Philip slept in separate rooms.

However impressive her composure and her businesslike stewardship of the House of Windsor, her style seemed increasingly at odds with the modern world during the 1980s and 90s – not least in her and Philip's advice to Charles over his failing marriage to Diana: pressurizing them to patch up their differences, just as Philip had initially pressurized Charles to propose.

Described by the Queen as her "annus horribilis" (horrible year), 1992 was meant to be a celebration of the fortieth anniversary of her accession; instead it was the year when everything went wrong. That March, Prince Andrew and his wife Sarah separated; in April, her daughter Anne divorced Captain Mark Phillips. During a state visit to Germany in October, angry demonstrators in Dresden threw eggs at her, and in November Windsor Castle suffered severe fire damage. In a major misjudgement of public opinion, the palace expected that the nation would foot the repair bill. In an unusually personal speech, Elizabeth said that any institution must expect criticism but suggested it might be done with "a touch of humour, gentleness and understanding". Two days later, Prime Minister John Major announced reforms of the royal finances, including the Queen paying income tax for the first time and a reduction in the civil list. Finally, in December, Charles and Diana formally separated, while the year ended with a lawsuit as the Queen successfully sued *The Sun* newspaper for breach of copyright when it published the text of her annual Christmas message two days before its broadcast.

Five years later, the standing of the royal family was given a further battering following the palace's response to the death of Princess Diana. In another misreading (or ignorance) of the nation's mood, the adherence to protocol in refusing to fly the Buckingham Palace flag at half mast and the seeming reluctance of the Queen to make a public statement of commiseration was seen as cold and unfeeling.

That the Queen's standing in the eyes of the public has recovered so much since then is a tribute to either her integrity or the skill of her spin doctors – or a measure of how quickly people forget. Certainly the media are now less interested in Elizabeth's kids than her grandchildren, and the younger royals are in turn a lot more media-savvy than their parents. The wedding of Prince William to Kate Middleton proved a great PR success and the perfect curtain-raiser to the Queen's diamond jubilee in 2012.

Prince Philip (1921–)

Public opinion seems to veer between considering the Duke of Edinburgh a national embarassment and a national treasure. The role Prince Philip has made for himself within the current royal family isn't entirely clear. He is famously brusque and impatient – two qualities that are hardly surprising when you consider his upbringing. His childhood was traumatic and itinerant: his family were banished from Greece in 1922, following the Greco-Turkish war, and he had little contact with either of his parents, being brought up by a combination of grandparents, distant uncles and boarding schools. He was educated at the "progressive" school of Gordonstoun, in Scotland, where punishing runs before breakfast, cold showers and Spartan discipline were part of the curriculum.

Prince Philip of Greece and Denmark was born at Villa Mon Repos on the Greek island of Corfu on 10 June 1921, the only son and fifth child of Prince Andrew of Greece and Denmark and Princess Alice of Battenberg. After school, Prince Philip joined the Royal Navy, graduating from the Royal Naval College, Dartmouth, as the top cadet in his course. It was there that he first met the young princess Elizabeth, when King George VI and Queen Elizabeth took a tour of the institution. During the visit, the Queen and Earl Mountbatten asked Philip to escort the King's two daughters.

The meeting may well have been partly engineered by Dickie (Louis) Mountbatten, Philip's avuncular mentor. Philip was eighteen years old at the time, while Elizabeth was only thirteen. She was by all accounts quite taken with him. At the time Philip was, in the words of his cousin Princess Alexandra of Greece, like "a huge, hungry dog; perhaps a friendly collie who never had a basket of his own and responded to every overture with eager tail-wagging". According to Marion "Crawfie" Crawford, the princesses' governess, Elizabeth "never took her eyes off him the whole time".

There were a few other women in his life – he had a few innocent teenage liaisons with an American actress named Cobina Wright and a Canadian debutante called Osla Benning, but neither were serious relationships. Philip and the princess exchanged letters throughout the war, and he spent several of his rare leaves at Windsor. He was commissioned as a midshipman in January 1940 and over the course of World War II was promoted to first lieutenant – one of the youngest in the Royal Navy. During the invasion of Sicily, in July 1943, as second-in-command of HMS *Wallace*, he saved his ship from a night bomber attack, devising a plan to launch a raft with smoke floats that successfully distracted the bombers and allowed the ship to slip away unnoticed.

Over Christmas 1943, the 22-year-old Philip attended the annual royal pantomime, *Aladdin*, in which the two princesses had starring roles. Elizabeth was reportedly highly excited at the prospect of Philip's attendance and Crawfie recalled that many noticed a "sparkle about her". Rumours began about a possible marriage. Initially the King and Queen were unhappy, considering Philip too boorish and uneducated. His reputation was not enhanced by his membership of an all-male drinking club, the Thursday Club, which met weekly in a Soho restaurant and whose members included the royal photographer Baron, Philip's old naval chum Mike Parker, his cousin the Marquess of Milford Haven and the actor James Robertson Justice. The prince's louche showbiz connections during this period inevitably fuelled rumours of affairs both before and after his marriage.

Nevertheless, the King and Queen gradually warmed to him; George VI told his mother that Philip "thinks about things in the right way". In the summer of 1946, the King granted Philip's request for his daughter's hand in marriage, providing any formal engagement was delayed until her twenty-first birthday the following April. At the prompting of Dickie Mountbatten, who saw it as an impediment to the marriage, Philip became a naturalized British subject, renouncing his Greek and Danish royal titles, as well as his allegiance to the Greek Crown, and converted from Greek Orthodoxy to Anglicanism. He took the surname Mountbatten as his own. After an official engagement of five months, Lieutenant Philip Mountbatten married Elizabeth on 20 November 1947.

A more-than-able seaman, Philip might well have been anticipating an exciting career in the navy before Elizabeth acceded to the throne. However, the unexpected death of George VI, just five years into his marriage, put paid to that. The Duke was no longer allowed to do the things he was best at and needed a new occupation. His attendance at a House of Commons debate was a one-off, as a result of the indignant objections of Cabinet members. His feelings of impotence were exacerbated by the stipulation of Winston Churchill and Queen Mary that the royal line must retain the Windsor surname. His much-quoted response was, "I'm nothing but a bloody amoeba" (although he has denied ever saying it).

Once installed at the palace, he embarked on modernizing the running of the palace, attempting to loosen some of the more rigid and antediluvian protocols. In this he was helped by Mike Parker, now installed at the palace as the prince's private secretary. Unfortunately both men had

THE GAFFER

A self-proclaimed "cantankerous old sod", Prince Philip has been known to put his foot in it. It's hard to know how much of this is crassness on his part, and how much is a knowing playing-to-the-gallery. National and racial stereotypes seem to be his stock-in-trade. In 1986, in a private conversation with British students in China, Philip joked, "if you stay here much longer, you'll go slit-eyed". In 1995 he asked a Scottish driving instructor, "how do you keep the natives off the booze long enough to pass the test?". He observed, of a Briton he met in Hungary in 1993: "You can't have been here that long – you haven't got a pot belly." In one interview in the late 1960s, he admitted "I would like to go to Russia very much – although the bastards murdered half my family." The duke is also clearly not over-awed by celebrity. He once enquired of Tom Jones: "what do you gargle with – pebbles?" Neither does his own family escape his candour: "if it doesn't fart or eat hay, she isn't interested," he once said of his daughter, Princess Anne.

However, when, in 1999, newspapers reported that Philip had commented to children from the British Deaf Association (who happened to be standing near a loud pop group), "no wonder you're deaf, listening to this row!" he denied it. In a letter to Gyles Brandreth, he suggested that "the story is largely invention" pointing out that his own mother "was quite seriously deaf".

enemies among the old guard, and when the prince set off, with Parker in tow, for a four-month trip to Australia aboard the royal yacht *Britannia*, rumours began to circulate about Philip's estrangement from the Queen. These were fuelled by Parker's wife accusing her husband of adultery, which in turn led to his summary dismissal. Undeterred, the prince continued to make regular solo tours during the 1950s. As consort to the Queen (though never officially Prince Consort), Philip also supported his wife in her royal duties, accompanying her to ceremonies such as the state opening of parliament in various countries, state dinners and tours abroad. He has, as he promised at her coronation, been her "liege man of life and limb".

It's hard to say whether Philip has been quite so supportive of his children. He can clearly be overbearing and it's evident that he made a few poor judgement calls with regard to his eldest son's upbringing – not least in his insistence that Charles be sent to Gordonstoun School, whose routine he was clearly unsuited to. When Prince Edward quit his gruelling Marine training in 1987, Philip (Captain General of the Royal Marines since 1953) did not hide his irritation with his youngest son. Relations appear to be more amicable with his more robust and extrovert middle children.

As well as his official duties, Prince Philip has been active with several charities. In 1956 he and Sir John Hunt (the leader of the 1953 Everest expedition) started the Duke of Edinburgh's Award. The organization aims to develop the potential of young people with a programme that includes volunteering, physical activity, the development of social skills and taking part in some kind of expedition. He has also been extremely active with the World Wildlife Fund (WWF), a leading environmental organization dedicated to the conservation of the natural world. Prince Philip was president of the WWF from 1981 to 1986, although his support for the preservation of endangered species has never prevented him from being an enthusiastic advocate of blood sports.

Not all that he seems? The Duke of Edinburgh visits a Sikh temple in West London in 2004.

Until the age of fifty, the prince was a regular polo player, but since then he has turned his attention to the marginally more sedate sport of carriage driving, often in competition, an activity that has involved him in a number of accidents. His least-known hobby is art: he paints in oils, and collects artworks, including contemporary cartoons, which hang at royal residences. The architect Hugh Casson once described Philip's oil paintings as "exactly what you'd expect ... totally direct, no hanging about. Strong colours, vigorous brushstrokes."

Prince Charles (1948–)

When his mother became Queen on 6 February 1952, Prince Charles automatically became the heir to the throne. He was just over three years old. Sixty years later he's still waiting to take over the top job, an even longer wait than that of his great-great-grandfather, Edward VII. In that time his popularity has fluctuated alarmingly, reaching an all-time low when details of the failure of his marriage to Princess Diana became widely known. Never fully at ease in the public eye (he has described himself as "not very good at being a performing monkey"), his ability to be king has been questioned frequently. A 2010 ICM poll suggested that 64 percent of the British population felt that the succession should pass him by in favour of Prince William.

Much of this popular rejection stems from the fact that the prince is perceived as an eccentric: a campaigner for a variety of causes – organic farming, complementary medicine, traditional architecture – that fail to chime with the wider public. His supporters, on the other hand, see the fact that he's prepared to stick his head above the parapet and extol the ideals that he passionately believes in as a virtue. The problem for the prince has always been what to do with his life until he became king. His education (which included the Spartan regime of Gordonstoun School and an undistinguished stint at Cambridge University) was followed, in predictable royal fashion, by military service divided between the RAF and the Royal Navy. When that ended in 1976 it was briefly suggested that Charles become Governor-General of Australia. He was enthusiastic about the idea, but it came to nothing. Meanwhile, he was rapidly establishing a reputation as a playboy, indulging his passion for polo, skiing and fox hunting, and no less enthusiastically pursuing a succession of good-looking, upper-crust young women.

It wasn't all hedonism, state visits and being waited on hand and foot, however. Shortly after leaving the navy, Prince Charles used his £7400 severance pay to set up a new charity, The Prince's Trust, which aimed to help disadvantaged young people make a fresh start. The late 1970s was a time of great social unrest in Britain, and Charles's intervention was seen by some as an implicit critique of government shortcomings and therefore far too political for a senior royal to be involved in. He carried on regardless and today the Trust is the country's leading youth charity, providing financial support and training for thousands of young people and organizations. It is, arguably, his most enduring legacy. But for the great British public and a voracious tabloid press, the prince's love life has always proved a far more fascinating subject.

Of Charles's many girlfriends before his marriage, the one who made the greatest impact on him was Camilla Shand, whom he met in 1970 (see p.24). More than a year his senior and considerably more sexually experienced, Camilla was – we now know – the love of Charles's life. But marriage seems not to have been an option and, in 1973, she became Mrs Parker Bowles. Charles continued "sowing his wild oats" (encouraged by

Keeping smiling. Charles and Di tripping the light fantastic on their Australian tour of 1988. Both were already involved in extra-marital affairs.

his great-uncle, Lord Louis Mountbatten), embarking on a series of relationships including one with Lady Sarah Spencer, daughter of a former Royal Equerry, the 8th Earl Spencer. But it was Sarah's younger sister Diana (see box opposite), some twelve years Charles's junior, who finally got the prize – if prize it was. Some would describe their marriage as the biggest disaster of both their lives. Despite the successful production of "an heir and a spare", there seemed almost nothing the Prince and Princess of Wales had in common, and the marriage began to flounder almost before it began. It wasn't helped by Charles's continued closeness to Camilla, and a mere three years after the glittering royal wedding in St Paul's Cathedral in 1981, shortly after the birth of Prince Harry, the two resumed their affair.

LADY DIANA SPENCER (1961–1997)

She may have only married into royalty, but Diana Spencer achieved an iconic status and near-mythic celebrity that none of the current British royal family are likely to match. Daughter of John and Frances Spencer, Diana gained the courtesy title "Lady" when her father inherited the honorific "Earl" in 1975. She grew up in London after her parents separated, and was educated at boarding school, attending Institut Alpin Videmanette, a Swiss finishing school, when she was sixteen. There she first met Prince Charles, who was at the time seeing her older sister Sarah. Diana wasn't exactly a bright student, having twice failed all her O-levels: she once famously described herself as "thick as a plank" and incapable of using a parking meter. On her return to London, she worked briefly as a dance instructor, then a playgroup teacher and nanny. Charles first started to show an interest in Diana in the summer of 1980, when he was 32 and she was 20. The pair were both guests at a country weekend, where Diana described the prince as being "all over [her] like a rash", and they began seeing each other in London afterwards. Diana was invited to Balmoral, where she met "the firm". Charles popped the question in February 1981.

Their marriage was a famously unhappy one, despite the birth of their two sons. According to Andrew Morton's biography *Diana: Her True Story*, Diana attempted suicide no fewer than five times while married to Charles. She threw herself into charity work, becoming particularly associated with HIV/AIDS and leprosy charities. While Charles resumed liaisons with Camilla Parker Bowles, Diana began an affair with Captain James Hewitt, her former riding instructor, in the mid-1980s: Morton's book, with the princess's sanction, made both affairs public in 1992. The Prince and Princess of Wales separated soon afterwards but did not divorce until 1995: the Queen wrote to the pair advising them to officially end their marriage following a television interview Diana conducted with Martin Bashir, in which she spoke frankly about both Hewitt and Parker Bowles, and commented that she wasn't sure kingship would suit Charles's temperament.

"It is better to be poor and happy than rich and miserable," Diana once observed. "But how about a compromise – like moderately rich and just moody?" That might well have summed up her post-Windsor existence. She had a serious but brief relationship with Hasnat Khan, a leading heart surgeon, and began dating Dodi Fayed, son of the Egyptian business tycoon Mohammed Al Fayed, soon afterwards. In 1997, she became the figurehead for the International Campaign to Ban Landmines, and visited post-civil-war Bosnia in August. On 31 August she and Fayed were killed in a car crash in Paris. Her chauffeur, Henri Paul (the head of security at the Ritz Hotel where the couple had stayed), lost control of their car in the Pont D'Alma tunnel while attempting to elude the paparazzi. Blood tests revealed he had been drinking, and that his drunkenness may have been compounded by anti-depressants. Over a million mourners lined the streets on the day of Diana's funeral (see p.149).

The Prince and Princess's London home was Kensington Palace but Charles was finding more and more excuses to spend time at Highgrove, the Gloucestershire estate he had purchased in 1980, which just happened to be a few miles from the Parker Bowles's home. As his marriage disintegrated, with Charles almost always coming off worse in the media war waged by his wife, he became increasingly bold about speaking out on issues close to his heart. At the British Medical Association's 150th anniversary dinner in 1982 his speech was a thinly veiled critique of conventional medicine, advocating a more "natural" approach to healing. Two years later he weighed in to modern architecture, trashing the winning entry for an extension to the National Gallery, memorably describing it as "a monstrous carbuncle on the face of a much-loved and elegant friend." These interventions infuriated his critics who saw them as undemocratic and an abuse of his privileged position. He has persisted to this day, however, and the recently published diaries of Tony Blair's spin doctor Alastair Campbell suggest that Charles tried directly to influence government policy on such issues as GM foods, fox-hunting and hereditary peers.

With the death of Princess Diana in 1997, and the public hysteria that followed, the standing of the royal family – and Prince Charles in particular – reached its nadir. Their subsequent gradual rehabilitation has survived such rumours that Charles has a flunky to squeeze his toothpaste for him (he doesn't) and that he "happily" talks to plants and trees. His reputation recovered sufficiently enough for him to marry Camilla – something of a public hate figure after Diana's death – in 2005, with her assuming the title of HRH the Duchess of Cornwall. As to whether he will ever become King Charles III, there is no reason why he shouldn't – short of predeceasing his mother. His succession is enshrined in law and, however popular Prince William is, it would take an act of parliament for William to leapfrog his father.

Camilla, Duchess of Cornwall (1947–)

She may have been born a commoner, but Camilla's background is extremely posh. Her father, Bruce Shand, was a British Army major who twice won the Military Cross and later worked for an upmarket wine merchant, and her mother was the Honourable Rosalind Cubitt, daughter of Roland Cubitt, 3rd Baron Ashcombe. Brought up as something of a tomboy among the hunting, shooting and fishing set of East Sussex, Camilla was educated locally and then at the exclusive Queen's Gate School in

London, followed by finishing school in Switzerland. As a teenager she was fascinated by the fact that her great-grandmother, Alice Keppel, was the favourite and most devoted of King Edward VIII's mistresses, and she would regale her school friends with family stories of her royal connection. Legend has it that on first meeting Prince Charles, at a polo match in 1970, Camilla propositioned him with the line "My great-grandmother was your great-great-grandfather's mistress – so how about it?" It was an offer that Charles was unable to resist, and they embarked on a passionate and remarkably public affair.

Never conventionally good-looking, Camilla was a highly confident good-time girl who, at the time she met Charles, was five years into a relationship with dashing Household Cavalry officer and notorious ladies man Andrew Parker Bowles. Some have suggested that her play for Charles was revenge for her boyfriend's infidelities (his many amours included Princess Anne). Certainly the naïve and relatively innocent prince was rather more smitten than she was. But they had a lot in common: as well as the obvious country pursuits – hunting in particular – she shared Charles's enthusiasm for the anarchic comedy radio series *The Goon Show*, to the extent that their nicknames for each other, Gladys and Fred, derived from the show. Several romantic trysts took place at the stately Hampshire house Broadlands, with the connivance of its owner and Charles's great-uncle Lord Mountbatten ("Uncle Dickie"), who saw Camilla as ideal mistress material until his granddaughter, Lady Amanda Knatchbull, became old enough to marry the prince. Did Charles propose to Camilla in 1973? If so, she turned him down, and a few weeks after he left for naval duty, Camilla and Andrew Parker Bowles finally got engaged. Charles was apparently devastated but the friendship continued, and he even agreed to be godfather to the Parker Bowles's first child, Tom.

Camilla now assumed the role of the prince's confidante-in-chief, and was a particular comfort and support when Charles's much-loved Uncle Dickie was blown up by the IRA in 1979. She was also one of a handful of people (the Queen Mother was another) who encouraged Charles to think of the teenage Lady Diana Spencer as a potential royal bride – despite Charles's own misgivings about their difference in age. But even in the early stages of their courtship, Diana was disturbed at the almost ubiquitous presence of Camilla at royal social events and the attention Charles paid to her. She had good reason to be fearful, since Charles never abandoned his close relationship with Camilla, sending his mistress presents and even, according to Stephen Barry (the prince's valet), sleeping with her on the eve of his wedding. It's little wonder that

Diana developed a hatred for her rival, whom she referred to as "The Rottweiler". In fact, after the wedding Charles and Camilla put a halt to their sexual relationship in order for the Prince and Princess of Wales to make a go of their marriage. It was a vain hope and after a few years the royal mistress was reinstated.

To all intents and purposes, Andrew Parker Bowles was unconcerned that his wife had resumed the affair. He'd indulged in extra-marital affairs of his own so never thought of himself as the wounded party. But his sang-froid was almost certainly tested by the publication in 1993 of the transcript of the "Camillagate" tape, a recording of a late-night intimate conversation between Charles and Camilla during which the prince expressed his desire to "…feel my way along you, all over you and up and down you and in and out" and went on to compare himself to a Tampax. Though Charles and Diana were already officially separated, the nation, the press and his family were appalled, and he was advised to sever his connection with his mistress or run the risk of never becoming King. He agreed but the separation only lasted a few months. Camilla and her husband were also leading largely independent lives, although Andrew Parker Bowles only decided to divorce his wife after Charles's public confession of adultery in a BBC television documentary aired in June 1994.

Despite the fact that Charles and Camilla were now both divorced, she was still reviled by the tabloids as the most hated woman in Britain. Plans to normalize the relationship in the public eye now began in earnest, master-minded by the prince's new media-savvy private secretary, Mark Bolland. Princess Diana's tragic death was a major setback to Camilla's public acceptance, but gradually she was eased into the limelight and arguments about whether it was right for the heir to the throne to marry a divorcee began to subside. She met Prince William in 1998 but it was another two years before the Queen agreed to meet her at a family function. Charles and Camilla were finally married on 9 April 2005 in a civil ceremony at the Guildhall, Windsor, followed by a service of dedication at St George's Chapel, Windsor Castle. Mrs Parker Bowles was now HRH The Duchess of Cornwall, Duchess of Rothesay and Countess of Chester. She was also entitled to use the title Princess of Wales but preferred not to.

Happily ever after? On the surface it would seem so, with Camilla's easy and relaxed manner going a long way to reconciling all but the most ardent Dianaphiles. But there are rumours that she finds the formality and fastidiousness of Charles's Highgrove existence too stuffy for her taste and will often retreat to her own house, Ray Mill, at Lacock in Wiltshire. Of course, this may simply be an indication of how difficult it is for two independent and – by all accounts – very different people to make the change from secret lovers to a very public married couple. Or could it be that there are yet more dramatic chapters waiting to unfold in the ongoing Charles and Camilla saga?

Prince William (1982–)

Ever since the royal wedding of April 2011, the House of Windsor seems to have had a spring in its step. It's a rare day when the Duke and Duchess of Cambridge are absent from the glossy covers of the magazine racks. The second-in-line to the throne likes football and drives a Ducati motorbike. He was nicknamed "Steve" by his fellow students at university, "Billy the Fish" by his RAF colleagues (a punning reference to his future Prince of Wales status via *Viz* comic's half-human, half-piscine goalkeeper) and simply "Wills" by the tabloids. He may have been privately educated at Britain's top schools, and he may be stupendously wealthy, but when he is photographed nattering with David Beckham, you can actually believe that they have a few things to chat about.

William Arthur Philip Louis made his first public appearance at the age of nine (an occasion that revealed he was left-handed when he signed the visitors' book at Llandaff Cathedral in Cardiff). His mother, Diana, Princess of Wales, was keen that her children should have as "normal" a childhood as possible. So they holidayed at Walt Disney World, and were photographed shopping and eating at McDonalds. Diana dismissed the royally appointed nanny, opting for one of her own choosing, and apparently managed her royal engagements to fit in around her children's lives, rather than the other way round. Once they were older, Diana would often take Harry and William with her while carrying out her charity work, and the brothers visited homeless shelters and HIV/AIDS charities.

Wills went to Eton, alma mater of Diana's brother and father – not Gordonstoun, the school where Prince Charles had had such an unhappy time. A pact was agreed with the tabloids: in return for regular updates on the prince's life, the media promised a lack of paparazzi intrusion into it. "Prince William is not an institution; nor a soap star; nor a football hero," pointed out John Wakeham, chairman of the Press Complaints Commission, helpfully stating the obvious for anyone unaware what a prince is. The circumstances of his mother's death, when Wills was fifteen, put any possibilities of aggressive tabloid attention out of the question. He passed three A-levels and was accepted at St Andrews University in Scotland, to read History of Art.

St Andrews underwent a temporary blip in the number of female applications after the announcement.

Before starting his degree, he took a gap year, which in many ways was the making of him – or, at least, the making of his public image. For ten weeks, as part of the Raleigh International programme, he taught children in the town of Tortel, in Patagonia, southern Chile. There he had to muck in with other young teachers, doing his share of household chores like cleaning the toilet. At one point he was the guest of Radio Tortel, the local radio station, and was given a short DJ's slot. "Hello all you groove jets out there!" Wills huzzahed. "This is Tortel Love and we are in the mood for some real groovin'!" (One wonders if this is what we are to expect from any future King's speeches.) He went on to play an enjoyable selection of tunes, including "High and Dry" by Radiohead, "Heroes" by David Bowie, Duran Duran's "A View to A Kill" and "Good Vibrations" by the Beach Boys. It was raining, and when it stopped he slipped in "Sun is Shining" by Bob Marley (such observational skills are a credit to the officer class), before rounding off his stint on the decks with Babybird's "You're Gorgeous", which he dedicated to "any of you people who are in the mood for lurve". His gap year also saw him gain his first armed forces experience, when he took part in training exercises in Belize.

The happy couple, en route from Westminster Abbey to their wedding reception.

THE ROYAL WEDDING OF 2011

As William is not the heir apparent, his wedding was not a state occasion – there were, therefore, no heads of state invited (other than the British one). Prince William had, however, invited all of his former girlfriends from school and university, while Kate also invited an old flame from St Andrews. Celeb guests included David and Victoria Beckham, Elton John and Guy Ritchie. (The Beckhams were invited on account of David's work with Prince William on England's 2018 World Cup bid.)

In a break with royal tradition, the groom had a best man (Prince Harry) rather than a "supporter", while the bride chose her younger sister, Pippa, as maid of honour (and the tabloids predictably drooled over her). The couple also wrote their own vows and a prayer, which featured this rather New Age imprecation: "In the busy-ness [sic] of each day, keep our eyes fixed on what is real and important in life, and help us to be generous with our time and love and energy."

After the reception, William drove his new missus out of the palace back to Clarence House, his official London residence, in his dad's blue Aston Martin Volante (very James Bond); Harry had pimped his ride with the rear number plate "JU5T WED". The evening meal was rumoured to have put the Buckingham Palace kitchen's nose slightly out of joint, as it was provided by chef Anton Mosimann, rather than being in-house. The royal couple also brought in a DJ, lighting and a sound-system for a late-night disco: they picked the music themselves.

Back in the UK in 2001, he started his degree. In terms of the royal's story, St Andrews is most famous for being where Wills met his future wife Kate Middleton, and where he achieved a 2:1 (after a shaky start in which he swapped History of Art for Geography), making him the most academically qualified of the current royal family. Post-university, he entered the military. He was commissioned as a lieutenant in the Blues and Royals regiment of the Household Cavalry – serving with his brother Prince Harry – and, two years later, earned his wings by completing pilot training at Royal Air Force College Cranwell. The prince transferred to the Royal Air Force, was promoted to flight lieutenant and underwent helicopter flying training in order to become a full-time pilot with the Search and Rescue Force. News of one or two of his adventures were recounted by the press as daredevil exploits: in 2008 he took part in an airborne patrol to catch drugs smugglers in the Caribbean, contributing to the seizure of £40m of cocaine.

He married his long-term girlfriend, Kate Middleton, in April 2011 at Westminster Abbey (see box above for the full story) and since then the pair have settled into the royal routine apparently effortlessly. Wills and his wife are thoroughly modern royals: they seem wholly at ease in front of the cameras and in public. What's more, they seem to be genuinely happy – which isn't something that can always be said about their older relatives.

Catherine, Duchess of Cambridge (1982–)

Much has been made of the fact that the future Queen Consort is a "commoner". Catherine Middleton is the first non-blueblood to wed a prince so close to the throne in more than 350 years, since Anne Hyde married James II in 1660. William and Kate are, in fact, very distantly related: fifteenth cousins via a common descent from Sir Thomas Fairfax and his wife Agnes Gascoigne, daughter of Sir William Gascoigne and Lady Margaret Percy. Kate's parents, Carole and Michael Middleton, are the owners of Party Pieces, a children's party supplies company, and met when they both worked for British Airways: Carole was a flight attendant while Michael was a flight despatcher. Their careers took them to Amman, Jordan, where Kate was born, and spent the first two years of her life, before the family returned home to Berkshire.

Kate attended several private schools, most notably Marlborough College, a mixed boarding school. She was said to have been a serious and quiet student, though she was sporty and enthusiastic in school activities. "I never once saw her drunk," pondered one of her schoolfriends to the *News of the World* newspaper. "Even after our GCSEs finished, she only drank a couple of glugs of vodka." Kate was also rumoured to have been a bit of a fan of Prince William long before they met. She was said to have once joked that "there's no one quite like William" and conjectured that he seemed very kind. That's not to suggest she was determined to bag a prince: after all, some of her Marlborough friends from the Cotswolds county set already knew William, so it's hardly surprising he might have cropped up in conversation once or twice. Prince William once joked that Kate had "about twenty" pictures of him, to which Kate replied: "He wishes. No, I had the Levi's guy on my wall, not a picture of William. Sorry."

She met William at the University of St Andrews in Scotland, where she studied History of Art, and roomed in St Salvator's – the same halls of residence as the prince. The pair were friends for a year or so before they became an item, and Kate is thought to have convinced William to stay at university when he was considering packing it in, following what was by all accounts a lonely first year for him; he then switched courses to Geography. She is thought to have first caught the prince's eye when she modelled a see-through dress at a university fashion show; the prince had a front-row seat. In an interview to mark his 21st birthday, the prince insisted he had no steady girlfriend, saying that he didn't want to rush into marriage until he was at least "28, or maybe 30". The prince dated a few other girls but, while sharing a house in Kate's second year, they discreetly became a couple. By and large, the press kept their distance, and the couple carried on living together during Kate's last two years of university: they shared an old farmhouse on the edge-of-town Strathyrum estate with two friends.

William and Kate have been together – with one small blip – ever since. In April 2007, *The Sun* newspaper broke a "world exclusive" suggesting that Prince William and Catherine had split up. The couple had indeed decided to break up during a holiday in the Swiss resort of Zermatt; the separation didn't last long. On 16 November 2010 it was announced by Clarence House that William and Kate were engaged. The Prince of Wales said he was "thrilled", adding that "they have been practising long enough". The engagement ring was Diana's: "My way of making sure my mother didn't miss out on today," said William on the day. The wedding took place on 29 April 2011 in Westminster Abbey; the day was made a national holiday. Estimates of the global audience range from 300 million to two billion people; the cost of the wedding was reportedly £20 million. The couple asked for charity donations instead of traditional wedding gifts – presumably they already had enough silverware. The honeymoon was in the Seychelles, before the newlyweds went to live on the Isle of Anglesey in Wales, where Wills is based with the RAF. The Duchess of Cambridge seems to have taken to her position like a duck to water, taking meet-and-greets with the Obamas in her stride, with not a hair out of place.

Prince Harry (1984–)

The smallest and frailest-looking of the main mourners at his mother's funeral caused many to wonder what further troubles might lie ahead for the youngest and potentially most fragile member of a shattered family. They needn't have worried. As "the firm" regrouped after Diana's death, Henry Charles Albert David Wales (his preferred surname) matured into a sporty, party-loving military man. Probably the least fusty of the royals, Harry has earned a reputation for being a popular, sometimes hard-drinking bloke, or as he might put it, just "one of the guys". Sharing understandable reservations about his royal destiny with his brother, he has a persona that to many looks admirably unbuttoned. To others

Harry Wales, this time not in fancy dress.

it looks merely boorish: behaviour that's fine on the rugby or polo field but falls short of the discretion needed in an era that demands respect, tolerance and maturity even from royals.

More rugged-looking than his brother (whom he followed to Eton) and distinctly less cerebral than his sometimes angst-ridden father, Harry excelled at rugby, the Eton Wall game and then polo. But he emerged from Eton with distinctly underwhelming academic results, leaving with a D in Geography and a B in Art. Luckily Harry's leadership skills on the field seemed to transfer easily to a military career that has included spells as a tank commander, helicopter pilot and army captain. Things got messier, however, with outraged tabloid reports of him smoking cannabis and binge-drinking, and there were further concerns that the royals had another liability on their hands when fisticuffs with the paparazzi and an ill-advised fancy dress choice as a Nazi officer received maximum publicity. No fan of the press, Harry faced further criticism for the epithets addressed to a couple of his military colleagues that included choice items such as "our little Paki friend" and "rag-head". Tory leader David Cameron joined the chorus of voices pronouncing the former unacceptable even as apologies were made.

In between spells of martial activity, Harry has also caught the headlines for his frequent and confident flirtations with a variety of women (usually blonde) as well as a long-term relationship with Chelsey Davey (daughter of a Zimbabwean millionaire businessman), which some had expected to end in marriage. This was not to be. Following his brother's wedding Harry pronounced himself "100 per cent single" before being linked with motor racing driver Jenson Button's ex-girlfriend, the lingerie and swimwear model Florence Brudenell-Bruce (known as "Flee"). A few weeks later the relationship was "off" and the press can look forward again to several more years of speculation about Britain's "most eligible bachelor". In this context it is not surprising the prince seems to value the army – said to be a cause of the break-up with Chelsey – not only for its camaraderie but also for the opportunity to mingle with other servicemen on an equal basis. It is thought that both brothers enjoy the security of an environment that allows them go about their daily business without the kind of press intrusion that once fuelled speculation that the rusty-haired Captain James Hewitt, a lover of Harry's mother, was in fact his true father, a theory now conclusively disproved.

As for weightier matters, Harry has managed to appeal to both ends of the political spectrum with his military and charitable activities. The prince's determination to serve in Afghanistan in 2007 as a Forward Air controller for Helmand Province was terminated after two months only due to an Australian newspaper leak breaching a coordinated press blackout. (He had to be recalled.) In April 2011 he was awarded the Apache Flying Badge, which would once again make him liable for deployment in Afghanistan, if the UK Chiefs of Staff felt it safe and appropriate. Serving others has taken other forms with his support and founding of Sentable (with Prince Seeiso of Lesotho), a charity assisting HIV/AIDS orphans in Lesotho. He has made several visits to the Mants'ase children's home where he again pursued his personal mission to encourage the playing of rugby and, more poignantly, expressed a desire to perpetuate his mother's humanitarianism.

Only a few years after delivering a dignified tribute to the "best mother in the world", it was the wedding of his brother that fixed a happier image of Diana's younger son in the public's mind and permanently erased that of the tearful twelve-year-old. His was a cheeky, blokey presence in the Abbey, joshing with his brother and teasing his new sister-in-law Pippa Middleton: a picture of informality and irreverence, though still with its uniform on.

Prince Andrew (1960–)

While Charles is known to have played the field in his bachelor days, and young Harry seems to have an eye for a blonde, not for nothing was Queen Elizabeth's second son known as "Randy Andy" in the 1980s. He trod the established path of the male Windsor-Mountbattens – Gordonstoun boarding school, followed by a long career in the armed forces – but distinguished himself by becoming the playboy prince. Models, actresses, yachts, golf and helicopters remain his abiding interests.

Andrew left school with four A-levels, but opted for naval college rather than university, joining the Royal Navy in 1979. He saw active service in the Falklands war as a helicopter pilot on board the aircraft carrier HMS *Invincible*, flying on several anti-submarine and anti-surface warfare missions. By all accounts, he was a very good pilot, and evidently he was happy enough in his job to remain in active service until 2001. Over the course of his career he was promoted to the rank of Commander, decorated for his war record, and ultimately awarded the honorary position of Rear Admiral in 2010.

His first public love affair, with an actress named Koo Stark, ended soon after it was revealed that she had once acted in a soft-porn film. He married Sarah Ferguson in 1986, about a year after they first met. The couple had two daughters – Beatrice (b. 1988) and Eugenie (b. 1990) – and appeared to be happy. However, in 1992 the pair announced plans to separate; the tabloids ran photos of the duchess in rather intimate association with her financial advisor, John Bryan. Their split seemed amicable and the duchess even continued to live at the duke's home, Sunninghill Park, until 2004. It's really only in the years since their breakup that their association has been controversial (see box opposite).

The single life clearly seems to be more to his taste: the prince has been linked to a succession of women, including former *Playboy* model Denise Martell and Ghislaine Maxwell, daughter of the late publishing tycoon Robert. The rock star Courtney Love once claimed Andrew turned up late one night at her house in Hollywood "to look for chicks".

In 2001 Andrew took on a new role as Special Representative for International Trade and Investment, for which he was fulsomely recompensed. "Airmiles Andy" was routinely criticized for his use of private jets and helicopters (rather than ordinary scheduled flights) for his meetings around the world and within Britain. He seemed to enjoy the hospitality of unelected foreign leaders and their families far more frequently than one might expect of a trade ambassador, while his overseas meetings often happily coincided with major sporting events. According to Tatiana Gfoeller, the US ambassador to Kyrgystan, Andrew could be a bumptious presence at meetings, on one occasion railing "at British anti-corruption investigators, who had had the 'idiocy' of almost scuttling the al-Yamama deal with Saudi Arabia".

In July 2011, he stepped down from the role; four months previously he had come under severe criticism for his association with the US billionaire

SARAH FERGUSON, DUCHESS OF YORK (1959–)

While cashing in on a royal connection is practically a British national pastime, Sarah Ferguson has taken it further than most. Mainly to the US, where she can flog her Moissante jewellery, Bath & Body Works scented candles, and heraldic spoons without infringing her agreement not to do business in Britain. However, in May 2010, a *News of the World* reporter filmed Fergie claiming that, if she were paid £500,000, Prince Andrew would agree to a meeting to pass on useful top-level business contacts; she was caught on camera receiving $40,000 in cash as a down payment. Andrew's entourage denied he knew of this situation.

Fergie claims that she is still very close to Andrew – although clearly not so close that she is invited to family weddings anymore. "I really love the feeling that sort of Diana and I both weren't there," was her staggeringly crass observation to Oprah Winfrey concerning her lack of invite to the Wills 'n' Kate bash. Still, it gave her time to finish off her latest book, a "my spiritual journey" type affair titled *Finding Sarah*, stuffed with such pearls as: "Become aware of your mind chatter. Sit at the end of the bed and talk to your imaginary friend." Her way with words has long been one of her strongest assets. When she was still married, she penned a series of children's stories describing the adventures of an anthropomorphized rotorcraft called Budgie. Doubtlessly inspired by Andrew's airborne escapades in Lynx and Sea King choppers, the *Budgie the Little Helicopter* books are among the best illustrated children's books ever written by a British royal – right up there with Prince Charles's *The Old Man of Lochnagar*.

It's too early to say what qualities Beatrice and Eugenie have inherited from mater and pater. They've been to school; they've graduated from university; they've begun taking on royal duties here and there. At their much more important cousin's wedding, they wore a pair of silly, insectoid hats that even Lady Gaga might have thought twice about. And one of them once had her BMW (parked in Kensington) nicked after she left her keys in the ignition.

Jeffrey Epstein, who was convicted for solicitation of prostitution. Andrew had visited the financier at his Florida home several times over the years; newspapers published photographs of him with his arm around the waist of Virginia Roberts, then seventeen, who has made further allegations against Epstein. Matters were made worse when Sarah Ferguson admitted having accepted £15,000 from Epstein to help pay off her debts.

In recent years, Andrew has developed strong links with the energy-rich Kazakhstan and is a regular goose-hunting companion of the country's president. In 2008, Timor Kulibayev, the president's son-in-law, purchased Sunninghill Park from Andrew for £15 million, £3 million more than the asking price (despite the fact it had languished on the market for five years).

Following the downgrading of the prince's position, he clearly felt he needed a holiday. In August 2011, *The Mirror* reported that he had been seen enjoying the company of a young lady in a leopardskin-print bikini on a luxury yacht moored off the island of Calvi, near Corsica. The boat belonged to a Middle–Eastern billionaire. Buckingham Palace declined to comment.

Prince Edward (1964–)

It must be rather depressing to know that no matter what you achieve, and whatever good works you do for charity or industry, you will always be best remembered for *It's a Royal Knockout*. This was a one-off episode of a long-running TV series and featured Edward, Prince Andrew, Sarah Ferguson and Princess Anne, all clad in Elizabethan costume, presiding over a tournament of silly games, attempted by a rogues' gallery of 1980s celebs (Sheena Easton, Toyah Willcox, Rowan Atkinson, Meat Loaf and Paul Daniels, among others). It made an indelible mark on the public consciousness of a generation of Britons: years later, the comedian Sean Lock made the observation that *It's a Malarial Dream* would have been a more appropriate title. After all, the programme featured such surreal spectacles as John Travolta wrestling a man dressed as an onion, and contestants Anneka Rice and Tom Jones (also dressed as vegetables) throwing stage-prop hams at each other.

Edward had produced the programme when he was 23, fairly fresh out of university, and having flunked his Marine training (to his father's utter disgust). It turned out to be both the high and low point of his showbiz career. He had thrown himself into theatre at school and at Cambridge (where he read History, despite having only scraped a C and two Ds at A-level). "I love the razzmatazz of show business," Edward said in 1987. "It's a wonderful world of fantasy and make-believe." Indeed. A cynic might point out that too much of Edward's life had been spent in that world. Undeterred by the critical mauling that *The Grand Knockout Tournament* (to use the official title nobody remembers the programme by) received, Edward landed himself a job with Andrew Lloyd Webber's Really Useful Company. It was there that he met actress Ruthie Henshall, whom he dated for two years. For his mother's sixtieth birthday, he answered the question "what do you give the person who has everything?" by commissioning the 1986 mini-musical *Cricket* from Lloyd Webber and Tim Rice (bits and pieces of which were ultimately regurgitated as *Aspects of Love*).

SOPHIE, COUNTESS OF WESSEX (1964–)

Sophie Helen Rhys-Jones is the only member of the royal family to have appeared topless on page three of *The Sun*. No, she has never been a glamour model: a few months before her wedding to Prince Edward, a photo (taken eleven years earlier) showing radio DJ Chris Tarrant hoiking up Rhys-Jones's bikini top was sold to the newspaper for thousands of pounds by Kara Noble, a fellow DJ. It provoked numerous complaints (and incurred the immediate sacking of Noble from Heart FM): less than two years after Diana's death, the public had little appetite for the tabloid's zoom-lens approach to royal-watching. *The Sun* duly apologized. However, this was not to be the last time Sophie would find herself in the middle of a tabloid controversy.

Sophie is not an aristo: she's the daughter of a tyre salesman and a secretary. She met Edward via her job in PR (during which she had spent four years at Capital Radio, where she first encountered the ungallant Tarrant). Like her royal hubby, she started her own business, forming RJH Public Relations in 1996, and continued to work after marrying into "the firm". But she stepped down as chairman in 2001 after an embarrassing sting by an undercover *News of the World* journalist, posing as a sheikh and a wealthy prospective client. Sophie herself was lucky in that she said nothing horrifically damning about her royal status and her PR interests – it could have been a lot worse. However, her colleague Murray Harkin was less reserved, embarrassing Team Windsor by casting aspersions on Edward's sexuality ("there's no smoke without fire") and suggesting ways the royal couple might lend the sheikh's leisure complex project a higher profile. Buckingham Palace released a statement saying that Sophie's reported comments were "selective, distorted and in several cases, flatly untrue". Whatever she did or did not say, damage was done and, like her husband, Sophie's daily routine today rarely veers from the traditional royal orbit of good works and charity.

Edward decided to strike out on his own, forming the TV company Ardent Productions in 1993. Ardent produced a number of poorly received documentaries and dramas, very few of which were commissioned, although *Edward on Edward*, a documentary about Edward VIII, sold reasonably well. The recurring theme of Ardent's work was, surprise surprise, royalty: programmes about the restoration of Windsor Castle after its fire, English royal warships, royal retainers, royal residences and royal family members. Granted, there was a series on the obscure sport of real tennis, and a political soap opera which was cancelled after ten episodes. Edward was accused in the media of using his royal connections for financial gain (despite Ardent losing money hand over fist): the sole year the company reported a profit was the year Edward did not charge it £50,000 for the rent of office space at his Bagshot Park residence). Edward didn't exactly endear himself to the British media. In an interview with the *New York Times*, he said of them that "they hate anyone who succeeds", effusing that Hollywood was, in contrast, a "breath of fresh air", and that "America is where the money is". He also annoyed his big brother Charles when an Ardent two-man crew filmed Prince William in September 2001 while he was studying at St Andrews, contradicting the agreement with the media regarding the teenage royals' privacy.

When Ardent collapsed in 2009, it had assets of just £40; Edward does not appear to have any further ambitions in broadcasting. Today he channels his ardency into charity work, alongside his wife Sophie, whom he married in 1999, and with whom he has two children – Louise (b. 2003) and James (b. 2007). One day the current Earl of Wessex will inherit the title Duke of Edinburgh from his father, and Edward accordingly plays an active role in the Duke of Edinburgh's Award, the scheme for young people set up by Philip.

Princess Anne (1950–)

Credited with possessing both the acerbic manners of her father – she once famously told obtrusive journalists to "naff off" – and the indefatigible industry of her mother, Anne is currently tenth in line to the throne (having once hit the dizzying heights of third after her mother Elizabeth's accession).

PETER AND ZARA PHILLIPS

Despite her somewhat haughty looks there's a good case to be made that Anne has something of a common touch, twice marrying out of the aristocracy – the second time to a man who once worked as an attendant of the Queen. Anne's son, Peter Mark Andrew Phillips (b. 1977), became the first direct grandchild of a monarch to be born without a title for 500 years – after his parents were said to have refused offers of a peerage from the Queen – and he carries out no royal duties. After his degree (Sports Science at the University of Exeter), he worked in sports sponsorship for the Bank of Scotland in Hong Kong, before relocating to London where he stays out of the media spotlight. He married a Canadian called Autumn Kelly; his daughter Savannah is twelfth in line to the throne.

Anne's daughter, Zara Anne Elizabeth Phillips (b. 1981), is much better known. Zara won the Eventing World Championship in 2006 and, just like her mum, also

She first caught the public eye on the back of her horse, winning an individual title at the European Eventing Championships. In a more deferential age, she was a (horse) shoe-in for the BBC's Sports Personality of the Year award shortly after. When, two years later, she married fellow equestrian Captain Mark Phillips, she was the focus of worldwide media attention, pipping Charles to the post. Her previous love affair with debonair man-about-town and off-limits Catholic Andrew Parker Bowles was nixed by his marriage to one Camilla Shand – who had at that early age already caught the eye of Anne's brother Charles. The love triangle (or should that be heptagon?) was redrawn by *Daily Mail* columnists in 2010, gleefully speculating that Anne's friendship with Parker Bowles was back on, following a supposed cooling of her relationship with her solidly reliable second husband Sir Timothy Laurence. Anne had first met Laurence when he was an equerry to the Queen, though he was a naval commander at the time of their marriage in 1992.

Anne is a royal with an edge. In 1974 she and Phillips escaped a kidnapping attempt when armed assailant Ian Ball, a disturbed 26-year-old gunman, ambushed their car on The Mall in London. Four people were shot by Ball, yet files reveal Anne was more angry than scared, straining hard not to lose her temper. She responded to Ball's gun-wielding demand that she "come with me for a day or two" with a "not bloody likely". She may also have needed to summon all the phlegmatic reserve at her disposal on two other occasions: first, when the police charged her for a speeding offence (93 mph on a dual carriageway); and later, in 2002, when magistrates fined her £500 for letting her bull terrier Dotty run out of control in Windsor Park,

carried off the BBC Sports Personality of the Year award. In 2011 her unlikely marriage to Shrek lookalike rugby star Mike Tindall seemed to cap a perfect double wedding year for the royals. Until "dwarfgate", that is. For a member of the extended royal family to be found blind drunk in the middle of professional tour duties is certainly unusual; to be revealed with his head in the breasts of a young blonde woman on CCTV footage might be considered even more unfortunate. But when this story comes wrapped up with the revelation that the occasion Tindall was attending, drinks-in-hand, was a dwarf-throwing contest, the story tipped into glorious farce. The media frenzy was casually shrugged off by Phillips; less comfortably by the English authorities who later fined Tindall £15,000. Zara had also been marked out as a royal rebel by the media for having her tongue pierced (since removed). She does undertake charitable activities and assignments but her air of duty is lightly worn.

The Princess Royal, competing at the cross-country section of the Eridge Horse Trials, East Sussex, 1971.

biting two boys – the first time a senior member of the British royal family had been convicted of a criminal offence. Another of Anne's dogs, Florence, was subsequently thought to have been the culprit when one of the Queen's corgis was killed only a year later.

Anne's public image is steely, a persona that has sometimes chimed better with the public mood than that of her brother – at one point during Charles's marital difficulties, some commentators called for Anne to step forward to succeed the Queen. Her own divorce certainly seems to have been more adroitly handled and her level of commitment impressive. Of the more than 200 charities and organizations she has worked with in some capacity – from Save the Children and St John's Ambulance to the University of Edinburgh, of which she is Chancellor – none has attracted the levels of criticism received by Charles's architectural lobbying or Prince Andrew's role as business ambassador.

Prince Richard, Duke of Gloucester (1944–)

The Duke and Duchess of Gloucester are the most low-profile of the senior royals. As Prince Richard he only became heir to the dukedom after his more dashing elder brother, Prince William, was killed in 1972 when the light aircraft he was piloting crashed. He inherited the title two years later on the death of his father Henry. As the Queen's first cousin (their fathers were brothers), he is currently twentieth in line to the throne.

Educated at Eton, he studied architecture at Magdalene College, Cambridge, and practised as an architect up until his brother's death. His career since then has been as a full-time royal, standing in for the Queen and taking part in official engagements both at home and overseas. His particular interests are in the areas of architecture and conservation, and his public duties often relate to these. In exchange for his activities as a royal he and his family enjoy rent-free accommodation at Kensington Palace.

Along with the dukedom, Prince Richard inherited the family home of Barnwell Manor in Northamptonshire, which had been purchased by his father in 1938. In 1995 he decided that its annual upkeep was too expensive and let the property out, initially to an antiques business, moving his 93-year-old mother Alice into the family apartments at Kensington Palace. She had lived at Barnwell all her married life and the duke was criticized by the press and, apparently, other family members for insisting that she move out. His handling of the family estate hit the headlines again in 2011 with

FRIENDS AND MORE RELATIONS

Within the inner circle of the Queen and Prince Philip, there have been a handful of intimates with whom they can be completely at ease. Some of these have had specific roles within the royal household, others have been relations and a few have been both. Here are ten of them.

1. **Lord Lichfield** (1939–2005) A cousin of the Queen (his mother, Anne Bowes-Lyon, was the Queen Mother's niece), the dandyish 5th Earl of Lichfield was a successful photographer, learning his craft as a fashion and society snapper in the Swinging Sixties, after a brief spell in the Grenadier Guards. His easy-going charm enabled him to produce some of the most spontaneous images of the royals, including the official pictures of Charles and Diana's wedding.

2. **Lord Harewood** (1923–2011) George Lascelles, 7th Earl of Harewood and a first cousin of the Queen (his mother was George VI's sister), was without doubt the most cultured of the royals. After service in World War II, which included a spell in Colditz, he moved into the arts, briefly running the Edinburgh Festival before becoming managing director and then chairman of English National Opera, a company he forged into a world-class ensemble.

3. **Lord Carnarvon** (1924–2001) The Queen is a passionate follower of the turf, and from 1969 to his death Henry Herbert, 7th Earl of Carnarvon ("Porchie" to his pals), was her racing manager. Under his management several royal horses achieved success, including wins for Dunfermline in the Oaks and the St Leger in Jubilee year (1977). His lordship was less popular with the sporting press, who regarded his sacking of the royal trainer, Major Dick Hern, as unnecessarily ruthless.

4. **Lord Brabourne** (b. 1947) Lord Mountbatten's grandson, a cousin of Prince Philip, as well as a friend of Prince Charles, Norton Knatchbull, 8th Baron Brabourne, was a key insider until his recent flit to the Bahamas in the company of new girlfriend, the fashion designer Lady Nuttall. He was apparently disenchanted with the responsibility of running the Mountbatten pile, Broadlands, but has subsequently returned to England.

5. **Lady Brabourne** (b. 1953) When her husband of thirty years walked out on her, Penny Brabourne put on a brave face and simply took over the running of their £100m estate. Senior royals have been equally staunch in their support of her. She is particularly chummy with Prince Philip and was, until recently, his regular carriage-driving companion. The Brabournes are no strangers to family troubles: their daughter, Leonora, died of leukaemia at the age of five, while their son and heir, Nicholas Knatchbull, has struggled with drug problems since his teenage years.

6. **Lady Pamela Hicks** (b. 1929) Lord Mountbatten's youngest daughter and Prince Philip's first cousin, Lady Pamela was a bridesmaid at Philip and Elizabeth's wedding and was with the royal couple in Kenya when news arrived of George VI's death. As a long-standing lady-in-waiting, she was close to the Queen, who she describes as "a very private person; a loner". In 1960 she married David Hicks, an interior designer who went on to decorate an apartment for Prince Charles at Buckingham Palace. She is currently working on her memoirs.

7. **The Hon Margaret Rhodes** (b. 1925) The nearest thing the Queen has to a big sister, Margaret Rhodes is another Bowes-Lyon cousin, the daughter of explorer and big game hunter Lord Elphinstone and his wife Mary (the Queen Mother's sister). A playmate to the princesses Elizabeth and Margaret, during World War II she lived first at Windsor Castle before getting a job at MI6. She married the writer Denys Rhodes in 1950, and was a bridesmaid at Philip and Elizabeth's wedding. A lady-in-waiting to her aunt, the Queen Mother, from 1991 she was with her when she died. Her recent memoirs, *The Last Curtsey*, were candid but ruffled no feathers.

8. **The Duchess of Abercorn** (b. 1946) If you want to counter the received opinion of Prince Philip as a tactless grouch then Sacha Hamilton, the wife of the 5th Duke of Abercorn, would be the person to speak to. A friend since the 1960s, she and Philip apparently bonded while discussing the psychoanalyst Carl Jung: "Prince Philip is always questing, exploring, searching for meaning, testing ideas. We had riveting conversations about Jung. That's where our friendship began." She is related to the prince and is also, more surprisingly, a descendant of the Russian poet Pushkin.

9. **Commander Mike Parker** (1920–2002) Philip's cousin, David, 3rd Marquess of Milford Haven, was his best man but was dropped soon after for various indiscretions. A better choice might have been the prince's wartime chum Mike Parker who, shortly after the wedding, became his private secretary. The two had served on sister ships in World War II, and had enjoyed some fairly raucous shore leave together. Prince Philip appreciated Parker's Australian directness, and he became a key figure in attempts to modernize life at the palace. Marital problems led to Parker losing his job but the two men continued their friendship up to his death.

10. **William Stamps Farish III** (b. 1939) A mild-mannered Texan and a family friend of George W. Bush, who made him ambassador to Britain, Will Farish is also a good friend to the Queen and Prince Philip. Their shared passion is for horses, which Farish breeds and trains at his two Lane's End Farms in Kentucky and Texas. The Queen has sent mares to stud at the Kentucky farm, had horses trained there and has visited several times. Reputedly one of the richest men in Texas, Farish inherited his money from his grandfather's oil dealings, which included dubious transactions with the Nazis, resulting in accusations of treason from Harry Truman.

another money-making scheme. This time he proposed leasing farmland close to Barnwell Manor to an energy company, who planned to erect five wind turbines. The predictable outcry was supported by two local MPs and several environmental groups, as well as the National Trust and English Heritage – extremely embarrassing for a man who is patron of the UK branch of the International Council on Monuments and Sites.

In 1965 the duke met Birgitte van Deurs (b. 1946), a young Danish woman, while he was an undergraduate and she was studying at a language school in Cambridge. They were married at Barnwell Parish Church in 1972. The couple have three children: Alexander, Earl of Ulster (b. 1974), the heir to the dukedom; Lady Davina Lewis (b. 1977), who is married to New Zealand builder Gary Lewis; and Lady Rose Gilman (b. 1980). The Earl of Ulster's son, Xan Windsor, who holds the courtesy title Lord Culloden, was born in 2007.

Prince Edward, Duke of Kent (1935–)

The Duke of Kent, currently 28th in the line of succession, is a cousin of the Queen and a first cousin once removed of the Duke of Edinburgh, to whom he bears a strong resemblance. He inherited the dukedom in 1942 at the age of seven after his father Prince George – King George VI's youngest brother – was killed when his RAF plane crashed on its way to Iceland on a secret mission. Educated at Eton and then at Sandhurst, the duke pursued a career as a soldier, serving with his regiment, the Royal Scots Greys, from 1955 to 1976. He represented the Queen at several of the independence celebrations of former British colonies in Africa during the early 1960s and has continued to carry out royal duties. His best-known public role, however, is as president of the All English Lawn Tennis and Croquet Club; every year he can be seen at the Wimbledon tennis tournament presenting the trophy to the winner of the men's final. More controversially, he is a leading freemason – Grand Master of the United Grand Lodge of England – although he likes to stress freemasonry's charitable activities, and insists that the organization's secrecy and the tendency of its members to look out for each other at the expense of others is a thing of the past.

While stationed at Catterick Army Camp, the Duke met Katharine Worsley, the only daughter of Sir William and Lady Worsley of Hovingham in Yorkshire. They were married, with much pomp, at York Minster in 1961. The duchess trained as a musician and music remains one of her most

EIGHT ROYAL RESIDENCES

Successive monarchs have occupied a surprisingly large number of royal residences over the centuries, several of which, such as Henry VIII's magnificent Nonsuch Palace, no longer exist. Here are eight that the royals still call home:

1. **Buckingham Palace** This is the big one, the monarch's main London residence since 1837, the place the tourists all want to see, and the HQ of the whole royal enterprise – from grand ceremonials to entertaining foreign dignitaries. The addition of a new frontage in 1913 increased the number of rooms to 775.

2. **Windsor Castle** Begun by William I, the castle was enlarged throughout the Middle Ages and includes the magnificent fifteenth-century Chapel of St George. Both an official residence and a private home, it's where the Queen spends most weekends. Nine of the main state rooms were destroyed by fire in 1992.

3. **Palace of Holyroodhouse** The monarch's official residence in Scotland was founded as an abbey in 1128 and became a royal home in the fifteenth century. Mary Queen of Scots witnessed the brutal murder of her secretary Rizzio while living there. Close to Edinburgh Castle, it is now used for state ceremonials.

4. **Balmoral** The private holiday home of the royal family in Aberdeenshire, Scotland, was built on the site of a fourteenth-century castle. Purchased for Queen Victoria in 1848, it was largely remodelled with the close involvement of Prince Albert. The Queen spends most of August and September at the house.

5. **Sandringham** This Norfolk estate was bought in 1861 as a country house for the Prince of Wales (later Edward VII). Following his marriage two years later, he almost completely rebuilt it so that he could socialize there on a grand scale. The house is where the royal family usually spends Christmas.

6. **St James's Palace** Built by Henry VIII in the 1530s on the site of a hospital, this red-brick complex of buildings is actually the sovereign's official residence, although its plush interiors are now mostly used for official functions. For the London Olympics, the Queen is planning to rent out some of the state rooms.

7. **Clarence House** Designed by John Nash, this was built within St James's for the Duke of Clarence, who continued living there when he became William IV in 1830. It was the home of the Queen Mother for nearly fifty years and is now the London residence of the Prince of Wales.

8. **Kensington Palace** A Jacobean mansion purchased by William III in 1689, it was the monarch's principal residence until the death of George II. Since then it has been home to an assortment of royals, including Princess Diana and Princess Margaret. The Duke and Duchess of Cambridge plan to move there in 2013.

abiding passions; for many years she was a member of the highly regarded Bach Choir. She has regularly presented the women's trophy at Wimbledon, famously comforting a weeping Jana Novotna when she narrowly lost the final in 1993.

The duchess has had her share of hardship. Suffering from depression after two failed pregnancies, she scaled down her public duties during the 1980s and was later diagnosed with an illness similar to ME. In 1994 she was received into the Roman Catholic Church and since then has lived more or less separately from her husband. Remarkably, for about twelve years she managed to teach music – virtually incognito – at a state primary school in Hull, where she was known as Mrs Kent. This "absolutely amazing" experience led her to set up a charity, Future Talent, with the aim of helping disadvantaged young people fulfil their musical potential.

The Kents have three children: George, Earl of St Andrews (b. 1962), Lady Helen Windsor (b. 1964) and Lord Nicholas Windsor (b. 1970). Only Lady Helen is in the line of succession, both sons were excluded: the Earl for marrying a Catholic, his brother for becoming one. The allegedly shy Lord Nicholas, who studied theology at Oxford, is a high-profile Catholic who married a member of the Croatian nobility in 2006; the service was held in the Vatican followed by a lavish reception at the Palazzo Doria Pamphili. Lord Nicholas is a vehement anti-abortionist, regarding abortion as a bigger danger to civilization than al-Qaeda and "the single most grievous moral deficit in contemporary life".

Prince Michael of Kent (1942–)

Prince and Princess Michael of Kent have an unenviable record for hitting the headlines for the wrong reasons. He is a business consultant, she is an author, and there have been frequent accusations of exploiting royal connections. The prince once advertised kitsch "House of Windsor" gifts on US television and his wife has earned herself the nickname "Princess Pushy" for her relentless self-promotion. But despite their commercial activities, they seem to struggle to make ends meet. Family life has been divided between Gloucestershire and London. Nether Lypiatt Manor was acquired and refurbished after the prince picked up a string of directorships in the 1980s before being sold for £5.75 million in 2008. While in London they have had the run of an apartment in Kensington Palace, living there virtually free of charge until 2010, when they were finally charged a commercial-rate rent.

Prince and Princess Michael of Kent on their way to the Queen's eightieth birthday in 2006.

As the younger brother of the Duke of Kent and Princess Alexandra, and the third child of the late Prince George, Duke of Kent, Prince Michael's early life was similar to that of his brother: Eton followed by Sandhurst and then twenty or so years as a soldier. Like the duke, he is also a leading freemason and a linguist but, while both brothers excel at French, Prince Michael is good enough at Russian to have acted as a military interpreter. Russia is one of his great enthusiasms. He is the patron of the Russo-British Chamber of Commerce and supports a number of Russian charities, several related to children's welfare. In fact, in Russia (where he's known as Mikhail Kentski) the prince is taken rather more seriously than he is in Britain. His resemblance to Tsar Nicholas II – a first cousin to three of Prince Michael's grandparents – undoubtedly helps. When the remains of the Russian royal family were interred in St Petersburg in 1998, the prince represented the British royal family.

In 1978 Prince Michael married interior designer Baroness Marie Christine von Reibnitz, the daughter of Baron von Reibniz, a Nazi Party member and friend of Göring. Her descent from several of the royal houses of Europe prompted the Queen to remark to Lord Mountbatten that "she sounds a bit grand for us". She is also a Catholic (albeit a divorced one), which meant the prince gave up his place in the succession when he married her. Six feet tall and haughty, she is apparently known as "our Val" within the royal family, short for Valkyrie (after the Nordic warrior maidens immortalized by Wagner). If not quite as gaffe-prone as the Duke of Edinburgh, Princess Michael's activities have raised eyebrows. There were perturbing similarities with another writer's work found in the first of her three books about European royalty (she blamed the mistake on researchers); misunderstood remarks to noisy African-American fellow diners in a Greenwich Village restaurant; snide comments to an under-cover reporter about Princess Diana; and, in the same interview, a defence of Prince Harry for dressing as a Nazi at a fancy dress party.

The couple have two children, Lord Freddie Windsor (b. 1979) and Lady Gabriella Windsor (b. 1981), both of whom were brought up as Anglicans and so remain in the line of succession. Lord Freddie, who worked as a model before joining JP Morgan as an investment banker, recently married English actor Sophie Winkleman (Big Suze in the TV comedy *Peep Show*) and now lives in Los Angeles. His sister, known professionally as Ella Windsor, is a freelance journalist who writes for several publications including *The Spectator* and *Monocle*.

Princess Alexandra (1936–)

The middle child and only daughter of George, Duke of Kent, Princess Alexandra is one of the most popular royals of the Queen's genera-tion. Brought up by her mother Princess Marina at the family home of Coppins in Buckinghamshire, she was educated at Heathfield, a private girls' school near Ascot, and at a finishing school in Paris. More charming and personable than her two brothers, she was an ideal stand-in for the Queen in an increasingly televisual age, and has been carrying out royal duties since the age of seventeen. She undertook a number of tours in Commonwealth countries and the Far East, and in 1960 was the royal who attended Nigeria's independence celebrations. In 1963 she got mar-

GEORGE, DUKE OF KENT – THE FAMILY BAD BOY

According to those close to the family, Prince George was the most charming and cultured of George V's four grown-up sons. But despite his many artistic talents – which included dancing and playing the piano – he was still made to follow the usual Windsor course of training for the navy, a career which he hated, not least because he suffered from seasickness.

To alleviate the grind of royal and naval duties, George played very hard indeed, with a constant round of partying among the high and low life of 1920s London, often in tandem with his beloved big brother, Edward, Prince of Wales. He also embarked on a series of love affairs with both women and men, proposing to the banking heiress Poppy Baring – a match stopped by his father. A heavy drinker, George was introduced to morphine by Kiki Preston (another lover) while hanging out with the decadent Happy Valley set in Kenya. His ensuing addiction only ended following the intervention of the Prince of Wales, one of the few unselfish acts of Edward's life.

Getting Prince George to settle down was now a priority; prospective brides were checked out, but in the end he made his own choice, falling for and courting the ultra-stylish Princess Marina of Yugoslavia. Soon after meeting her, he was given the title Duke of Kent. The couple married in 1934; their first child, Edward (see p.44), was born a year later and a daughter, Alexandra (see opposite), in 1935. George's closeness to his eldest brother ended with the abdication crisis and his refusal to honour the promise he made to be Edward's best man. Then, with the advent of World War II, he was faced with the usual royal frustration of how to make himself useful. He wanted a proper job, but was fobbed off with inspectorates – first of bomb sites and later of factories.

When the war came, George resumed naval duties but in 1940 switched to the RAF. Given the rank of Air Commodore, his main task was to tour RAF stations assessing welfare arrangements both in Britain and overseas. In August 1942 (a few weeks after the birth of his son Michael) he set off on a Sunderland flying boat from Scotland to Iceland on what was, officially, a morale-boosting visit to troops stationed there. Departing from Invergordon on the east coast, the plane flew off course and crashed into a hillside in the far northeast of Scotland. The Duke and all the crew were killed, with the exception of Flight Sergeant Andrew Jack.

This tragedy for the duke's family has given rise to a number of conspiracy theories. Like many upper-crust Brits, the duke had leaned towards appeasement with Germany, and had had meetings with Nazi officials in the 1930s. Some have even connected him to the mysterious arrival in Scotland of Hitler's deputy, Rudolf Hess, in 1941. Was the Iceland flight a secret mission to broker a peace deal with Germany or, as some have suggested, an attempt to appear to do so? Key documents that might shed light have been lost, others locked away, and whatever Sergeant Jack may have known went with him to the grave.

ried in Westminster Abbey to businessman Angus Ogilvy (1928–2004), the second son of the Scottish aristocrat and high-ranking courtier the Earl of Airlie. The couple refused the usual grace-and-favour home and instead purchased the lease on Thatched House Lodge, a Crown property in Richmond Park. Their two children, James and Marina, were born in 1964 and 1966.

Princess Alexandra and the Right Honourable Angus Ogilvy were regarded as an exemplary royal couple. But in 1973 Lonrho, the mining company of which Ogilvy was a director, was accused of sharp practice, and of breaking the sanctions the British government had imposed on Rhodesia. To avoid causing embarrassment to the Crown, Ogilvy felt obliged to resign many of his directorships, even though he thought he had been unfairly criticized. With his business activities now severely reduced, he took on a greater role supporting his wife and involving himself in various charities, many of them concerned with the welfare of young people.

In 1989 the couple hit the gossip columns again when their daughter Marina Ogilvy, a talented musician, became pregnant by photographer Paul Mowatt. Her parents' allegedly horrified reaction prompted Marina to sell her story to a newspaper, appear on various chat shows and pose for some mildly raunchy photographs. Despite the bad feeling, Sir Angus (as he now was) gave away his daughter the following year at a wedding ceremony at which no other royals, apart from the mother of the bride, were present. The wedding pictures duly appeared in *Hello!* magazine. Marina has continued to be – by royal standards, at least – something of a bohemian. In 2003 it was revealed that she was living in a cottage on the Queen's Windsor estate with her two children, Zenouska and Christian. Despite her parents' wealth (not to mention that of the rest of the family), she was receiving housing and child benefit – prompting moral outrage in the tabloids. Her Eton-educated brother, publisher and founder of upmarket *Luxury Briefing* magazine, has managed to maintain a rather lower profile. His wife Julia (née Rawlinson) was a successful business woman but gave it all up after a partial breakdown. She subsequently launched a charity, ProjectScotland, which aims to transform the lives of young Scots through volunteering projects. She and her husband have two teenage children, Flora and Alexander.

2

A British dynasty?

Loyalty to the queen (or the king) is seen as a sign of patriotism, yet how often over the centuries were the monarchy actually foreigners? The Normans and Plantagenets were French, the Tudors were Welsh, the Stuarts Scottish and the Hanoverians German. The original name of the current Windsor dynasty (Saxe-Coburg-Gotha) is a reminder that British monarchs have not always been as British as their subjects. Here we give an account of the international connections of the monarchy past and present.

Early royals: Anglo-Saxons and Danes

The problem with delving into Britain's early history is that it's virtually impossible to tell who's a native and who's a foreigner. There is a tendency to see the Anglo-Saxons as the true ancestors of the English, yet genetic studies suggest that most modern Brits are descended primarily from Celts who came from the Basque region of Spain in the Neolithic period. These same Celts, or ancient Britons as the Romans called them, then had to cope with (and survived) waves of immigration of Angles, Saxons and Jutes from Germany and Denmark after the collapse of the Roman Empire. By 600 AD, the island was a patchwork of competing Anglo-Saxon and Celtic kingdoms, including central Mercia, East Anglia, Wessex in the south, Kent in the southeast, and Northumbria in the northeast.

From the end of the eighth century onwards, the Vikings or Norsemen began to raid the coastline of Britain, massacring the locals, demanding

THERE IS NOTHING LIKE A DANE

The Queen is descended from the Danes who ruled over England thanks to James III of Scotland, who married one of Sweyn Forkbeard's descendants, Margaret of Denmark. Sweyn's Danish blood was thus introduced into the Scottish royal family and eventually, via James VI – who became James I of England in 1603 – into the English royal family.

protection money and eventually colonizing the north of the country. It's probably fair to say the Danes weren't the most popular folk in England by the end of the tenth century. In 1002, Æthelred the Unready (978–1016) ordered the St Brice's Day Massacre, a sort of ethnic cleansing of Danes in Oxford, justifying it afterwards by complaining that they were "sprouting like cockle amongst the wheat". Unfortunately, Gunhilde, sister of the Danish and Norwegian king, Sweyn Forkbeard, was believed to be among the victims, a fact which provoked renewed Viking raids and then a full-scale Norse invasion in the summer of 1013 under Sweyn Forkbeard's command. By winter, Sweyn was in control of the country and Æthelred had fled to Normandy. On Christmas Day 1013, Sweyn became the first Dane to be proclaimed King of England, but his reign lasted only five weeks when he died suddenly on 3 February 1014 at his base in Gainsborough, Lincolnshire.

Cnut and sons

Sweyn's son, Cnut (1016–1035) – whose mother is actually thought to have been Polish – was initially forced to flee to Denmark to escape Æthelred the Unready who'd been recalled from exile. However, in the summer of 1015, Cnut returned with an even larger army of Vikings. After over a year of sporadic warfare, during which both Æthelred and his son Edmund Ironside conveniently died, Cnut was proclaimed King of England. Æthelred's only surviving son, Eadwig, fled, but Cnut had him killed anyway, and to shore up his position he married Æthelred's widow, Emma of Normandy. Cnut's attempt to build an Anglo-Danish North Sea Empire might well have succeeded in the long term had he not died at the age of just forty, followed within a few years by his two sons, Harold Harefoot and Harthacnut. The last of the Danish kings, Harthacnut, choked to death at a wedding feast in Lambeth in 1042, and the two kingdoms were divided, with Denmark going to Magnus I of Norway, and England to Edward the Confessor, the son of Æthelred and Emma.

The Vikings try again

The Norsemen had one more serious shot at regaining the English throne when the King of Norway, Harald Hardrada, formed an alliance with Tostig, the disgruntled brother of King Harold of England. Harald Hardrada invaded in 1066, sailing up the Humber with a fleet of at least 300 ships and taking York. However, at the Battle of Stamford Bridge, the Norse army was utterly defeated by King Harold, and Harald Hardrada and Tostig were both killed. Just three days after Harold had secured this decisive victory, William the Conqueror landed in the south of the country, and three weeks later Harold himself was killed at the Battle of Hastings, paving the way for the Normans to claim the English throne. Neither the Danes nor the Anglo-Saxons were prepared to give up entirely, however. So in 1069, King Sweyn II of Denmark (Cnut's nephew) teamed up with Edgar Atheling (Æthelred the Unready's great-grandson) and invaded England, sailing up the Humber (again) and taking York (again). On this occasion, Sweyn was bought off by William and, despite two more raids in 1075 and 1085, the Viking threat to England was over – although of course the Normans themselves were just Norsemen who'd settled in northern France in the tenth century.

French connection: the Normans

As every school child knows, William the Conqueror, Duke of Normandy, invaded England in 1066 and defeated the English King, Harold II, at the Battle of Hastings. Norman (a northern dialect of Old French) became the language of the nobility, and would remain so until the fourteenth century. So for nearly three hundred years, England was basically run by French-speaking princes. These French rulers were in a slightly awkward position, since, to keep their French possessions, they had to pay homage to the King of France, although as kings of England, they were nominally equals. It was a complicated relationship which was at the root of most Anglo-French tensions in the Middle Ages.

The Norman influence on the English court actually predated the Battle of Hastings, harking back to 1002, when Emma of Normandy (William's great-aunt) married King Æthelred the Unready. Their son, Edward the Confessor, spent more than 25 years in exile in Normandy (while the Danes were in charge of England) before becoming King of England himself. Understandably, Edward felt a great deal of gratitude towards his Norman hosts and was heavily influenced by his sojourn there. He went on to build England's first Norman cathedral, Westminster Abbey, and – according to the Normans – to choose William (the bastard son of his first cousin) as his successor.

Unlike Cnut, the Danish King of England, who simply rewarded his followers with money, William the Conqueror decided to displace the native landowners and reward his Norman chums with titles and land. By the time the Domesday Book was completed in 1086, the country's wealth was concentrated in the hands of around 250 individuals, nearly every one of whom had been brought in from across the Channel by William – of the country's sixteen bishoprics, only one was held by a non-Norman. Within five years of the Conquest, William was secure enough to return to his homeland of Normandy, where he spent most of the rest of his reign. His youngest son, Henry I (1100–1135), followed suit, continually crisscrossing the Channel, dividing his time equally between the two.

French connection II: the Angevins

With the marriage of William's granddaughter, Matilda, to Geoffrey Plantagenet, Count of Anjou, and the accession of their son, Henry II (1154–1189), to the English throne, it was the Plantagenet family's turn to dominate the English throne. Born and brought up in France, speaking only French and Latin, Henry would be astonished to find himself thought of as one of the great English kings. He spent two-thirds of his reign in France and most of his energies protecting his vast French territories, which stretched from the Pyrenees to the Channel and centred on Angers, the capital of Anjou (hence Angevin). At their zenith, the Plantagenets had more land in France than the King of France himself. Henry was buried in France, as was his son, Richard the Lionheart (1189–1199), who spent half his reign crusading with the King of France, and half hanging out in the French territories of his childhood – he was in England for just seven months.

King John (1199–1216) was the first king since before the Conquest to spend the majority of his reign in England, but only because – as his nickname "Lackland" suggests – he had lost nearly all his French estates to the King of France. Long after the English had any significant possessions in France, the influence of foreigners at the royal court continued to cause resentment. The boy-king Henry III (1216–1275) was crowned by a Frenchman, Peter des Roches, Bishop of Winchester, who became

Henry's tutor and protector. On coming of age, and marrying Eleanor of Provence, he increasingly relied on his in-laws from Provence and Savoy, appointing three of his wife's uncles to be ministers, and lavishing land and titles on his four French half-brothers. However, it's a sign of the times that when the barons finally rebelled in 1258, they turned to another Frenchman, Simon de Montfort, as their leader.

Edward III (1327–1377) was the first king to speak English fluently and played a large part in turning the Plantagenets into a truly English dynasty at the same time as fostering a nascent English national identity. Edward had mottos emblazoned in English – although his best-known one, *Honi Soit Qui Mal Y Pense* (evil to him who evil thinks), is French. In 1362, Edward decreed that, in addition to French, English could now be heard in courts of law; the same year he opened parliament with a speech in English. When Charles IV of France died in 1328, leaving no male heirs, Edward stepped in, as his nephew, and claimed the French throne, giving himself the title "King of England and France" and kicking off the Hundred Years' War. His son, Henry IV (1399–1413), was the first monarch since the Conquest whose mother tongue was English: he took the coronation oath in English and wrote his will in English.

Even with the end of the Hundred Years' War, the French connection with the English crown didn't fade entirely. Calais remained in English hands until 1558 (the Channel Islands still do), and it wasn't until 1802 that the British monarchy gave up the pretence of being kings of France and dropped the title altogether. Even today, English legal terminology is littered with French words and phrases – culprit, force majeure, parole – that are a reminder of the country's Norman roots.

A kingdom of kingdoms

The people whom the Romans found living on the island when they invaded in 43 AD are generally thought to have been Celts. The Romans called the island Britannia, and are therefore ultimately responsible for the term "British". However, a British national identity was only really forged after the United Kingdom was created in 1707 and the British Empire began to expand. Even today, "Britishness" is still something felt more keenly in the English heartland than in the Celtic fringe. However, the royal family are keen to portray themselves as thoroughly British, and not simply English, so they claim descent from just about every royal house in the British Isles.

KING LOUIS I OF ENGLAND

One name that tends to get missed off the roll-call of English kings is Louis I (son of King Philip II of France and himself the future Louis VIII), lorded it as King of England for a full year before giving way to Henry III. His successful invasion of England in 1216 rarely gets a mention in the school history books, though it provides the main plot of Shakespeare's seldom-performed play *King John* (Louis appears as "Lewis the Dauphin"). Yet Louis set sail for England with a fleet almost as strong as that of William the Conqueror and a much larger army. He landed on the Isle of Thanet, off the north Kent coast, on 21 May 1216, and marched more or less unopposed to London.

Louis's claim to the throne was pretty tenuous (his wife was one of Henry II's granddaughters), but he had been invited over by the English barons, who'd had enough of King John reneging on the promises he'd made when signing the Magna Carta the previous year. At a grand ceremony in St Paul's Cathedral, in the presence of numerous English clergy and nobles, the Mayor of London and Alexander II of Scotland, Louis was proclaimed King of England. And in less than a month, Louis controlled a third of the country and enjoyed the support of two-thirds of the barons.

By October, King John was seriously on the run, famously losing the crown jewels at high tide in the Wash, and dying of dysentery (and a surfeit of peaches and cider) a few days later. Paradoxically, King John's death did for Louis, too – with King John gone, the rebellious barons had no more need for Louis. John's nine-year-old son was hastily crowned King Henry III using some of his mother's jewellery (since the crown jewels were lost), in Gloucester Cathedral (since Louis held London and Winchester). The barons quickly began to desert the French usurper in favour of the elderly William Marshal, a popular former jousting champion who had been appointed regent. Marshal fought at the head of the young king's army and defeated Louis' forces at the Battle of Lincoln in May 1217. And then in August, French reinforcements were intercepted by an English naval force off the Kent coast, who blinded the French with lime dust and beheaded their commander, Eustace the Monk, on the deck of his flagship.

By signing the Treaty of Lambeth in September, Louis gained 10,000 marks but wrote himself out of the history books by agreeing he had never been the legitimate King of England.

The Scots

The independent Scottish monarchy is usually calculated from Kenneth MacAlpin (843–858) on, though it's unclear as to whether he was a king of the Picts or a king of the Gaels, or both. In any case, a strong Scottish national identity didn't really exist until the "Braveheart" period of the late

King Louis I of England – reigned for one year, forgotten for many more.

thirteenth century. Even then, the origins of the two dynasties that have come to represent Scottish patriotism lie largely in the Anglo-Norman world of the English court, rather than the Scottish Highlands. King David I (1124–1153), for example, spent much of his childhood in England, and only took power with the backing of King Henry I. Once in power he dispensed huge estates in southern Scotland to his Anglo-Norman followers, one of whom, Walter FitzAlan, took the name "Steward" from the office of High Steward that he held. These hereditary Stewards eventually transformed themselves into the Stuart dynasty. That other great Scottish hero, Robert the Bruce, also had a distinctly mixed, mostly French heritage: his father's family originated from Normandy and his mother was of Franco-Gaelic stock.

Whatever the Anglo-Norman influences on the Scottish crown, it was the Scots who had the last laugh because when Elizabeth I died in 1603 leaving no heir, the Scots were asked to step in and save the day. King James VI of Scotland, Elizabeth's nephew, succeeded to the throne, and became James I of England. The new monarch moved down to London, proclaiming himself "King of Great Britain", although Great Britain didn't yet exist, rarely bothering to return to his Scottish homeland. However, the Stuart dynasty, which had reigned in Scotland since 1371 (and in England since 1603) came to an abrupt end when the 1701 Act of Settlement was passed. This law meant that when Queen Anne, the last Stuart, died childless, the crown passed to the German Protestant George I, rather than any of the 57 (much closer) Stuart Catholic claimants. With the 1707 Act of Union, the Kingdom of Scotland ceased to exist as a separate kingdom.

The Welsh

Gruffydd ap Llewelyn (1055–1063) was the first (and pretty much the only) Welsh monarch that could claim to hold sway over the whole of Wales. However, while under attack from the future English king, Harold, and his brother Tostig, he was assassinated in his hideout in Snowdonia by one of his own men. Wales remained weak and fragmented until Llewelyn ap Gruffydd, the last prince of an independent Wales, died fighting the English in 1282, and Edward I annexed the country (see p.172).

Like the Scots, however, the Welsh nobles made something of a comeback when one of their own, Henry Tudor, came to the English throne as King Henry VII (1485–1509). A member of an old-established Anglesey family, which claimed descent from Cadwaladr, the legendary seventh-century king of Gwynedd, Henry won the Battle of Bosworth in 1485, despite having arrived with only a tiny French invasion force, and with at least 29 people alive with a better claim to the throne.

Coat of arms of Henry VII, combining the lions of England with the fleur de lys of France. The supporters on either side are the dragon of Cadwaladr and the greyhound, associated with the House of Richmond. Henry's father, Edmund Tudor, was Earl of Richmond.

The Irish

If the Welsh monarchs were rarely in control of their national destiny, Ireland was even more famously fragmented, with the country divided into a multiplicity of kingdoms and dynasties. Nevertheless, the Queen claims descent from the High Kings of Ireland (who claimed to have lordship over the whole of Ireland) via Robert the Bruce, whose ancestor, Aoife MacMurrough, was the daughter of Dermot, King of Leinster. It was Dermot who fatefully asked Henry II for help recovering his kingdom; Henry used the excuse to invade Ireland in 1171. After the Norman invasion of Ireland, the monarchs of England gave themselves the title Lord of Ireland, and ruled over areas of Ireland that expanded and retreated over time. Following his break with Rome, Henry VIII declared himself and his successors Kings of Ireland in 1542. The kingdom came to an end as a separate entity under two Acts of Union passed in 1801 that established the United Kingdom of Great Britain and Ireland.

Going Dutch: William of Orange

Forget 1066 and all that. The last foreign invasion of Britain took place in November 1688 when Willem van Oranje (William of Orange), Stadtholder of the United Provinces, was invited over by parliament to help overthrow James II, the unpopular Catholic king of England. William landed at Torbay and, after a spot of tourism – he went to see the formal gardens and the Van Dycks at Wilton House near Salisbury – marched to the capital unopposed. Following this popular, bloodless, "Glorious Revolution", William and his wife Mary Stuart (James II's daughter) were declared King and Queen. Or at least that's what the Protestant propagandists would like to have you believe.

In reality, William had been planning an invasion for some time as a pre-emptive strike to prevent James II forming a Catholic alliance with Louis XIV of France. What forced the issue was the birth in June 1688 of a son and heir to James's second wife, Mary of Modena – which meant that William's wife Mary was no longer the heir apparent. William immediately requested an "invitation" from his supporters in the English parliament and organized nationwide distribution of his Declaration, which portrayed the invasion as an altruistic act aimed at restoring law and order – a piece of propaganda any US president would be proud of, aimed firmly at winning over English "hearts and minds". Predictably, the Declaration said nothing about the compelling political and economic reasons why the Dutch themselves might want to invade.

In the end, it was less a "Glorious Revolution" and more an unopposed military invasion by the Dutch, with whom we'd at war three times in the last forty years. William sailed across the Channel with a Dutch fleet of 450 ships carrying 20,000 crack Dutch troops, and, blown off course, landed in Devon. He rode into Exeter dressed in white on a white charger, with 200 black soldiers from Suriname forming a guard of honour, also dressed in white, with turbans and feathers. After a minor skirmish at Reading, a contingent of elite Dutch Blue Guards was sent ahead to secure key buildings across London, including St James's Palace, while all English troops were told to withdraw from the capital and James II was whisked off to Rochester. Only then did William enter London along a two-mile route lined with the Dutch Blue Guard. London remained under Dutch military occupation until the spring of 1690 and, taking no chances, William retained the Blue Guard as his personal bodyguards until his death in 1702.

In the end, the English people accepted William and Mary as joint monarchs because they considered it was better to have a foreigner than a

WHICH MONARCHS DIDN'T SPEAK ENGLISH?

Following the Norman Conquest, William the Conqueror made this dialect of Old French the official language of the English court. William himself is thought to have made some attempt to learn Anglo-Saxon, but few of his followers bothered. No king could even speak English until Henry III (1216–1272), and French remained the mother tongue of all English monarchs until Henry IV (1399–1413). The first royals to speak the kind of English comprehensible to modern ears were the Tudors, who presided over the first flowering of English literature.

William of Orange (1689–1702), although a native Dutch-speaker, was brought up in a bilingual Dutch–English household, dominated by women who were native English-speakers, including his mother. So it came as something of a shock to the English court when the 54-year-old George I (1714–1727) arrived from Hanover knowing so few words of English that the coronation was conducted mostly in Latin to aid his comprehension. George never bothered mastering the language, and had to make do with getting himself understood in French and Latin, but his son, George II (1727–1760), although born in Germany and a native German-speaker, was fluent in English. George III (1760–1820) was the first Hanoverian to be born in England – in fact, he never even visited Hanover, and was more or less bilingual in English and German by the age of eight.

Queen Victoria's early childhood was spent with her German mother, Victoria of Saxe-Coburg-Saalfeld, her German half-sister Theodore, and her German governess, Baroness Lehzen. In later life, Victoria claimed that as a child she was only allowed to read German and speak English, but, although her public image as an "English" child was carefully cultivated by her mother, she must have been pretty much bilingual at home in Kensington Palace. She was also taught French, Italian and Latin and, later in life, as Empress of India, she learnt Hindi. When she married Prince Albert, they conducted their relationship in German, and spoke German to the kids, six of whom went on to marry Germans (see p.62).

Catholic on the throne, or perhaps, as historian Lisa Jardine puts it, simply because "regime change was preferable to another civil war". The idea that it was a "Bloodless Revolution", however, is manifestly untrue. It may have been bloodless in London – aside for the anti-Catholic rioting – but resistance to the foreign invasion continued for several years and much blood was spilt across the British Isles. In July 1689, "Bonnie Dundee" rallied 2400 Highlanders and scored a bloody victory at the Battle of Killiecrankie, only to die during the proceedings. William subsequently demanded an oath of allegiance from the Highland clans, butchering those who refused to cooperate. In Catholic Ireland, resistance was even stronger, culminating in the Battle of the Boyne in July 1690, where William III's army of foreign mercenaries defeated James II's Irish and French troops. James II fled the British Isles never to return.

Axis Germania

The arrival of the Hanoverians brought a German flavour to the British monarchy which has never really disappeared. The first two Georges were German-born and German-speaking, and all four Georges married Germans. Even Queen Victoria's miserable childhood in Kensington Palace had a distinctly German flavour. Her father, the Duke of Kent, died when she was very young and she was brought up by her German-born mother, Princess Victoria of Saxe-Coburg-Saalfeld, alongside her older, German-speaking half-brother and half-sister, Carl and Ann (both of whom went on to marry Germans). Victoria herself married a German, Prince Albert of Saxe-Coburg and Gotha (see p.112), and produced 9 children and 42 grandchildren, 26 of whom married into noble and royal families across Europe, many of them German. The family tree opposite indicates the extraordinary extent to which consanguinity was common among married couples within the royal family, with marriage between first cousins not regarded as unusual. Unsurprisingly, Queen Victoria was known as the "Grandmother of Europe" and when Europe went to war with itself in 1914, her grandchildren inevitably, found themselves on opposing sides.

World War I created a huge rift between the British and German sides of the royal family, pitting royal cousin against royal cousin. As well as being the first cousin of Tsar Nicholas II (their mothers were sisters), George V was also first cousin to his war-time foe Kaiser Wilhelm II and the Kaiser's brother Prince Heinrich, commander of the German Navy's Baltic Fleet. Both Wilhelm and Heinrich were sons of Queen Victoria's firstborn daughter, also called Victoria. George had attended the Kaiser's wedding in Berlin as recently as 1913, and was himself married to the British-born Mary of Teck, whose German parents were, somewhat fortunately, no longer living. However, during World War I Queen Mary kept up a weekly correspondence with her aunt in Germany, using the Crown Princess of Sweden as an intermediary, until her aunt started expressing such fiercely pro-German sentiments that she had to stop writing. Rising anti-German feeling prompted the royal family to change its name in an

Some descendants of Queen Victoria's first three children

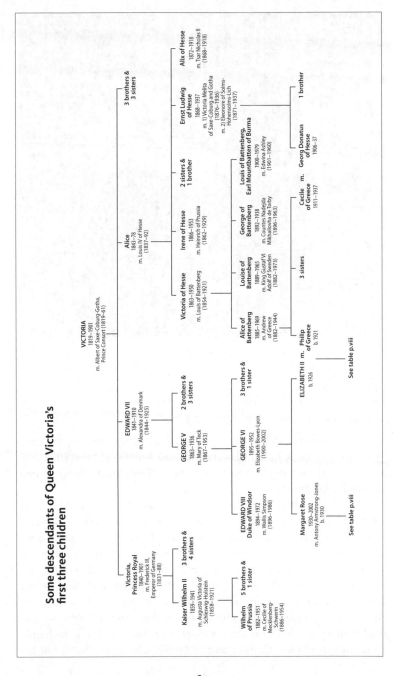

VICTORIA
1819–1901
m. Albert of Saxe-Coburg-Gotha,
Prince Consort (1819–61)

Victoria, Princess Royal
1840–1901
m. Frederick III,
Emperor of Germany
(1831–88)

EDWARD VII
1841–1910
m. Alexandra of Denmark
(1844–1925)

Alice
1843–78
m. Louis IV of Hesse
(1837–92)

3 brothers & 3 sisters

Kaiser Wilhelm II
1859–1941
m. Augusta Victoria of
Schleswig-Holstein
(1858–1921)

3 brothers & 4 sisters

GEORGE V
1863–1936
m. Mary of Teck
(1867–1953)

2 brothers & 3 sisters

Victoria of Hesse
1863–1950
m. Louis of Battenberg
(1854–1921)

Irene of Hesse
1866–1953
m. Heinrich of Prussia
(1862–1929)

2 sisters & 1 brother

Ernst Ludwig of Hesse
1868–1937
m. 1) Victoria Melita
of Saxe-Coburg and Gotha
(1876–1936)
m. 2) Eleonore of Solms-
Hohensolms-Lich
(1871–1937)

Alix of Hesse
1872–1918
m. Tsar Nicholas II
(1868–1918)

Wilhelm of Prussia
1882–1951
m. Cecilie of
Mecklenburg-
Schwerin
(1886–1954)

5 brothers & 1 sister

EDWARD VIII Duke of Windsor
1894–1972
m. Wallis Simpson
(1896–1986)

GEORGE VI
1895–1952
m. Elizabeth Bowes-Lyon
(1900–2002)

3 brothers & 1 sister

Alice of Battenberg
1885–1969
m. Andrew
of Greece
(1882–1944)

Louise of Battenberg
1889–1965
m. King Gustaf VI
Adolf of Sweden
(1882–1973)

George of Battenberg
1892–1938
m. Countess Nadejda
Mikhailovha de Torby
(1896–1963)

Louis of Battenberg, Earl Mountbatten of Burma
1900–1979
m. Edwina Ashley
(1901–1960)

Margaret Rose
1930–2002
m. Antony Armstrong-Jones
b. 1930

See table p.viii

ELIZABETH II
b. 1926

m. **Philip of Greece**
b. 1921

See table p.viii

3 sisters

Cecile of Greece
1911–1937

m. **Georg Donatus of Hesse**
1906–37

1 brother

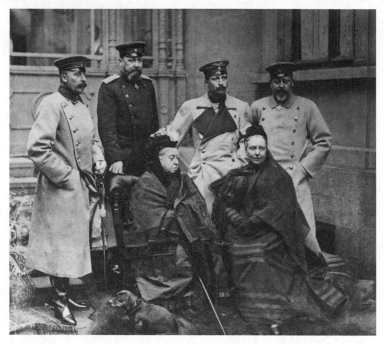

A German family. Queen Victoria sits with her eldest child, Princess Victoria (Dowager Empress of Germany), and (from left to right) Arthur, Duke of Connaught (the Queen's seventh child), Duke Alfred of Coburg (her fourth child), Kaiser Wilhelm II (Princess Victoria's son) and the Prince of Wales (the Queen's second child, later Edward VII). Even the dog, a dachsund, is German. Photographed at Coburg in 1894.

effort to reinvent itself (see box opposite) and to renounce all the family's Germanic titles. In 1915, several German Knights of the Garter were struck off the rolls, but to deprive anyone of their British titles required an Act of Parliament.

In 1917, the Titles Deprivation Act was passed and four of George's relations, who supported the German side, were stripped of their peerages, among them the Eton-educated Duke of Saxe-Coburg and Gotha, yet another of George's first cousins and a favourite grandson of Queen Victoria. George V had two more male first cousins of fighting age resident in Germany: Prince Albert of Schleswig-Holstein was a serving officer in the Prussian army but was excused service in World War I by the Kaiser – perhaps because his older brother, Prince Christian, had died fighting for the British in the Boer War. The other was the highly cultured Ernst Louis, Grand Duke of Hesse, who spent the war at the

THE WINDSOR NAME

Not that the Queen needs a surname as such, but the whole idea of the House of Windsor is a complete invention. As World War I dragged on, anti-German sentiment reached such a peak that there were stories of dachshunds being stoned to death in the streets of Berkhamstead. With Gotha aircraft bombing London, the royals decided that it was time to dump their embarrassingly German surname, Saxe-Coburg and Gotha. By royal proclamation, in 1917, the family name was changed to the more PR-friendly Windsor, after their castle in Berkshire. On hearing the news, Kaiser Wilhelm apparently said he was looking forward to seeing Shakespeare's play *The Merry Wives of Saxe-Coburg-Gotha.*

Others followed suit, with Prince Louis of the Battenberg branch of the family changing his name to the more reliable-sounding Mountbatten, while at the same time being ennobled as the 1st Marquess of Milford Haven. During World War II Prince Philip, whose mother Alice was the Marquess's daughter, decided to adopt the Mountbatten name in preference to the more cumbersome, and decidedly Germanic, Schleswig-Holstein-Sonderburg-Glücksburg (see box on p.66). After Philip's marriage to Princess Elizabeth, there was a dilemma over whether the family name should be Windsor or Mountbatten-Windsor. Churchill, the then prime minister, urged the Queen to choose Windsor. The only sop to Philip was the order the Queen issued in 1960, which states that those of her descendants who do not reign and have no other title may use the surname "Mountbatten-Windsor".

Kaiser's headquarters in Berlin. As well as being a cousin of George V and Wilhelm II, the Grand Duke was also the brother of the Tsarina Alexandra of Russia and the brother-in-law (and first cousin) of Prince Louis Battenberg, the First Sea Lord of the British Navy. Who amongst this hugely complex network of relations supported the Nazis in World War II is covered on p.180.

Foreign spouses

England's first post-Conquest queen, Matilda of Flanders, set the trend on several counts. For a start, she and William the Conqueror were cousins and only got papal approval retrospectively – a further twenty or so royal marriages would subsequently be guilty of consanguinity (bride and groom sharing a common ancestor), including the present Queen's. Matilda also aided and abetted her eldest son, Robert Curthose, when he

PHILIP OF SCHLESWIG-HOLSTEIN-SONDERBURG-GLÜCKSBURG

Prince Philip may appear an archetypal upper-class English gent, but in fact his family background is German-Danish from the House of Glücksburg. Despite being known in his youth as Philip, Prince of Greece – or "Pog" to his navy chums – he isn't the slightest bit Greek. "If anything, I've thought of myself as Scandinavian", he himself has said. His grandfather, Prince Wilhelm of Denmark, was asked to become King of the Hellenes at the age of just seventeen, after the previous incumbent had been deposed. His father, Andrew, spoke only Greek with his parents, but Philip's mother, Alice of Battenberg, was deaf from birth, and could lip-read and speak only English and German. English, French and German were spoken almost equally within the house – in his ninetieth-birthday interview, Philip says he was brought up speaking French. At the age of ten, his mother was diagnosed with schizophrenia and was committed to a Swiss sanatorium, after which she became a Greek Orthodox nun, while his father moved to Monte Carlo, leaving the English-based and German-based sides of the family to fight over who should take charge of Philip, who until then had been schooled in France.

In 1933, Philip was sent to Schloss Salem in Nazi Germany for a couple of terms, before following the German-Jewish educationist Kurt Hahn out of the country and off to Gordonstoun in northern Scotland. Philip's four older sisters all married Nazis in the early 1930s. Philip attended each wedding, and the funeral of Cecile and her German family, who died in an air crash in 1937. During his wartime service in the British Navy, Philip could only communicate with his sisters by writing to the Queen of Sweden, who happened to be his Aunt Louise – "[his sisters] would write to her," according to one of Philip's German relatives, "and she would copy out the letter and send it on to him." In 1946, in order to facilitate his engagement to Princess Elizabeth, he converted to Anglicanism and became a British citizen with the name Philip Mountbatten. However, when the wedding took place the following year, Philip was severely limited as to whom he could invite without causing offence: none of his sisters and their families were invited, only his mother.

decided to wage war against her husband. This became a regular feature of medieval queen consorts, with Eleanor of Aquitaine, wife of Henry II, probably the most rebellious and powerful of all the foreign spouses. She actively encouraged three of her sons to do battle with their father and in 1173 became the first (but by no means the last) queen consort to be imprisoned, in her case for supporting the future Henry III's revolt against her husband, for which she spent the next sixteen years incarcerated in various castles across England.

Most queen consorts were the object of a great deal of curiosity and, as foreigners, frequent animosity. After all, it was easier (and safer) to criticize a foreign-born queen than to criticize a king. Eleanor of Provence, wife of Henry III (from 1236), was lambasted for surrounding herself with a large retinue of greedy foreigners from her homeland and neighbouring Savoy. On one occasion, whilst sailing down the Thames, she was pelted with stones, rotten eggs and vegetables and had to take refuge at the home of the Bishop of London. Isabella of France, wife of Edward II (from 1308), was so unpopular that she was nicknamed the "She-Wolf of France". In 1326, she conspired with her lover Roger Mortimer, invaded England from France, and overthrew her husband, Edward II. For four years, she ruled the country with her lover before her son Edward III took control, executing Mortimer and briefly imprisoning Isabella.

It wasn't until the Reformation, however, that queen consorts began to attract criticism not simply for their foreignness, but for their religion. Henrietta Maria, wife of Charles I (from 1625), was very French and very Catholic at a time when it wasn't a good idea to be either. She refused to attend her new husband's coronation on religious grounds, and was seen "frisking and dancing" with her French ladies-in-waiting in Whitehall Palace instead. Charles II's wife, Catherine of Braganza, was Portuguese, Catholic, and like Henrietta Maria, spoke virtually no English. She was not destined to be a popular queen consort, and when she failed to produce a male heir, she paved the way for Charles's Catholic brother James II to take the throne. James's second wife, Mary of Modena, shared his religious preferences, and the two of them proved such a disaster that leading parliamentarians actually asked the Dutch to invade in 1688 (see p.60) and overthrow the monarchy. After that, no monarch was permitted to marry a Catholic, although in 2011 it was announced that the law would be changed (see p.6).

Few kings married for love, though one or two did find love within their arranged marriages to foreign princesses. Richard II was so devastated by the death of Anne of Bohemia that he had Sheen Palace, where she died, torn to the ground. More recently the modern expectation of marrying for love has caused enormous ructions in the royal family. Edward VIII was pressurized into abdicating because the object of his love, Wallis Simpson, was not only a foreigner and a commoner, but had also been twice divorced.

Before the recent wedding of Prince William, much attention was paid to the fact that Catherine Middleton was a "commoner" – that is neither royal nor a member of the nobility. When William becomes king, this – it was claimed – would make her the first queen born a commoner since Anne Hyde married James, Duke of York (later King James II). In fact a commoner is, simply, someone who isn't royal. Which makes Elizabeth Bowes-Lyon (the late Queen Mother) and Diana, Princess of Wales, both commoners, even though their backgrounds were aristocratic. George V was the last British monarch to marry a princess, Mary of Teck in 1893, while the last royal to do so was George, Duke of Kent in 1934 (see p.49).

In the past, precisely who royal princes married was an obvious cause for concern. James, Duke of York, had married Anne Hyde against the wishes of both his brother, King Charles II, and her father. When two of George III's brothers married commoners without even consulting him, the king instigated the Royal Marriages Act of 1772. This specified that no descendant of George II could marry without the monarch's consent, unless they were over 25 and had given one year's notice to the Privy Council (official advisers to the sovereign). The Act was regarded by many as tyrannical and was flouted by the king's son, George, Prince of Wales, when he illegally married the Catholic widow Maria Fitzherbert in 1785 (see p.89). The Act remains in force but is under review following the announcement in 2011 regarding the laws of succession.

Footnote: Two foreign queen consorts never even made it across the Channel. The most obscure is Berengaria of Navarre, whom Richard I married. It was never going to be a match made in heaven, given that Richard preferred the company of men. She was married and crowned in Cyprus, and remains the only English queen never to set foot in the country. The other queen never to make it to England was George I's wife, Sophia Dorothea of Celle, who was unwise enough to have an affair with a Swedish count (see p.165).

3

Heroes, villains and maverick monarchs

Here, in alphabetical order, is a selection of the brightest and best, wickedest and worst ever to have sat upon the British throne. From Alfred the Great to William and Mary, these are the iconic figures of national legend sitting alongside the more notorious characters of recent centuries – priapic princes, querulous queens and charismatic kings.

Alfred the Great (c.848–899)

Uniquely among all their kings, the English call Alfred "the Great". This is chiefly because he laid the foundations of England itself. He drove out the invading Danes (for a while). He strengthened the monarchy, making it a little less like a tribal overlordship and a little more like a sacred institution. And even if he wasn't actually the first king of all England, he was the first to gain ascendance over the seven micro-kingdoms of Anglo-Saxon times. His early biography reveals the makings of an unlikely military hero. Born in either 848 or 849, Alfred was a sickly and scholarly youth who apparently prayed for a disease to cure him of lust. He was rewarded with what sounds like a case of piles – although after marriage he developed what was probably an intestinal disorder, perhaps Crohn's Disease.

Three of his elder brothers rose to the throne of Wessex, a territory that waxed and waned in size but was centred on modern-day Hampshire, Wiltshire and Dorset. All three died, however – two of them in fighting the Danes, who were fast changing at this time from being booty-seeking "Viking" skirmishers to armies of conquest and colonization. Ascending to the throne in 871, Alfred bought himself time: first by fighting (the battles were inconclusive); and then by bribing the Danes to go away. This didn't mean going back to Denmark, however: by this time the Danes, under their overlord Guthrum, were firmly settled in the Danelaw, a huge swathe of England covering much of the Midlands, East Anglia and the northeast. There was little reason for them not to return to Wessex, and return they did, routing Alfred's forces in a surprise attack in January 878.

As the *Anglo-Saxon Chronicle* described it, "with a little band he made

his way by wood and swamp" into the Somerset marshes. This was the nadir of his reign. It was at this point that, careworn, he supposedly failed even to keep proper watch over an old woman's stove, and "burned the cakes". (In fact, the legend is a Germanic one that predates Alfred, and probably only got itself attached to his name after his death. Disappointingly the cakes in question weren't some kind of Saxon proto-brownie but a kind of ash-baked bread, more like oatcakes.)

In May 878, Alfred summoned the *fyrds*, or local militias, to a place called Egbert's Stone, and then marched to inflict a ringing defeat on Guthrum, forcing him not only to surrender but to convert to Christianity – a triumph that, for the devout Alfred, would have been far more gratifying than any military conquest, or even the treaty that he eventually made Guthrum sign.

A statue of Alfred the Great, erected in Winchester in 1901 to commemorate the 1000-year anniversary of his death. (Historians now believe he died in 899.)

Now there was time to do all the things for which he is now most famous. He devised a coherent military strategy, building and garrisoning some thirty *burhs* (forts), probably with wooden palisades on earth walls, and creating a standing army in place of the ad hoc *fyrd*. He also enlarged the royal fleet with new fighting ships that were developed to be twice the size of the Viking longboats: for this he is often celebrated as the founder of

ÆTHELRED THE UNREADY (C.968–1016)

Surprisingly few English kings have received epithets, the way so many continental monarchs do. The best ones are martial: William I "the Conqueror", Edward "Hammer of the Scots" and Richard I "the Lionheart"; though the pious-sounding Edwards of the Anglo-Saxon era aren't too bad – "the Martyr" and "the Confessor". There are oddities, such as "Longshanks", "Ironside" and "Crouchback", but the name that really stands out is Æthelred the Unready.

He was said to be "graceful in manners, beautiful in face and comely in appearance". But his reign was unfortunate. It began with his mother's (probable) murder of his half-brother Edward, who subsequently became the posthumous focus of his own martyr cult – which didn't help Æthelred. Then, in 980, Danish raiders came back to England for the first time in a century. Æthelred paid vast tribute to buy them off, and even fought a major battle at Maldon in 991 (celebrated in an epic poem, one of the classics of Old English literature).

In 994 a huge Viking fleet sailed against London. Æthelred's response to the chaos was to order the massacre of all Danish men (some say women and children too) in the English kingdoms. It took place on St Brice's Day, in November 1002 – and only made matters worse. By 1009, Danish war bands were roaming freely across the country that was only then just beginning to be called "Englalond", and in 1013 King Sweyn of Denmark launched a full-scale, vengeful invasion, his warriors plundering and raping unchecked for five months. Æthelred fled into exile in Normandy, returning a year later to find his kingdom in ruins. His own son, Edmund Ironside, had revolted, allowing Sweyn's heir, Canute, to conquer England.

Æthelred died in 1016. It was a reign "cruel at the outset, pitiable in mid-course and disgraceful in its ending", as William of Malmesbury put it in the 1120s. Yet the name "Unready" is undeserved. It's actually a mistranslation of an Anglo-Saxon pun: *Æþelræd* means "nobly advised" in Old English; adding *unræd* to it, as in the original *Æþelræd Unræd*, makes it "Nobly Advised / Ill-advised". So either his counsellors were dodgy or his policies were hopeless. Either way, it doesn't imply he wasn't *ready* for the Danes. He just couldn't cope with them when they came.

the English navy. Although Danish attacks continued through the 880s, he was able to enter London in triumph in 886. "All the English people who were not subject to the Danes," his tenth-century biographer Bishop Asser proudly wrote, "submitted to him". Asser added that he became "King of the Anglo-Saxons" – not quite King of England, but not far off it.

None of this, however, was what Alfred himself regarded as lastingly valuable. "I desired to live worthily," he wrote, "and to leave after my life, to the men who should come after me, the memory of me in good works." He tried to unify the English law code (with mixed success), and attracted scholars from across England to his court, where he sponsored a kind of academy for literacy and godliness. Armies were not the only way to defeat the Danes, Alfred believed: the king had to prove to God that the English were worthy of divine protection. He joined in the effort to translate key works from the Bible and the writings of the Church fathers from Latin into Old English. His writings are still read today and his name is remembered with significantly more pride and admiration than his fellow pious-yet-murdersome Anglo-Saxon kings.

Charles I (1600–1649)

On 30 January 1649, Charles I stepped out from a first-floor window of Whitehall's Banqueting House and onto a scaffold draped in black cloth. In the middle stood the axe and block. "It might have been a little higher," Charles said, on seeing the block. He tucked his dark locks up inside his cap. "Is my hair well?" Charles asked the masked executioner. He looked up to heaven, and then stooped down and laid his head on the block. He stretched his arms out to the side, the executioner swung his axe, and the King of England's head fell to the floor. The crowd groaned.

How did it go so horribly wrong for Charles? The second son of James I, "Baby Charles" was small, shy, and suffered from a stammer. Soon after his accession in 1625, he married the French Catholic princess Henrietta Maria, with whom he had six children. He had a weakness for beautiful things, and an eye for expensive clothes and Italian art. He collected Titian and Raphael and he patronized some of the seventeenth century's greatest artists: Van Dyck, Rubens, Bernini.

But Charles had an inflated sense of his position. Although he could be an attentive king, he liked the pomp and loftiness of majesty and carefully restricted audiences to his sacred person. He was too easily swayed by his counsellors (his chief minister and favourite George Villiers, Duke of

Buckingham, was loathed by the public) and he supported Archbishop William Laud's unpopular affection for Popish rituals. As the asset-stripped churches began to be restocked with crosses and candles, the Puritans feared that their beloved Reformation was being slammed into reverse. Charles's greatest flaw was his unshakeable belief – inherited from his father – in his divine right to rule. "Kings are not bound to give an account of their actions but to God alone," he said. When faced with a House of Commons that criticized his policies and refused to finance his ill-advised wars on the continent, Charles's solution was to simply dissolve parliament and go it alone.

From 1629 to 1640, Charles ruled without once summoning parliament. With the help of a team of top lawyers, he financed this "eleven years' tyranny" by imposing illegal taxes. In 1637, Charles infuriated the Presbyterian Scottish Kirk by trying to force them to accept the English prayer book. When his Scottish subjects resisted, Charles sent in his army. "I will rather die," he said, "than yield to their impertinent and damnable demands." But Charles was decisively beaten and had to grovel to parliament for money in order to crush the rebels. The disaffected MPs took this opportunity to vent their own grievances and claw back power. Charles was willing to compromise on some things, but refused to give way on religion. On 22 August 1642, after months of failed talks, the king raised the royal standard at Nottingham. England was at war.

For the next seven years, Royalists (Cavaliers) fought Parliamentarians (Roundheads) on bloody battlefields all over England. The Civil War did not set out to abolish monarchy, but Charles failed to see that he could regain authority by conceding some of his power. Instead, he tried to bargain with both the Scots and the English, and made false promises to each. This risky strategy backfired. When Charles fled to Scotland in 1646, the Scots handed him back to the English parliament, who were now running the country. From his cell in Carisbrooke Castle on the Isle of Wight, Charles then hatched a plan with the Scots: in return for invading England and putting him back on his throne, he promised to establish Presbyterianism in England. But Charles underestimated the might and fervour of the New Model Army, headed up by Oliver Cromwell. After their spectacular victory at the Battle of Preston in 1648, the most radical of the army leaders now pushed to put the king on trial for waging war against his own subjects. Charles was a tyrant, "the grand author of our troubles", who should be brought to justice for the "treason, blood and mischief he is guilty of".

But from the moment Charles went on trial, during which he behaved with dignity and resolve, he was transformed in the minds of many from tyrant to martyr. He was canonized in 1660, and the day of his execution remained a feast day in the English Church until 1894. Charles may have defied England's ancient laws by his, er, cavalier attitude to parliament, but he was still an anointed king. It's a measure of how the monarch was still regarded that, during his reign, thousands of sick Englishmen and women had flocked to his court to be cured by his supposedly magic, healing hands. His death horrified many, even his enemies. Those who had fought so hard for liberty definitely did not want Charles. But did they really want Cromwell instead?

Charles II (1630–1685)

His subjects called him the Merry Monarch for his jovial nature, ready wit and constant partying. But Charles II had little to be merry about. His enduring reputation was a triumph of relentless good humour over bitter experience.

Charles was born on 29 May 1630, the son and heir of King Charles I of England. He was titled Duke of Cornwall and Duke of Rothesay, and granted lands, wealth and servants to match. But trouble was coming: in 1642 war broke out between King Charles I and his parliament.

Young Charles was fitted out in a miniature suit of armour and sent off to Devon to become "commander" of the King's forces in the West Country (real authority lay with Sir Ralph Hopton). Nevertheless, Charles trotted about bravely enough until the disastrous Battle of Torrington in February 1646, after which Hopton sent him packing to France to avoid capture. Charles was still on the continent three years later, when his father was beheaded in London by the Parliamentarians.

Charles tried to regain his throne by force, but the venture ended in bloody defeat at the Battle of Worcester in 1651. He went on the run, famously hiding up an oak tree to escape Roundhead cavalry who were searching the thickets. After weeks of great hardship, Charles made it to France, where he lived on the charity of his French relations. He consoled himself by having an affair with Lucy Waters, daughter of a fellow exile, and indulging in sports and heavy drinking. Lucy gave Charles an illegitimate son: James, the future Duke of Monmouth.

Back in England, the rule of parliament and its army had become increasingly unpopular. Cromwell died in 1658 and within a year a group of nobles, merchants and MPs had decided that Britain's future was best served by a monarch ruling with the advice of parliament. They sent a

Absolutist Charles II, in all his finery.

message to Charles asking if he would accept the Crown on their conditions. Charles arrived in London on 19 May 1660 and cheerfully agreed to everything asked of him in constitutional and political terms. He requested two things in return: that the nine men he blamed most for his father's death should be executed; and that those who helped him escape from Worcester should be rewarded. His return was blighted by the death of his beloved younger sister Mary and their brother Henry from small-pox, caught in London.

As king, Charles took care not to argue with parliament. He worked tirelessly to be popular with the middle classes who had shown their political muscle in the Civil War. He ostentatiously favoured popular entertainments such as going to the theatre – where he met the notorious Nell Gwyn, the most infamous of his mistresses. Charles developed a precursor to the three-piece suit, by mixing the old formal court dress with the simpler woollen outfits worn by country gentlemen. He founded the Chelsea Hospital for old soldiers and was the patron of many other charitable institutions.

The stories of Charles's love of a good time were many: typically tales of epic dinners accompanied by copious drinking. At one such feast, Charles announced that the joint of roast beef in front of him was the finest meat ever served. He demanded to know what cut it was, to be told it was a loin. Charles lurched to his feet, whipped out his sword and knighted the beef, declaring: "This is a simple loin no more, now it is a Sir Loin." And so the cut known as sirloin was born.

In his later years, Charles's life was blighted by the inability of his wife, the Portuguese princess Catherine of Braganza, to produce children. This was unfortunate, as it meant that Charles's unpopular younger brother James, Duke of York, remained heir to the throne. Charles was dragged into a series of political squabbles and predicted disaster for James after his death. Then young James, Duke of Monmouth, began claiming that Charles had in fact married Lucy Waters, which would have made him heir to the throne. Monmouth's documents turned out to be forgeries, but the affair can't have done his father's blood pressure any favours.

On 2 February 1685, Charles suffered a sudden fit and was taken to his bed. Death was coming, but Charles faced his end with his usual wit. "I am sorry, gentlemen, for being such a time a-dying", he quipped at the mournful faces around him. Then his thoughts turned, as they so often had, to women. He called his brother James to his side, gripped his hand and begged "Let not poor Nell starve". They were his last words.

Edward I (1239–1307)

Edward was tall, muscular and had a ferocious temper. He could reduce grown men to tears; it was said that the Dean of St Paul's dropped dead of a heart attack during a heated argument with Edward. Unsurprisingly, Edward's reign was characterized by warfare, violence and disputes.

Born on 18 June 1239, Edward had a quiet childhood. In 1254 he married Eleanor of Castile as part of a political treaty arranged by his father Henry III. Edward and Eleanor remained devoted to each other until Eleanor's death in 1290, and together had sixteen children. Edward was given Gascony, an English possession in southwestern France, to rule. He acquitted himself well, but fell out with his father in 1259 when he announced that he supported the aims of the "reformist" barons, led by Simon de Montfort. (While their complaints lay in the amount of power wielded by the king, they were ultimately out for themselves.) Once war broke out, however, Edward fought for his father. He was defeated at Lewes in 1264, and de Montfort became ruler of England. But he only held onto power for a year; Edward bested and killed de Montfort at Evesham in 1265, having disguised his army by flying de Montfort's colours. He executed the chief rebels, but urged his father to accept many of the main "democratic" reforms that de Montfort had championed.

With England pacified, the restless Edward decided to go on crusade. He recruited a thousand men, and in August 1270 arrived in Tunis, just as the French made peace with the local Emir. He next sailed off to Acre, again arriving just as a truce was agreed. With no fighting left to do, Edward went to Sicily where he met a messenger bringing news of the death of his father. But Edward saw no need to hurry home, with England at peace. He spent two years touring Italy and France before returning to London, and was crowned in August 1274.

Once crowned, Edward began an extensive and far-reaching series of legal reforms. The particulars of all land holdings were put on a firm written basis, along with the taxes pertaining to them and the rights that went with them. Local officials were made subject to periodic investigation by royal officials, who came down hard on corruption and laziness. Assorted new laws brought the regulation of trade under royal justice, giving merchants enforceable rights in business dealings.

In 1282 a war with Wales broke out when Dafydd ap Gruffydd, Prince of Wales and a former English ally, led a rebellion against Edward. Earlier kings of England had been content to enforce an overlordship on the Welsh princes and noblemen, leaving them more or less to themselves. But Edward took a more dictatorial view, seeking to impose English law on Wales, a hardline stance that lent Dafydd's stance broad popularity among Welshmen. Edward campaigned energetically, eventually defeating the Welsh after a series of battles. He built a network of impregnable castles and fortified towns, inhabited by English immigrants, to enforce

English rule over Wales. Finally he appointed his own son, the future Edward II, to be Prince of Wales. While there continued to be sporadic uprisings, Welsh independence had effectively ended.

In 1290 the royal dynasty of Scotland died out with the death of Margaret, "Maid of Norway". No fewer than fourteen Scottish noblemen announced that they had a claim to the Scottish throne. Civil war loomed, so the nobles took the fateful decision to ask Edward to decide who had the best claim to be king. Edward consented and in 1292 chose John Balliol, who owned large estates in England and had agreed that Edward would be his feudal overlord.

Edward took this promise literally and interfered in Scottish affairs so much that in 1296 Scottish nobles raised an army, ousted Balliol and invaded England. He responded with a massive invasion of Scotland, crushing opposition at the Battle of Dunbar on 27 April 1296. He then loaded the coronation Stone of Destiny (also known as the Stone of Scone) on a cart and took it to London, hoping that no future King of Scotland could be crowned without his permission. The Stone remained in Westminster Abbey until 1996 (with one temporary removal, after it was stolen in 1950), when it was moved to Edinburgh.

Back in England Edward now ran into his first serious domestic problems. The cost of the wars in Wales and Scotland had been immense, and Edward's talented chancellor, Robert Burnell, had died in 1292. Edward tried to introduce new taxes and financial demands, but met determined opposition from the Earls of Norfolk and Hereford. Parliament was in uproar and even the Church turned against the king. Edward's problems were made worse when he fell out with his son, Edward Prince of Wales. The younger Edward was spending money he did not have and lavishing gifts on his favourite, a young Gascon knight named Piers Gaveston.

The threat of civil war in England was averted only by the news from Scotland that an upstart named Robert Bruce had proclaimed himself King of Scotland and defeated the English army at Stirling Bridge. England pulled together to meet the threat and Edward mustered a new army for war. He marched north with his son in tow, Gaveston having been exiled to France. In 1307, Edward was within seven miles of the border when he fell ill with dysentery. It soon became evident he was dying.

Edward's final act was to summon the Earls of Lincoln and Warwick to his bedside. He made them promise to advise the new king, to oversee the national finances and above all to make sure Piers Gaveston never returned to England.

Edward II (1284–1327)

Edward II was in many ways everything a good medieval king ought to be: tall, muscular, good looking, witty, intelligent and proficient with sword and lance. At the same time, he was averse to hard work, detested the hardships of military campaigning and preferred growing flowers to checking government paperwork.

On becoming king, Edward called off the campaign in Scotland and hurried back to London. There he sent for his great friend (and reputed lover) Piers Gaveston. This dashing young Gascon knight wielded an untoward amount of influence over the king in the early years of his reign: Edward had quickly repealed Gaveston's banishment to France and made him Earl of Cornwall. Like Edward, Gaveston was handsome, witty and dedicated to having a good time. His wit was often cruel and he delighted in teasing and cracking jokes about English nobles and prelates. In 1308 Edward travelled to France to marry Isabella, daughter of King Philip IV of France, and left Gaveston as acting regent. He managed to annoy almost everyone.

In 1311 the barons and bishops confronted Edward and demanded he agree to a list of 41 ordinances. These, for the first time, drew a distinction between the king's personal wealth and the finances of government, as well as between government officials and the king's personal appointments. They also provided for a council of nobles – the Lords Ordainers – to oversee the decisions of the king and for annual meetings of parliament to allow merchants and knights to have their say as well. Article 20 exiled Gaveston from England for life.

Edward agreed to the ordinances, but played for time over the exile of Gaveston. Finally, in November 1311, Gaveston left England, but returned two months later, whereupon Edward once again declared his exile unlawful and restored his lands. This was too much for the Lords Ordainers, who, under the leadership of the Earl of Lancaster, decided to take Gaveston captive and then negotiate with the king. In the end, an assembly of barons condemned the upstart Gascon to death for breaking his exile; he was killed and beheaded on Lancaster's land. The murder enraged Edward and split the Ordainers. Edward began to claw back royal powers.

Then, in the spring of 1314, news arrived from Scotland. The last English stronghold, Stirling Castle, was under siege. Sensing an opportunity to win glory, gain popularity and undermine the Ordainers, Edward gathered a large army of some 2500 knights and 20,000 infantry and marched to Stirling. On 22 June the Scots, led by nobleman Robert Bruce (who had declared himself King of Scotland in 1306), launched a dawn assault on the English camp. Edward's army were taken by surprise in the cramped space between the River Forth and the Bannock Burn; they were destroyed piecemeal by the Scots. Edward escaped unharmed, but his reputation was shattered.

Back in England, Edward became increasingly reliant on Hugh, Baron Despenser. Although a talented administrator, he was also corrupt and siphoned royal lands into his own hands. Despenser's son, Hugh the Younger, was by 1318 Edward's new favourite (and possibly lover). He outdid his father in grabbing lands by questionable means and fell out with the popular Roger Mortimer, Earl of March, who led a post-Ordainers style rebellion against the king, known as the Despenser War. The attempted coup was unsuccessful, and Mortimer escaped execution by fleeing to France.

Edward appeared to have triumphed over his domestic enemies. He then made a fatal error, sending his long-suffering wife Isabella and eldest son Edward to France as a peace envoy between the two countries. However, once in France, Isabella began to raise an army with which to invade England, and began an affair with Roger Mortimer. In September 1326 they landed in Suffolk with Prince Edward in tow, announcing that they had come to restore good government and destroy the Despensers. Mortimer's men quickly rounded up Edward and his relatively few followers. The Despensers were put through a quick trial and executed, along with a number of their sympathizers and followers.

Isabella summoned a parliament and asked it to pass an act deposing Edward II in favour of his son, Edward. Instead it passed an act that removed the powers of the monarch from the elder Edward, yet left him as king. Mortimer sent the news to Edward along with a message inviting him to abdicate or risk the consequences. Edward abdicated at Kenilworth on 20 January 1327, then moved to one of Mortimer's castles at Berkeley. In October the news of his death was announced – from natural causes, according to Mortimer. Rumours abounded that the former king had been murdered on the orders of Mortimer. One account said he had been suffocated, another that he was strangled and a third that he had died following horrific tortures, involving a red-hot poker being inserted into a private place. Some historians believe he wasn't executed at all, and that he may have died in Italy around 1341.

Edward VII (1841–1910)

The oldest monarch yet to have inherited the British crown, Edward had to wait until he was sixty years old before he could sit on the throne. After the long wait, his actual reign was something of an anticlimax. Yet he still managed to give his name to the Edwardian era.

Edward was born on 9 November 1841 and was granted the title of Prince of Wales one month later. He received army training, but his mother, Queen Victoria, felt that a military career was too dangerous and insisted he be removed from any significant duties. Instead she wanted Edward to undertake the "public good will" appearances expected of a royal, while she herself got on with the more serious monarchical duties.

Edward's first outing in this role was a visit to North America in 1860. He started off in Canada, opening a number of buildings and bridges, before moving on to the US to visit President Buchanan, pay respects at the tomb of George Washington and meet a wide variety of celebrities. The tour was judged to be a great success and, buoyed by Edward's public acclaim, Victoria began laying plans for Edward's marriage. She was keen on Princess Alexandra of Denmark and surreptitiously arranged for the pair to meet up in September 1861. The two got on very well.

It was therefore with great anger that Victoria learned that Edward had been caught in his tent with a woman when on military manoeuvres. The ailing Prince Albert was sufficiently annoyed to leave his sick bed to deliver a stern lecture to Edward. Albert died a few days later, and Victoria blamed Edward for his death. Mother and son never repaired their relationship.

Despite this incident, Edward and Alexandra married in March 1863. The marriage was to be a happy one, largely because both

Royal pomp, Edwardian-style: the first twentieth-century monarch.

greatly enjoyed a lively social life and regularly entertained at their home in Marlborough House. They had five children and, although he was happy at home, there were many rumours of affairs: Edward liked the company of pretty women. In 1870 Edward was called as a witness in the divorce proceedings of Sir Charles Mordaunt and it was suspected he was to be named as an adulterer, though in fact he bore witness only to household arrangements. It was not Edward's only appearance in a court. In 1891 he was called as a witness in a libel trial brought by Sir William Gordon-Cumming following allegations he had been cheating at cards. Again, Edward's evidence proved to be disappointingly unexciting.

Setting the template for the treadmill of royal tours and meet-and-greets that is the lot of today's royals, Edward continued with a busy schedule of visits to various parts of Britain and the Empire. He opened the Thames Embankment in 1871 and embarked on a lengthy tour of India in 1875. His special insistence on meeting a variety of local people, not just civic dignitaries, broke with tradition and largely endeared him to the press and public. The press picked up on his fashion sense. Among other sartorial innovations, he left the bottom button of his waistcoat undone, wore tweed, turned down the collar of his shirts and pioneered the black dinner suit as a more practical outfit than the previously fashionable white tie and tails.

Kingship finally came his way on 22 January 1901. He reintroduced much of the pomp and ritual of monarchy that his mother had neglected, donning a variety of splendid outfits to show himself off to his subjects during ceremonies. Interestingly, despite the lands and properties associated with monarchy, Edward was the first monarch to accede to the throne and not be in personal debt since the sixteenth century and, through astute financial management, he died in credit as well.

Edward enthusiastically engaged in reforms of the military, deeming them to be necessary after the poor showing of the British army in the Boer War of 1899–1902. His main role in politics, however, was in foreign affairs. He was, after all, related to almost every other European monarch. His visit to Russia in 1906 helped defuse an explosive situation between Russia and the UK. The two nations had been on the brink of war following the Dogger Bank incident of 1904: during the Russo-Japanese war, British trawlers in the North Sea had been attacked by Russian warships, which had mistaken them for Japanese naval vessels.

In March 1910 Edward collapsed while on holiday in Biarritz. He returned to London in April but on 6 May suffered a series of heart attacks. In the later afternoon he was told that his horse Witch of the Air had won a race. "I am very glad," replied the king, then lost consciousness.

Elizabeth I (1533–1603)

When Anne Boleyn was crowned Queen of England in 1533, visibly pregnant, the crowd cheered for the unborn boy in her belly. Unfortunately, the hoped-for he turned out to be a she. A baby girl, Elizabeth, was born in the afternoon of 7 September 1533.

Despite her parents' disappointment at her gender, nearly 500 years later Elizabeth has been the subject of countless films and television dramas, and is the most recognizable of all British monarchs. She ruled for a staggering 44 years and was mythologized as Gloriana, the Virgin Queen and Good Queen Bess – her name synonymous with the triumph of Protestantism, the defeat of the Spanish Armada and England's golden age of Shakespeare and maritime adventure. But Elizabeth is also the most misrepresented of all monarchs.

For most of the sixteenth century, the chances of Elizabeth becoming queen at all were pretty slim. It required both of her siblings to die without leaving any children and on Elizabeth being recognized as legitimate. Her father had branded her with the mark of bastardy when her brother Edward was born, and her sister Mary had desperately tried to block her from the succession. But, on 17 November 1558, hours after Mary's death, the 25-year-old auburn-haired princess, whose mother had been condemned as a whore, was proclaimed Queen of England at her home in Hatfield. She fell to her knees. "This is the Lord's doing; it is marvellous in our eyes," she cried out.

Elizabeth's first challenge as queen was to restore the Act of Royal Supremacy instigated by her Protestant father, Henry VIII (it had been repealed by her Catholic sister, Mary I). The English monarch was "the only supreme head on earth of the Church in England" once again. But Elizabeth's beliefs were relatively moderate and her keenness to retain certain Catholic rites and symbols were to bring her into conflict with many of her bishops and advisers – including her right-hand man Sir William Cecil, who wanted her to espouse a more austere version of Protestantism. The Act of Uniformity, passed in 1559, reinstated the English Book of Common Prayer and made church attendance compulsory. Those who refused to conform, however, were not severely punished. Elizabeth may be remembered now as the champion Protestant queen, but for many of her councillors and clergy, her reforms never went far enough.

England was not on the whole accustomed to queens regnant, whatever their religion. It was hoped by the inner circle that Elizabeth would listen to the men around her, particularly when it came to two major

Gloriana, the Faerie Queen, Good Queen Bess: the most mythologized monarch since Arthur.

concerns: her marriage and the succession. We cannot know whether Elizabeth really did intend to live and die "a virgin", as she herself prophesied, or whether some of her favourite courtiers were also her lovers, but the subject of her marriage was a hot topic for nearly twenty years. There were some serious contenders for her hand: her brother-in-law Philip II of Spain; her childhood friend and favourite Lord Robert Dudley; King Eric XIV of Sweden; the archdukes Ferdinand and Charles of Austria; and her "little frog", the Duke of Anjou. Elizabeth remained inscrutable.

Finally, it became clear that this ageing monarch would never marry, and would die childless. As a result, the succession crisis dogged Elizabeth's reign until her death. She never agreed to name her heir, even when she fell seriously ill with smallpox in 1562. Waiting in the wings and hoping to seize the crown was her Catholic cousin Mary Queen of Scots – whom Elizabeth later had executed in 1587 – and those usurping Greys, the descendants of Henry VIII's younger sister, Mary. (Lady Jane Grey had already tried to claim the throne in 1553.) Elizabeth's refusal to name her successor is, perhaps, an indicator of how insecure she felt on her own throne – and with some cause.

LADY JANE GREY (1536–1554)

Mary Tudor's toppling of Lady Jane Grey, after only nine days as queen, was the only successful rebellion in the entire Tudor period. Poor young Jane owes her "Nine Day Queen" epithet to a peculiar custom. Newly proclaimed monarchs had to take possession of the Tower of London and stay there for ten days before they could be crowned. When Edward VI died in July 1547, Jane was rushed to the Tower. During the next nine days, Mary – Henry VIII's first child and Edward's half-sister – rallied her troops, won over the privy council and was proclaimed the rightful Queen of England. Jane was never crowned. In fact, she never again left the Tower.

Before his death, Edward and the meddling and ambitious Duke of Northumberland had tried to overturn the acts of succession that Henry VIII had passed. Choosing to ignore Henry's reinstatement of his own daughters, Mary and Elizabeth, to the royal line, they jumped to the descendants of Henry's younger sister, Mary, because this line – the Suffolk line – was safely Protestant. And English. Jane was also young and already married, rather conveniently, to Northumberland's own son Guildford Dudley. Mary, of course, was Spanish, Catholic, unmarried and 37 years old. But to take the crown away from the legitimate Tudor heir, the "lawful and natural daughter of our King Henry VIII'", shocked even the most hardened of Protestants.

At first Mary was lenient, and spared her sixteen-year-old cousin's life. But, in the wake of Wyatt's Rebellion – an unsuccessful coup, led by Sir Thomas Wyatt, ostensibly out of concern over Mary potentially marrying Philip of Spain – the date of the execution was set. Jane and her husband were beheaded on 12 February 1554. She is now remembered as a Protestant martyr and tragic heroine who, in her final moments, stumbled blindfolded towards the block crying "Where is it? What shall I do?" She may have died at the hands of a Catholic queen, but it was her family who were more to blame: they sent her on a doomed attempt to claim the English throne, like a lamb to the slaughter.

Throughout Elizabeth's reign, Spain remained a major power, and a huge threat to Protestant England. In 1588, a fleet of Spanish ships sailed up the Channel and prepared to invade. Elizabeth, clad in silver-plated armour, addressed her troops at Tilbury in Essex, and uttered the stirring and much-quoted words: "I know I have the body of a weak and feeble woman, but I have the heart and stomach of a King, and a King of England too." What Elizabeth did not know was that by this point the Spanish Armada already had been driven off and were on their way home. Nevertheless, it was Elizabeth's finest hour.

Elizabeth's last years were marked by political factionalism, bad harvests, poverty and anxiety about the succession. Gloriana painted her face white and wore a wig. Artists ignored her wrinkles and smallpox scars and presented her as eternally young, and surrounded by the symbols of her now iconic virginity: pearls, a crescent moon and a sieve. She died, aged 69, on 24 March 1603, having finally given the nod that her council had been waiting for: James VI of Scotland, the son of Mary Queen of Scots, would inherit the throne. England would have a king.

Soon enough, however, as the Stuarts began to disappoint both courtiers and public, the English began to miss their Good Queen Bess – and the cult of Elizabeth was revived with a vengeance.

George III (1738–1820)

The life and achievements of King George III have been obscured by his periodic bouts of madness. Those episodes marked only the end of his life – for his first fifty years, he was perfectly healthy, and lived into his eighties.

George was born in London on 4 June 1738, making him the first of the Hanoverian dynasty to be born in Britain. From the age of ten he was studying chemistry, physics, astronomy, mathematics, French, Latin, history, music, geography, commerce, agriculture, constitutional law, dancing, fencing and riding. Of these, agriculture was his favourite and he took such an interest in the industry that he was often nicknamed "Farmer George".

When he was eighteen George fell in love with Lady Sarah Lennox, but was forbidden to marry her by his grandfather, George II. He then turned down a number of proposed political marriages, but when he became king in 1760 he accepted that he had to marry. His choice of bride was Princess Charlotte from the obscure German Duchy of Mecklenburg-Strelitz. The marriage would prove to be a success, with both partners remaining faithful to each other and fifteen children being born. However, the first few years were unhappy for Charlotte, who struggled to learn English and was confused by British manners. Eventually she found herself a role as a patron of the arts and of botany.

The early years of George's reign were dominated by the Seven Years War against France and by attempts to bolster royal finances. British allies in Europe fared badly in the war, but Britain triumphed. In India, Africa, the Caribbean and North America the French were defeated and stripped of profitable colonies. King George, meanwhile, solved his personal financial problems by surrendering the Crown Lands to parliament in return for fixed annual payments to himself and other members of the royal family. The civil list was the basis for the funding of the royal family for centuries, only replaced in 2013 with the Sovereign Grant.

For a decade following the war, British politics and George's family life were both fairly quiet. However, in the North American colonies trouble was brewing. The British government had imposed steep taxes to help pay the costs of the war, and had introduced regulations to control settlement and trade in the newly acquired French lands. The colonists resented paying the taxes and bridled at having to obey British regulations.

The simmering discontent came to a head in 1775, when British commanders in Massachusetts sought to disarm the local militia. Fighting broke out and before long the colonial militias were effectively at war with the British army. In 1776, thirteen of the British colonies declared their independence from Britain and the war became official. George was determined to win back control of the colonies, even when France and Spain joined the war against Britain. However, once America was well and truly lost, and George had signed the treaty recognizing colonial independence, he came to regard the new United States of America as a potential ally and trading partner. When the first US ambassador arrived in London, George greeted him very warmly.

In the years that followed, George was increasingly occupied by disputes with parliament. He believed that, as king, he was a better judge of the national mood than MPs were, each representing only a small area. He was not helped in these squabbles by the fact that, in the summer of 1788, he fell ill, suffering from memory loss, bouts of compulsive talking to himself and periods of severe confusion. He left London to rest at Cheltenham, but his mental illness baffled the royal doctors, as the symptoms were unlike that of other forms of madness they had encountered. Suddenly, in the spring of 1789, the king rapidly improved and by May seemed to be entirely sane.

War with revolutionary France had broken out, a situation that would cast a shadow over the rest of George's reign. He suffered recurrent bouts of mental illness in 1800, 1801 and 1804, but each time recovered. His doctors and ministers, however, were wary of involving the sexagenarian king too much in government business as he had become so unpredictable.

In 1810 his favourite daughter, Princess

One of numerous unflattering pictures of George III.

Amelia, died of tuberculosis. George again fell ill, and this time his madness was compounded by rheumatism and near blindness. Parliament passed a Regency Act transferring royal powers to Prince George (later King George IV) in 1811. George III never recovered and he died on 29 January 1820.

George IV (1762–1830)

One of the most colourful and extravagant individuals ever to sit on the British throne, George IV set the fashions for what became known as the Regency Period, and was famous for his wit and charm. Yet he managed to drag the prestige of the monarchy to one of its lowest ever levels.

George was born on 12 August 1762, the eldest son of King George III. His childhood was spent at home with his parents, where his tutors reported him to be clever but lazy. At the age of 21 Prince George left the nest and set up in London's Carlton House, with pocket money of £50,000 per year. He plunged into a lifestyle of heavy drinking, wild womanizing and excessive spending. He is rumoured to have fathered between one and four illegitimate children during these years. While his antics earned him the nickname "First Gentleman of Europe", they made his father furious.

Young George fell in love with the high-society girl Maria Fitzherbert, who was deemed unsuitable wife material on all fronts: a commoner, a widow and a Catholic. George married her anyway in December 1785 in the drawing room of her house in Park Street; the Prince paid off the £500 debts of one of his chaplains, springing him from the Fleet Prison, in order for him to wed the pair. The marriage was invalid in law as King George III had not given his permission. Two girls officially said to be Mrs Fitzherbert's nieces may have been her children by George.

George's debts continued to rise rapidly and by 1795 had reached £630,000. George III agreed to pay them off, but only if George married a suitable bride. The old king fixed on Princess Caroline of Brunswick, thereby securing the help of Brunswick and other German states in the war against revolutionary France. When the pair first met, George is said to have gasped: "Pray, give me a glass of brandy!" The wedding took place on 8 April 1795, and nine months later Caroline gave birth to Princess Charlotte. Thereafter Mrs Fitzherbert took up most of George's attention and the king and queen separated. Caroline's access to her daughter was restricted following rumours of infidelities on her part (which were found, after an official inquiry conducted by senior officials, to be groundless). In 1814, Caroline left England for Italy.

George was fond of the seaside town of Brighton, where he could party in a converted farmhouse away from the prying eyes of his father's servants. In 1815 George hired the famed architect John Nash to transform the farmhouse into an exotic palace – the Royal Pavilion – at enormous cost.

Meanwhile, in 1810, the prince's father was again suffering from mental health issues; the following year the Regency Act appointed Prince George as regent. George was generally happy to let his ministers and parliament get on with the business of running the country. It was under George that the custom was established that parliament recommend a prime minister to the monarch: before then it had been the other way round.

By the time George became king in 1820, his attitude to money, his dissolute lifestyle and treatment of his wife had made him deeply unpopular. Caroline returned to Britain, becoming the focus of a popular reform movement that opposed George. George attempted to divorce her via the introduction of a new measure to parliament, the Pains and Penalties

Bill, which was in essence nothing more than a convoluted way of declaring Caroline to have committed adultery. Following public outcry, it was abandoned before it could be debated in the House of Commons.

George planned a vast coronation celebration, costing ten times as much as his father's had. The day was marred when the estranged Queen Caroline arrived and hammered on the locked doors of Westminster Abbey, demanding to be let in. The following year, in July 1821, Caroline fell ill and died three weeks later, having alleged that George had poisoned her.

George's most significant interventions into affairs of state centred upon his resistance towards Catholic emancipation. He argued that his coronation oath to defend the Protestant faith precluded him from supporting any pro-Catholic measures. Influenced by his rabidly anti-Catholic brother, the Duke of Cumberland, George's to-ing and fro-ing

MINORS AND THEIR REGENTS

Regents have been appointed on numerous occasions when the reigning monarch has been unable to rule for reasons of absence, health or youth. But while absence or illness tend to be short-term problems, youth can last for years. In 1216 Henry III came to the throne of England at the age of twelve. His regent, William Marshal, was honest and hard-working, but he died after three years and was replaced by Hubert, Earl of Kent – just as hard-working but nowhere near as honest.

Henry VI became king in 1422, at the age of nine months. He had two regents, his uncles John, Duke of Bedford, and Humphrey, Duke of Gloucester. Both men did a reasonable if unspectacular job. Edward V was less lucky in his regent. His uncle, Richard of Gloucester, ousted the teenage king to take the throne for himself; he may well have been his murderer.

Scottish royals seem to get through a lot of regents. In 1286, thirteen-year-old Queen Margaret of Scotland had a council of six regents to rule Scotland while she was in Norway. She died before she ever arrived at her realm. In 1329 the five-year-old David II had the Earl of Moray as Guardian of Scotland. Moray then died and was replaced by the Earl of Mar, who was promptly killed in battle against the English. Next was Sir Andrew Murray, who was taken prisoner by the English, leaving the way open for Sir Archibald Douglas, also killed by the English. Then came joint guardians, Robert Stewart and John, the new Earl of Moray. They fell out, so Stewart resigned, while Moray tried to invade England and was killed in battle for his pains. Young King David was captured, doubtless despairing over the general uselessness of his so-called guardians.

over giving assent to the Catholic Relief Act so annoyed the cabinet that they resigned in protest – forcing the king into a U-turn.

George did not age well; he grew very fat, losing the athletic figure of his youth, and took rather more laudanum than was good for him, alongside heavy drinking. He became increasingly reclusive, his weight topping 17 stone; he suffered from gout, arteriosclerosis, dropsy and possibly porphyria. His beloved daughter Charlotte had died in childbirth in 1817, and many thought he never really recovered. He had also split from his mistress Maria, though he kept all her letters, reading and re-reading them frequently. By 1828 he would spend entire weeks in bed and suffered bouts of forgetfulness.

At 3am on 26 June 1830 George suddenly sat bolt upright in bed and grabbed the page who was sitting by his bedside. "Good God. What is this?" demanded the king. He stared for a while at something the page could not see, then declared "Oh. My boy, it is death".

George VI (1895–1952)

"Everything is going now. Before long I shall also have to go." These words, spoken by George VI in 1948, were addressed to the writer Vita Sackville-West, after she had told him that her ancestral home was being handed over to the National Trust. The king died just four years later. But his remark wasn't so much a reference to his own mortality as a pessimistic view of the future of the British monarchy. After all, his unanticipated reign had witnessed the end of the British Empire following the horrors and upheavals of World War II. He was the last Emperor of India and the first Head of the Commonwealth.

Christened Albert Frederick Arthur George, he was known as "Bertie" to his family. As a child, he suffered from ill health. His father, George V, was an arch-conformist and a stickler for form, and both parents were largely removed from their children's day-to-day upbringing. Bertie had a stammer, and was forced to write with his right hand although naturally left-handed; he also suffered from chronic stomach problems as well as knock knees, for which he was forced to wear painful corrective splints. Like two of his brothers, he trained for the navy, coming consistently near the bottom of his year while at naval college.

In his twenties, Bertie met Elizabeth Bowes-Lyon at various society balls and functions. A bright, popular girl, she was the ninth child of a prominent Scottish aristocrat, the Earl of Strathmore. Bertie, who was

Reluctant monarch George VI addresses the nation at the outbreak of war in September 1939.

now Duke of York, had to propose three times before Elizabeth finally said yes: on the first occasion, the famously shy prince had used a go-between. They were married at Westminster Abbey in 1923. His bride later wrote that she did not love Bertie when she married him, but grew to love him over time. A year after their wedding, the couple undertook an official tour of East Africa and the Sudan: two years after that their first child, Elizabeth, was born.

In the same year, 1926, the Duke of York decided to do something about his stammer following the painful ordeal of giving a public speech at the British Empire Exhibition. The therapy he received from Australian Lionel Logue boosted his self-confidence and went a long way to solving the problem, though his stammer never completely disappeared. As part of the treatment, the duke was given tongue twisters to practise, such as "she sifted seven thick stalked thistles through a strong, thick sieve".

On 11 December 1936, the Duke of York had kingship thrust upon him. He was a reluctant ruler: the day before his brother Edward VIII was to announce his abdication to the public, the duke went to London to see his mother, Queen Mary. He wrote in his diary: "When I told her what had happened, I broke down and sobbed like a child." He had had no preparation for the responsibility and had never even looked at a state paper, despite a year at Cambridge University in 1919 which included studying the British constitution. To maintain a sense of continuity, he was crowned as George VI rather than using his first name, Albert.

As a young man in World War I, Bertie had seen active service in the navy, manning a gun turret during the Battle of Jutland in 1916. World War II proved to be the public making of him as a monarch. After a shaky start, that is: he supported Neville Chamberlain's appeasement policy towards Germany and offered to make a personal appeal to Adolf Hitler to secure peace. (An offer the Foreign Office wisely declined.) It made his initial dealings with Chamberlain's successor, Winston Churchill, uncomfortable, although the pair eventually established a warm working relationship.

During the Blitz, the king and queen refused to leave London and the pair would regularly visit troops and bombed-out civilians on morale-boosting tours. While his first visits – to London's East End – were met with jeers and boos, his resilience made him increasingly popular among the British people, particularly after Buckingham Palace was hit by a bomb. "Now we can look the East End in the eye," commented Elizabeth.

The post-war years brought many changes to British life. Clement Attlee, the new prime minister, headed a Labour government committed to broad social change and the break-up of the Empire. Though such radical change was anathema to the king, the royal family settled into a routine of charity work and public appearances: a tour of South Africa in 1947, the opening of the Festival of Britain in 1951. But the king was dogged by ill health, and he died in his sleep in February 1952, after a battle with lung cancer, leaving the throne to his daughter, Elizabeth.

Henry V (1386–1422)

The English love to love Henry V. During his reign, the incessant dynastic fighting over the throne – conflicts that brought death and misery to tens of thousands of English people during the reigns of his father, Henry IV, and his son, Henry VI – was briefly interrupted by something quite different: war across the Channel for the throne of France.

Shakespeare memorably portrayed the young Henry as "Prince Hal", a roguish wastrel under the sway of the drunkard-lecher Sir John Falstaff. In truth, the young Henry was largely brought up (and brought up well – he could read Latin, French and English) by Richard II, after his father had been sent into exile (by Richard II). After his father returned to England, seized Richard's throne and was crowned as Henry IV, the young prince spent much of his time fighting the barons who rose up against the king, notably the Welsh ruler Owain Glyndŵr and the firebrand son of the Earl of Northumberland, Harry "Hotspur". At the Battle of Shrewsbury, in July 1403, Henry even took an arrow in the face and survived – no small feat in the fifteenth century.

Hal returned to England to take up a number of important government posts. But in 1411 he fell out with his father and was sacked from his positions. The disgrace did not last more than a year, for Henry IV was ill and, as a usurper himself, he was keen to ensure a smooth succession for his son. Young Henry became king on 20 March 1413 and quickly introduced bold new policies. In a frenzy of governing zeal, he raised new taxes, established English as the language of government (for the first time), attempted to re-establish the authority of the courts (which civil war had greatly weakened) and forgave many of his father's enemies. But he stamped hard on the Lollards (see box opposite) – Oldcastle was hanged in St Giles's Fields.

Henry might have been an effective king – if a ruthless one – but by 1415 he was already in thrall to the siren call of war in France. On 25 October, St Crispin's Day, he pulled off an outrageous victory over the French at Agincourt, where the heavily armoured French knights were bogged down in recently ploughed and rained-upon fields. They fell in their thousands to the arrows – and then the hand weapons – of the lightly armed English longbowmen on the wooded flanks. Those who survived were captured and murdered on Henry's orders; Henry notched up a dent in his helmet from an axe blow that left him a little dazed for a while.

In Henry's second fierce campaign, of 1417–19, the English conquered most of Normandy – for once concentrating not on plunder but on actually trying to bring the duchy back under English control. In 1419, as his army stood at the gates of Paris, with support from the mightily powerful Dukes of Burgundy, Henry forced the French to recognize him as heir to the French throne, and he married the beautiful Catherine de Valois, Charles VI's daughter, for good measure. Unsurprisingly, the Dauphin, or French crown prince, rejected the treaty that disinherited him, however, and in 1421 Henry launched a third, fierce campaign in northern France, while his wife was pregnant with his first child (the future Henry VI).

Henry made further gains against the Dauphin, but campaigning in the winter of 1421–22 was too much even for this iron-hearted soldier, and he became sick, finally succumbing to dysentery in August 1422.

SHAKESPEARE'S ROYALS

Shakespeare wrote history plays, not history, and bent the facts to fit his dramatic needs. He also bent them to suit the necessities of a writer working in the reign of Elizabeth I, the last monarch of the Tudor house. Among the most notoriously "spun" of his play's characterizations is that of Richard III, who is portrayed as a murderous, Machiavellian "bottled spider", and gets a hunchback thrown in (or on) for good measure. Richard, of course, was overthrown by Henry VII, the first of the Tudors – so he *has* to be a villain.

Most of the kings who get a bad press from Shakespeare – Macbeth, Hamlet's uncle, Henry VI, John – are rebels against a legitimate monarch. In most cases, historians have scrubbed off some of the black paint to reveal a more complex picture beneath. One of Shakespeare's most famous characterizations, however, is surprisingly accurate. He depicts Henry V emerging sun-like from behind murky clouds, throwing off his wild youth as "Prince Hal" and cruelly rejecting his former carousing partner, Sir John Falstaff.

It turns out that the young prince was in fact close to a certain Sir John Oldcastle, a leading figure in the proto-Protestant Lollard movement – and "Oldcastle" was probably Shakespeare's first choice of name for his Falstaff character. The Lollards believed in things like translating the Bible into English and reforming the clergy – and were not, therefore, reputable people.

There's more: in 1411 Prince Henry was thrown out of his father's council, seemingly for pressing his own desire to rule too hastily and too hard. Shakespeare's depiction of the young prince toying with his sleeping father's crown ("O polished perturbation! Golden care!"), then, is perhaps not as far-fetched as all that. Whether Henry V was the great English hero-king, as Shakespeare portrays him, or just another aristocratic warlord trying to expand his territory, however, is another question.

His only son, Henry, was one year old. Within a few years, the Dauphin – now Charles VII – reconquered much of the territory Henry had gained in France, with the help of the extraordinary warrior-saint Joan of Arc. Meanwhile, England's aristocracy went into fresh convulsions as the House of York challenged the House of Lancaster, under Henry VI, for the throne. The profoundly futile Wars of the Roses had begun.

Henry VIII (1491–1547)

"Everything is full of milk and honey and nectar," wrote Lord Mountjoy on Henry's accession in 1509. Henry was only seventeen years old when he was crowned king of England, alongside his pretty new wife – and former sister-in-law – Katherine of Aragon. Henry was tall, athletic, auburn-haired and, according to the awestruck Venetian ambassador, blessed with "a round face so very beautiful that it would become a pretty woman". Henry was the first king for nearly 100 years to inherit rather than seize the throne, and England was delighted. But he owed his Crown to chance. Henry's beloved older brother, Arthur, had died in 1502, aged fifteen and only a few months into his marriage with Katherine of Aragon.

Henry's legacy is the stuff of schoolroom history: he had six wives and got rid of the Pope. But the tyrannical Henry we all recognize thanks to Holbein's portraits – overweight, legs akimbo, codpiece dominating – was once the ideal of a Renaissance prince. Henry was cultured, devout, in love with his wife and presided over a splendid and pleasure-loving court. Intent on consolidating the teetering Tudor dynasty, he set about making peace with his murdering Yorkist cousins, cancelling debts and planning a French invasion. He was a hero in the tilt-yard and craved fame on the battlefield, modelling himself on his heroic ancestor, Henry V. In 1513, in defence of the Pope, Henry waged war against France, earning himself the accolade "Most Christian King" from the papacy. In 1517 he defended the Pope again, but this time in a battle of words with the young German heretic, Martin Luther. The Pope now named him "Defender of the Faith".

But just twenty years later this loyal if ambitious Catholic monarch severed all ties with Rome and named himself Supreme Head in Earth of the Church of England. His reign of terror then began. In the name of reform, monks were chased out of their homes, Church wealth was seized by the Crown, heretics were burned, and former friends and counsellors went to the block. What went wrong?

The answer is there in the beginning. The legitimacy of Henry's marriage to Katherine of Aragon rested on one of history's great unknowns. The Bible prohibited marriage between a man and his sister-in-law on grounds of consanguinity, but Katherine maintained until the day she died that she and Arthur had never consummated their marriage. The Pope issued the couple with a special dispensation anyway, but for Henry it was not so simple: "If a man shall take his brother's wife it is an unclean thing ... they shall be childless," Henry said, quoting the Bible. Katherine had had a son, Henry, but he died when only a few weeks old. In 1516, a daughter, Mary, had been born but there had been several miscarriages and Henry yearned for a son. For him, their marriage was "blighted in the eyes of God".

By the mid-1520s, Henry had also met Anne Boleyn. Henry had taken mistresses before – including Anne's sister, Mary – but Anne, it seems, was different. He was in love with her (and she refused to sleep with him unless he married her). Henry needed a divorce, so he turned to his Lord Chancellor and most flattering advisor for help: Cardinal Thomas Wolsey, the butcher's son from Ipswich.

But even Wolsey, hitherto the power behind the throne and de facto Pope in England, could not solve the king's "Great Matter". When the royal marriage first went on trial in secret in May 1527, with Wolsey in the judge's chair, Charles V, Emperor of the Holy Roman Empire and, crucially, Katherine's nephew, was effectively holding Pope Clement VII hostage. It was impossible for Wolsey to get Rome to authorize the divorce and he lost his job (and nearly his head). It took another five years for the divorce to come through, by which time Henry had a new team, managed by the brilliant Archbishop of Canterbury, Thomas Cranmer. Cranmer's ingenious move was to argue that Henry did not need the Pope, for did not the Bible itself declare that a king was ordained by God alone, and subject to no one but God?

There was now no stopping Henry. In 1532, he broke with Rome, and declared England "an empire". In January 1533, he married Anne Boleyn and on 1 June she was crowned Queen of England, already six months pregnant. But, fatally for Anne, the bump turned out to be a girl: Elizabeth. Three years later, Anne was beheaded for adultery, incest and treason. Henry then married Jane Seymour (who died), Anne of Cleves (who he divorced), Catherine Howard (who he beheaded), and Catherine Parr (who survived). Jane Seymour had given Henry a longed-for son (the sickly boy-king, Edward VI) but Henry's dogged pursuit of a male heir had irrevocably transformed what it meant to be king, and a subject, in England.

Henry's achievements were radical and astonishing. After all, he established a national church, authorized the first Bible in English, built up the navy, designed stunning palaces, wrote "Greensleeves" (well, actually this one is just a myth) and, by using parliament to force through his changes, increased their power. On the other hand, Henry destroyed thousand-year-old traditions and buildings, accrued enormous wealth, crushed rebellions, told people what to believe and how to worship and executed both wives and enemies. A Protestant hero for many, but a costly one.

James I (1566–1625)

"This is the son who, I hope, shall first unite the two kingdoms of Scotland and England!" So said Mary Queen of Scots on the birth of James in 1566. A little over a year later, her son was crowned James VI of Scotland. He had to wait until 1603 before he succeeded the childless Elizabeth I to become James I of England, but the succession was at least surprisingly smooth. Turning England and Scotland into one kingdom, however, would prove rather more tricky.

Elizabeth had only confirmed that her Scottish cousin should succeed her as she lay dying in her bed at Richmond Palace. But ever since the execution of his mother, Mary Queen of Scots, in 1587, James had known that he was the next legitimate heir. He was a direct descendant of Henry VII (through his great-grandmother, Margaret, Henry VIII's older sister), and, unlike his mother, he seemed perfectly fitted to become England's king. James was a Calvinist, having been brought up in the Scottish Kirk, and an experienced and diplomatic monarch. In April 1603, James set off for London, rather pleased to be leaving behind his power struggles with wilful kirkmen, heading south where monarchs were supreme governors of the Church and ruled by divine right (or so he thought). "Kings," James said, "are justly called Gods." He did not return to his first kingdom for fourteen years.

James brought with him a wife, Anne of Denmark, two healthy sons (Henry and Charles) and a daughter (Elizabeth). He promised peace and, in 1604, ended England's twenty-year war with Spain. He tolerated Catholics and foiled what would have been England's most significant act of religious terrorism to date, the Gunpowder Plot. The King James Bible – one of the most celebrated works in the English language, and a triumphant combination of puritan plainness and poetic flair – was commissioned at his request. Shakespeare's theatre company did well under James, and he employed Ben Jonson as his poet laureate. He was also a writer and thinker, composing poetry, writing a book about witchcraft and theorizing about the nature and duties of kingship. In 1617 he published his collected *Works*; the philosopher Thomas Hobbes described him as "our most wise king" (though whether this was a balanced assessment or simply sucking up to a royal is debatable).

James was criticized for being neglectful and absent. He shied away from public ceremonies and avoided attending to matters of state, preferring instead to hunt his stags (a sport at which he did not excel) and rampage through the countryside (one farmer threatened to accuse him of trespassing). He liked drinking wine and spending money.

Scottish King James VI became James I of England and united the two thrones.

Much to the annoyance of militant Protestants, he was reluctant to become involved in Europe's religious wars. Much of the animosity towards James stemmed from English xenophobia: James was, and remained, a Scottish king. English courtiers complained that Whitehall was filled with a "crew of necessitous and hungry Scots" who stood "like mountains" between them and the king.

Before James had come to England, it had been rumoured that he was "too much carried by young men that lie in his chamber". James's fostering, and subsequent dumping, of male favourites set some tongues wagging. The young flaxen-haired Robert Carr was knighted, made Gentleman of the Bedchamber and eventually Earl of Somerset, before he was disgraced, being convicted of the murder of Sir Thomas Overbury.

MARY, QUEEN OF SCOTS (1542–1587)

Mary was born on 8 December 1542 and inherited the throne six days later but grew up in France. She married François, heir to the French throne, at the age of sixteen. However, their marriage was short-lived; in 1560 François died.

Widowed at just eighteen, Mary returned to Scotland to rule her native land. Her arrival angered her half-brother, James Earl of Moray, who had been ruling Scotland perfectly well without her. Mary then made the foolish move of claiming the English throne, though she had no chance of taking it. Queen Elizabeth I of England understandably took a dim view of the claim and made a strategic alliance with Moray.

Mary then married the dashing Lord Darnley and in 1566 the couple had a son, James. Proving Mary had no luck in the husband department, Darnley arrogantly demanded precedence over all Scottish nobles, who promptly turned against him. He grew deeply jealous of his wife's male servants and murdered one, David Rizzio, in front of Mary. The royal couple's relationship utterly soured, and they began a vicious feud which ended only when Darnley was murdered on the orders of the Earl of Bothwell. A few weeks later Bothwell married Mary. Duff marriage number three: getting hitched to the suspected murderer of her husband turned Scottish opinion against Mary and rebellion broke out. Mary abdicated, then fled to England.

If Mary expected Elizabeth to raise an army to restore her to power in Scotland, she was much mistaken: Elizabeth favoured the Earl of Moray. Mary was put into comfortable, but very secure, quarters in England. This did, however, result in her becoming the figurehead for discontent among English Catholics who did not want to be ruled by the Protestant Elizabeth. In 1586 Mary began a secret correspondence with the politician Thomas Babington, in which she openly approved of a plot to kill Elizabeth and put herself on the English throne. But the letters were being intercepted by Elizabeth's chief spy, Sir Francis Walsingham. Mary was put on trial and denied everything but her letters condemned her. She was executed by beheading on 8 February 1587. While Mary had never come close to seizing the English throne, when Elizabeth died in 1603 she left the English crown to Mary's son, King James of Scotland.

Next, James met George Villiers, his "white-faced boy" with shapely legs. Villiers began as cupbearer to the king and rose rapidly through the ranks to end up as Duke of Buckingham. He accessed James's bedroom by a secret passage and led England into an expensive and unpopular war with Spain. Historians have speculated as to whether James was bisexual: whatever the truth was, he was hardly the only king to have patronized a string of favourites and had same-sex bedfellows.

James should really be remembered for managing an impossible coalition. Many of his clashes with the English parliament arose from conflicting ideas about kingship, and about his plans for a complete union with Scotland. The English baulked at the idea of being called Great Britain, at the introduction of a common currency and at the flying of the Union Flag.

On 27 March 1625 James died (with Buckingham at his bedside). His first son, Henry, had died tragically young, so it was his second son, Charles, who inherited huge debts, a court tainted by corruption, and a fractious relationship between king and parliament. James was too clever to ever assert that he was above the law and rule absolutely in the way that his son was to do. But Charles clearly learnt something from his father about the divine right of kings and the intransigence of English MPs.

King John (1166–1216)

Of all England's kings, John is inseparable from his bad reputation. He is the tyrant who usurped his brother, murdered his nephew, gave in to the barons, lost most of France to the French and, for good measure, persecuted Robin Hood. Only the last part, sadly, isn't true – it was the Victorians who attached the age-old Robin Hood legends to his reign.

John was never supposed to have been king. When his father, Henry II, divided his Angevin empire between his sons in the early 1170s, there was nothing left for the youngest, and he became known as Jean sans Terre, or "Lackland". Even when three of his elder brothers died, leaving John the heir of his last remaining brother, Richard I, he was disinherited in favour of Richard's nephew, Arthur of Brittany.

John had not deserved Richard's trust. While the Lionheart was away crusading in the Holy Land, John set himself up as a rival to his brother's regent, establishing his own parallel court and sending diplomatic overtures to the French king Philip II: he hoped to seize Richard's French territories with Philip's assistance, in return for acknowledging Philip as

ELEANOR OF AQUITAINE (1122–1204)

Eleanor of Aquitaine blazes out of the historical darkness that obscures the lives of most medieval women. She was powerful and independent, brilliant and potently sexual; she was the first great queen of England, and is regarded by many today as a proto-feminist hero.

Her patrimony, Aquitaine, was a vast and powerful duchy in the south-west of what is now France. Eleanor inherited the territory from her father in 1137, aged about fifteen, and was promptly married off to the monkish French king, Louis VII. He was a poor match for the sophisticated red-haired beauty from Aquitaine's cosmopolitan court. Louis' clerical friends grew to loathe her. By the time she had bought her way into the ranks of the Second Crusade, along with her female retainers – dressed in white and riding white horses, as legend would have it, much like Amazon warrior princesses – relations with Louis were poor. It didn't help that, on campaign in the Near East, she smartly avoided an attack on the French army while her husband was forced to scramble up a cliff to safety. It didn't help that she challenged Louis' military plans. It helped even less that her flirtatious intimacy with her notorious uncle Raymond of Poitiers, Prince of Antioch, was interpreted by many as evidence of an incestuous affair.

It may have been: Eleanor was known for taking lovers. On her return to France – a troubled voyage, with the couple in separate vessels – her marriage with Louis was finally annulled, on the grounds that they had been too closely related. By the terms of the marriage contract, which specified that only a son could inherit his mother's lands, Eleanor's patrimony was returned to her. The

Eleanor, beside Henry II, in their French tomb at Fontevraud.

seed of hundreds of years of conflict between England and France was sown: within weeks, Eleanor had married Henry Plantagenet, a French nobleman with a strong claim on the English throne. He was a lion of a man: charismatic, physically powerful, and twelve years her junior. With his wife's backing, he secured his hold on England and was crowned Henry II in 1154. It was said to be a ceremony of unprecedented splendour, Eleanor insisting that the vestments were of the costliest silks and gold-embroidered velvets.

She was now Queen of England. Eleanor had eight children with Henry but by the time the last one, John (later King John), was born, her marriage was ruptured, her husband having taken up with Rosamund "the Fair" Clifford. At Christmas 1167, Eleanor sailed for France, and her home city of Poitiers – which, like Eleanor herself, had always resisted Henry's authority. There she established a new court devoted to chivalry, song, romance literature and courtly pleasures. One source claims she established a Court of Love, where women ruled. In Poitiers, she also began plotting with her sons, inciting them to support her eldest, known as Henry "the Young King", in revolt against their father – and even encouraging them in an alliance with her first husband, Louis VII. The revolt failed, however, and Henry II took Eleanor prisoner.

She spent the next sixteen years effectively under house arrest in England. When Henry II died, however, in 1189, her eldest surviving son, Richard (the Lionheart), ordered her release. In her late sixties, she began the next phase in her extraordinary life. She acted as de facto regent for Richard while he fought in the Third Crusade, and when he was held hostage on his way home, Eleanor herself negotiated his ransom. Upon Richard's death, in 1199, Eleanor backed her youngest son, John, against the claims on her territories posed by Arthur of Brittany, her great-nephew. Arthur was supported by the new French king, Philip II, who wanted Eleanor's Aquitainian territories under his control.

Now in her seventies, Eleanor's political career still wasn't over. First, John sent her across the Pyrenees to Castile, to choose one of his nieces as the bride of the French crown prince – the price of a peace treaty. She was held hostage on the way home, but reportedly argued herself free, and continued her journey. On return to France, she attempted to retire to a nunnery at Fontevraud, in the Loire Valley, but in 1201 fresh conflict drew her south to Poitiers, to defend her ancestral capital against the French. Again, she was captured and, again, rescued – this time by John, who marched his army south to release her. Age and illness, however, had finally weakened her. She became a nun at Fontevraud (a refuge, incongruously, for abused women and former prostitutes) and died there in 1204. Her effigy still lies in the abbey, in glorious polychrome, alongside her husband Henry II and her son, Richard.

feudal overlord. For good measure, John repudiated his wife and agreed to marry Philip's sister, Alys (though his mother, Eleanor, eventually stepped in to stop the marriage – Alys had been betrothed previously to Richard and had probably had a child with Henry II).

In England, Richard's loyal followers rebelled against John and, when the king finally returned from the Crusades in 1194, John fled to Normandy. Astonishingly, he was forgiven, and even named once more as heir to the throne – at least, most of the English barons recognized John as king when Richard died in April 1199. Many of the French nobles demurred in favour of Arthur of Brittany. War broke out between supporters of the rival claimants, and only subsided when John again agreed to acknowledge Philip as overlord in France. By caving in to Philip, rather than fighting him, John thus earned himself another unflattering soubriquet: John Softsword.

The fragile peace in France was soon broken anyway. John fell in love with a young French heiress, Isabelle of Angoulême, and attempted to marry her in 1200 – thus alienating Hugh de Lusignan, the French nobleman to whom she was engaged. Hugh appealed to Philip II, who summoned John as his feudal vassal. When John refused to come, Philip took the opportunity to attack, sweeping through Normandy and winning the entire territory for France by 1204.

Of all the French lands brought to the English crown by Eleanor, only Aquitaine now remained. John repeatedly tried and failed to regain Normandy. At home, in 1209, John even managed to get England interdicted and himself excommunicated for attempting to resist papal interference in the election of the Archbishop of Canterbury. Humiliatingly, John backed down in 1213, acknowledging Pope Innocent III as another overlord, and paying for the privilege.

The greatest humiliation was still to come. A revolt in England by the so-called Army of God – a group of self-seeking nobles from the north, irked by taxation – was only suppressed by John agreeing to give the barons greater power. The "Great Charter", or Magna Carta, was signed by John on 15 June 1215: it acknowledged that the king, like other men, was subject to the law, and limited his ability to impose taxes without consent. Later generations of democrats would see this as a historic moment.

As usual, the treaty didn't stick. John's last year saw him still fighting with his barons, who had treacherously invited the French crown prince to help them. In a last, disastrous manoeuvre, John's army lost its baggage train while crossing The Wash – the chronicler Roger of Wendover tells us that the Crown Jewels were sucked into the sands.

John died of dysentery in October 1216. He left an empire in tatters and a kingdom divided among itself. He did, however, leave a legitimate son to succeed him – which was more than his lion-hearted brother managed. The Plantagenet line seemed secured.

Mary I (1516–1558)

Few monarchs have been as vilified as Mary I, England's first crowned queen. While history represents her sister, Elizabeth I, as majestic, powerful, even masculine, Mary has been portrayed as foreign, hysterical and cold. But Mary Tudor was just as accomplished, striking and, indeed, red-haired as Henry and Elizabeth and, before her parents' divorce, she was adored by her father and admired across Europe. As queen, Mary then set the precedent for female rule that future queens (who had the good fortune to rule for much longer) would follow.

Mary had to wait and fight to become queen. Even though Henry acknowledged Mary's claim to the throne before he died, he had, legally, declared her a bastard. And, in 1553, when it became clear that Edward VI was dying, he and his circle moved to shunt Mary out of the succession and proclaim Lady Jane Grey (of the Protestant branch of the Tudor family) as the next queen. But Mary mobilized her forces and moved swiftly, entering London to be declared England's rightful queen by Protestants and Catholics alike. England celebrated by ringing bells and lighting bonfires. "From a distance the earth must have looked like Mount Etna," ambassadors reported. On 3 August 1553, Mary rode into London in royal splendour, robed in purple velvet. Behind her, as part of the new queen's train, was her sister, Elizabeth.

It has often been said that Mary's gravest political – and personal – mistake was to marry an unpopular foreigner: Philip II of Spain. For Philip, it was not a marriage of love: "The marriage was concluded for no fleshly consideration, but to remedy the disorders of this kingdom," he said. But Mary insisted that she had been spoken to by God, and she married Philip against the advice and wishes of her council and country. She was determined and decisive.

In February 1554, she stirred Londoners to quash the rebellion led by Sir Thomas Wyatt against her forthcoming marriage with a powerful speech: "Good and faithful subjects, pluck up your hearts, and like true men stand fast with your lawful prince against these rebels both our enemies and yours, and fear them not, for I assure you that I fear them nothing at all." Wyatt was beheaded, and his body parboiled and quartered and put on display around the city as a warning to traitors. Elizabeth, accused of involvement with the plot, was thrown into the Tower of London, but there was not enough evidence to convict her.

Marrying the Spanish prince could, indeed, be seen as a shrewd choice. Philip was her husband, but was not crowned king (an English husband might have had more success in this regard) and Mary continued to rule as a sole queen. If her marriage had produced a child, then history might have judged it rather differently. But Mary was already 37 when she married Philip, and she had a troubled history of illness and irregular menstruation. She did not conceive the child she desperately wanted – and needed in order to secure a Catholic succession. A year after her wedding she was so sure that she was pregnant that she withdrew into her chamber to prepare for the birth. In anticipation of this child, parliament voted to abolish the Royal Supremacy and restore the Pope.

Mary remained devoted to the memory of her mother, Katherine of Aragon, and to the Catholic faith. In November 1554, Cardinal Reginald Pole arrived back from exile in Italy and together he and Mary set about rebuilding and reviving the Catholic Church. They sought out heretics and stamped on the "corrupt and naughty opinions" of the Protestants. Nearly 300 men and women died for their beliefs in Mary's five-year reign. But the failure of Catholic restoration was not inevitable: if Mary had borne a child, or even if she had reigned a little longer, the Protestant threat may have been quelled for good, however horrific the means.

In an age suspicious of female rulers, Mary was courageous, serious and hard-working. She crushed two rebellions, ensured that women could rule as kings, and reunited England with Rome (although she did lose Calais). Elizabeth had much to learn from her sister about being a queen. In January 1559, before her own coronation, she brushed down Mary's cloth-of-gold dress, adjusted the bodice, and wore it to the Abbey.

Richard the Lionheart (1157–1199)

Like so many of England's kings and queens, Richard Cœur de Lion, the "Lionheart", wasn't particularly English. He barely spoke the language and spent most of his life campaigning in the French Duchy of Aquitaine, or on crusade in Palestine – all the time milking England for money to pay for it.

He inherited Aquitaine via his mother, Eleanor, but only became its overlord when his father, Henry II, passed on the duchy to him in 1170.

It was a mistake worthy of King Lear: by 1173, Henry's sons had risen up against him, in league with the French king Louis VII, and egged-on by Eleanor. The revolt failed when the French king made peace with Henry in September 1174, however, and Richard had to beg his father for mercy. He was given the kiss of peace and control of just half of Aquitaine.

Peace didn't last. In 1187 Richard joined forces with the new French king, Philip II, driving his father's armies in flight across the Loire Valley. He forced Henry to name him as heir and (finally) allow him to marry his fiancée, Alys – who Henry had taken as his lover. Again, Henry kissed his son in peace, albeit audibly muttering "God grant that I may not die until I have had a fitting revenge on you." The prayer failed. As Henry lay dying at Chinon, in 1189, he learned that his only loyal son, John, had joined the rebels. He turned his face to the wall, shouting "Shame, shame on a vanquished king!"

Even as he campaigned against his father in France, Richard learned that Yusuf Salah ad-Din, better known in the West as Saladin, had reconquered Jerusalem. Richard "took the cross" in 1187, vowing to liberate the Holy Land, and began raising funds for his crusade (the Third Crusade, as it's now known). He set his mother up as regent, and sailed in 1190, occupying Sicily and conquering Cyprus on the way. (In Cyprus he married Berengaria of Navarre, though he hardly saw her afterwards, and they had no children.) Landing in Palestine in 1191, he quickly captured the fortress port of Acre, famously shooting down defenders from the walls with a crossbow, despite suffering from scurvy.

WAS THE LIONHEART GAY?

"At night their beds did not separate", claimed Roger of Howden concerning Richard I and Philip II of France, in 1187. Apparently, Philip loved Richard "as his own soul". The chronicler may only have been noting a public demonstration of alliance, but Richard did almost certainly have male lovers (as well as female: he had an illegitimate son, Philip). Richard reportedly did public penance for the sin of sodomy.

The later rumour that he had an affair with his Muslim rival, Saladin, is, sadly, baseless, though the two leaders were certainly impressed by each other. Shakespeare, intriguingly, seems to touch on Richard's sexuality in his play, *King John*. "I would not wish a better father", Philip the Bastard avows, upon discovering his father's identity; "He that perforce robs lions of their hearts/May easily win a woman's."

After coldly murdering almost 3000 Muslim prisoners in Acre, Richard confronted Saladin at Arsuf. Saladin was routed, Richard again playing a hero's role, pursuing the enemy with "singular ferocity", as a contemporary wrote, using his sword "as if reaping the harvest with a sickle". It was a spectacular start, but Richard was already quarrelling with his allies, notably Philip, and is even suspected of having murdered Conrad, the elected King of Jerusalem, using Ismaili assassins. The conquest of Jerusalem was abandoned and, in 1192, Richard made peace with Saladin, who guaranteed the safety of Christian pilgrims to the Holy City.

Richard returned home disguised as a pilgrim – he had to cross the lands of many of the crusaders with whom he had clashed – but was recognized. Taken prisoner by the Duke of Austria, he was ransomed to his mother in 1194, for a colossal sum. Richard sped home to confront his brother, John, who had seized power in his own name. ("Look to yourself," Philip of France famously wrote to John. "The devil is loose!") The brothers were quickly reconciled, however, allowing Richard to launch a new campaign in France against Philip. He was winning back his French territories when he was shot down in 1199 by an arrow fired by a bowman on the walls of a castle he was besieging. He died of a gangrenous wound a fortnight later, cradled by his mother, Eleanor.

Richard was undoubtedly a magnificent man: tall and powerful, red-haired and handsome, courageous and skilled as a general. The English tend to criticize him for not taking better care of his kingdom but, in truth, Richard was fierce in defence of his territories – he simply considered himself Duke of Aquitaine more than King of England.

Richard III (1452–1485)

Of all the men and women who have occupied the throne of England, none has a worse reputation than Richard III. In recent years, however, some historians have attempted to rehabilitate Richard, suggesting he was simply a man acting upon his family's royal claims, much like many monarchs before him. The fourth son of Richard, Duke of York, he was born on 2 October 1452. His father's staking a claim to the English throne was one of the main causes of the Wars of the Roses and in 1460 York and his second son Edmund were killed in the battle of Wakefield by supporters of King Henry VI. The orphaned Richard and his brother George were placed in the care of Richard Neville, Earl of Warwick. With Warwick's help, Edward, Richard's eldest brother, set about defeating Henry's men

Whatever its historical accuracy, Laurence Olivier's portrayal of Shakespeare's insidious Richard III has permanently coloured how we see him.

and seized the English throne – becoming King Edward IV in 1461 – decimating Lancastrian forces at the Battle of Towton.

Richard was loyal to Edward throughout his reign, which saw Edward briefly deposed by a resurgent Henry VI in 1470, in cahoots with Edward's former ally, the opportunistic Warwick. Richard proved his military mettle, commanding Yorkist troops against the Lancastrians at the Battle of

Tewkesbury in 1471, unleashing his men at a crucial moment to gain a decisive victory. Many of the defeated Lancastrians fled to Tewkesbury Abbey to seek sanctuary; Richard had them dragged out and killed.

Among the Lancastrian supporters that were then rounded up across the country was Anne Neville, Warwick's daughter. Richard treated her well and took her to a convent where she would be safe. The pair had known each other as children, and in July 1472 they married. Richard took his bride to Yorkshire, from where he governed northern England and patrolled the Scottish borders. In 1478 Richard's brother George,

GREAT PRETENDERS: PERKIN WARBECK, LAMBERT SIMNEL AND OTHERS

The death of Richard III in 1485 marked the extinction of the legitimate Yorkist dynasty. Those who opposed the rule of Henry VII had no obvious candidate to take his place. Until 1487, that is, when a ten-year-old boy approached the Earl of Kildare in Ireland to announce that he was the Earl of Warwick. Warwick was heir to King Richard, but had been imprisoned by Henry. Kildare accepted the tale and with the help of Warwick's aunt, Duchess Margaret of Burgundy, hired 2000 German mercenaries. The boy invaded England with the mercenaries, but Henry then announced that the Earl of Warwick was alive and well in the Tower of London. Few Englishmen turned out to support the invaders, who were defeated at the Battle of Stoke Field in Leicestershire on 16 June 1487. The boy turned out to be a baker's son named Lambert Simnel. He had been used by a priest, Roger Simon, to try to trick money out of Warwick's family. Simnel was pardoned and given a job in the royal kitchens. Simon was thrown into prison for life.

Three years later a teenager began claiming to be Richard, Duke of York, the younger of the two princes in the Tower who had vanished in 1483. "York" spent four years touring Europe trying to gain the recognition of various rulers and collecting money. In 1495 "York" arrived in Scotland where he was backed by King James IV, who mustered his army to invade England. After some border raiding, James made peace with Henry and expelled "York".

"York" moved on to Cornwall but was captured by royal troops. Under questioning he admitted that his real name was Perkin Warbeck and that he was the son of a Flemish merchant who had learned English when working for English masters. Everyone who met him agreed that he did look very like King Edward IV, and since Edward is known to have visited Warbeck's home town, it has been speculated that he may have been an illegitimate son. Warbeck was imprisoned in the Tower of London. He tried to escape in 1499 and was executed.

Duke of Clarence, was executed for treason against Edward IV. The details of his guilt are unclear and some historians have suggested Richard was to blame.

On 9 April 1483 Edward IV died, and his twelve-year-old son became King Edward V, taking up residence in the Tower of London, as was customary for the new monarch. Edward was too young to rule, and Richard rode to the capital, ostensibly to attend the coronation, but in fact to ensure that he became acting regent in place of the new king's mother. In the midst of this scramble for power, the Bishop of Bath and Wells announced that Edward V was in fact illegitimate, as his parents had never been properly married. Parliament met on 25 June, announced the boy-king was a bastard and asked Richard to accept the Crown. The coronation took place on 6 July.

Edward IV's widow, Elizabeth Woodville, sent her younger son, Richard, Duke of York, to live in the Tower of London with the now ex-king Edward V. What happened to the two boys is an enduring mystery. They stopped being seen in public around late August 1483. Richard's enemies later accused him of murdering the pair that autumn, but there is no firm evidence. The boy's mother remained on good terms with Richard, which would be odd (though perhaps politic) if she suspected he had killed them. Others have suspected the Duke of Buckingham or Henry Tudor (later Henry VII) of the crime. A few have suggested that Richard sent the boys to live with relatives in eastern Europe.

Richard then settled down to the business of ruling England. He continued the competent administration of his brother Edward. He suffered the loss of a son in 1484 and his wife died in 1485. Last of the Plantagenets, he had no blood heir, and first named his nephew, Edward, Earl of Warwick, as his successor; then John de la Pole, Earl of Lincoln.

Some of the gentry, in particular Henry Stafford, the Second Duke of Buckingham, believed Edward IV's son should have been king. They united and invited Henry Tudor, who had a claim to the throne through his mother, to return to England and take the crown. In August 1485, Henry landed in Wales with a force of mercenaries and sent word ahead to raise troops from loyal Lancastrian areas. He entered England at Shrewsbury with about 6000 men. Richard had meanwhile ordered his army, around 9000 strong, to meet at Leicester. Other nobles were converging on Leicester; among them brothers Lord Thomas Stanley and Sir William Stanley, with some 8000 men, were hedging their bets, reluctant to pick sides.

The battle took place near Market Bosworth on 22 August. At first Richard had the upper hand, but then the Stanleys joined the battle on Henry's side. Realizing he was losing, Richard led his bodyguards in a mounted charge at Henry Tudor. He himself slew Henry's standard bearer and was within ten feet of his opponent before he was driven off. Richard was unhorsed, but fought on until he was cut down and killed.

Queen Victoria (1819–1901)

For a large part of Victoria's extraordinarily long reign – she ruled from the age of 18 to 81, and presided over ten prime ministers – the monarchy was deeply unpopular. Republican ideas were spreading. In 1864, the great Italian revolutionary Garibaldi was received by tumultuously cheering crowds in England, much to Victoria's distaste. Republican clubs were springing up everywhere and, in 1871, the Liberal MP Sir Charles Dilke spoke out against the monarchy in the House of Commons. Attempts to assassinate (or at least assault) the queen, meanwhile, were made in 1840, 1842, 1849, 1850, 1872 and 1882 – though on at least two occasions the attackers' pistols were not loaded, and at the last attempt, two Eton schoolboys managed to beat the assailant off with umbrellas.

Looking back, however, Victoria's reign appears as a kind of silver age for the monarchy (not quite up there with Elizabeth I's supposedly golden one). It's intriguing that the most celebrated of English sovereigns were both women, and that both reigns ended much more happily than they had begun.

Victoria's uncle, William IV, had famously held on to life until Victoria's mother, the Duchess of Kent (and her mother's lover, Sir John Conroy), could no longer become regent. In an act of telling confidence, Victoria's first important command was to banish Conroy from court. The queen wasn't without her own influential advisors, however, notably the charming old prime minister Lord Melbourne – jeering crowds were heard to shout "Mrs Melbourne" after her. More sinisterly, in Ireland, where more than a million people died in the 1840s as a result of potato blight and British export policies, Victoria was dubbed the "Famine Queen".

Marriage was deemed crucial to protect the young queen. Unfortunately, Victoria fell passionately for a younger son from the minuscule German principality of Saxe-Coburg. The British public was unimpressed by the prospect of having a penniless German prince for a monarch. Victoria felt very differently. "It was with some emotion that I beheld Albert", she confessed to her diary in 1839, calling him "beautiful". She herself was a

A photograph of Queen Victoria in later life, turning the century with a smile.

rather dumpy, if perky, five-footer. Albert, by contrast, was a fine figure of a man, keen on fencing and shooting, but also principled and committed to reform, albeit of a certain paternalistic kind.

After they married on 10 February 1840 (and after a honeymoon night she called "a gratifying and bewildering experience … he clasped me in his arms and we kissed each other again and again") Victoria produced an astonishing sequence of children. The first, Victoria, was conceived within days. The second, the future Edward VII, was born eleven months later. By 1857, she had nine children – the last two born with the pain-killing help of chloroform.

Albert's influence grew alongside his family. He built a new home for them all at Osborne House, on the Isle of Wight, creating a kind of model household for wealthy, family-centred respectability. Soon after, he presided over an even greater national exemplar: the Great Exhibition of 1851, which placed much of Hyde Park inside a giant glasshouse, and exhibited within it all the crafts, trades, manufactures and machines on which the economic hopes of the kingdom – soon to be an Empire – were built.

Ten years later, however, Albert was dead, after catching a chill while attempting to put a stop to his eldest son's philanderings at Cambridge. Victoria collapsed in grief, retreating into deep mourning at Osborne House and refusing to come out even to open parliament. In the early 1860s, the "widow of Windsor" became a burden on the nation, and her reputation suffered further as a result of her deeply intimate, passionate friendship with her "Highland Servant" John Brown. (At her burial, Victoria was secretly interred along with a lock of Brown's hair, his photograph and his mother's wedding ring, which she used to wear on her right hand.)

What saved the monarchy, in the public eye, was the surprise recovery of the crown prince, "Bertie", from typhoid – the disease that had killed his father. The prime minister, William Gladstone, who Victoria detested, organized a triumphantly successful Day of National Thanksgiving. Soon after, his replacement Benjamin Disraeli (who Victoria adored) flattered her to perfection by obtaining for his "faery queen" the title of Empress of India, in May 1876. She was "in ecstasies", similarly, after Disraeli borrowed £4 million from Baron Rothschild to buy a majority of shares in the Suez Canal. As Disraeli told Victoria, unctuously, "you have it, Madam."

The last twenty-odd years of the reign were relatively uneventful, for Victoria at least. For Britain, it was a time of profound social and political change. As British power imperial waxed, with wars successfully pursued in the Crimea and South Africa, politics were transformed. In Victoria's own lifetime, voting rights were granted by parliament to millions of men, although women and unpropertied men were still excluded at the time of her death.

Victoria won admiration almost as a result of her unchangeability. In 1887, she weathered a storm over her beloved Indian servant, Abdul Karim. In 1896 she became the longest-reigning British monarch to date. In 1897 she celebrated her Diamond Jubilee in a riot of empire-themed celebrations. In 1901, having just made it into the twentieth century, she died, leaving a nation profoundly more royalist than it had been at her accession, an age before.

William the Conqueror (1028–1087)

That "William the Conqueror" has beaten "William the Bastard" as this monarch's enduring moniker is testament to his ambition and force of character. For he was both.

One day his father, Duke Robert of Normandy, had spotted a group of women dyeing leather in the town square of Falaise. One of the women was so stunningly attractive that Duke Robert at once sent for her. The young Herleva refused to consent to the duke's advances unless she was first given a white horse, a new dress and cloak and some fine jewellery. Slavering with lust, Robert agreed. As a result of this encounter Herleva gave Robert a son, William. When the duke died in 1035, William was his only surviving child and, despite his illegitimate birth, the boy inherited Normandy.

The nobles and churchmen of the region reacted in predictable fashion to having a seven-year-old of ignoble stock as their ruler. They stopped paying taxes, grabbed royal estates for themselves and began squabbling with each other. King Henry I of France supported William's position, and safeguarded it for twelve years of struggle, until the mature William finally gained control of Normandy.

His position relatively secure, the nineteen-year-old William then decided he wished to marry the young, attractive and very rich Matilda of Flanders. Negotiations between William and Matilda's father went well, until his twenty-year-old prospective bride sent a message saying she would not marry a bastard, even if he was a duke. Enraged, William is said to have stormed up to Matilda's bedroom, grabbed her by her long plaits and knocked her to the floor. Whether it was a result of this thuggish behaviour or not, Matilda reconsidered, and married William. Despite this unpromising start, the pair proved to be devoted to each other, producing four sons and two daughters.

In 1060 Count Geoffrey II of nearby Anjou died childless, so William seized the opportunity to grab the border county of Maine for himself. But Maine was not enough. Another neighbour of William's, albeit the ruler of a rather larger region, was childless and nearing death: King Edward the Confessor of England. In 1064, Earl Harold of Wessex – the leading nobleman in England and the favourite to succeed Edward – arrived in Normandy. What Harold was doing in Normandy is unclear, and what happened next is even murkier. William later claimed that Harold had voluntarily agreed to support William's claim to the English throne. Given that Harold had a stronger claim himself, this seems unlikely, but it was William's story and he stuck to it.

STEPHEN AND MATILDA
(1092–1154 AND 1102–67)

The overlapping reigns of King Stephen and his cousin (and rival) the Empress Matilda were not happy. They are known as "The Anarchy" or "The Nineteen-year Winter". One agonized contemporary chronicle even said it was a time "when Christ and his saints slept". The trouble all stemmed, as usual, from a succession crisis. Henry I's only son, William Adelin, had died when his vessel, the *White Ship*, foundered off Normandy in 1120. Some blamed drink, while William of Nangis thought the tragedy was a moral judgement on the passengers and crew all being "sodomites". (Quite how he could possibly have been so certain remains a mystery.) William of Malmesbury astutely wrote: "No ship ever brought so much misery to England." King Henry only had one other legitimate child, a daughter named Matilda – known as the Empress Matilda after her first marriage to Henry V, the Holy Roman Emperor. Matilda was clearly the heir to the throne, but the laws of succession at the time were not well established, so her father tried to bolster her position by forcing his barons to swear allegiance to her.

When Henry died in 1135 (famously after scoffing a "surfeit of lampreys"), his daughter and kingdom were left unprotected. Henry's wealthy favoured nephew, Stephen of Blois, crossed the Channel from Normandy (on a more seaworthy vessel than the *White Ship*), seizing his moment – and the throne. He gathered support from the barons, who had little enthusiasm for a female monarch despite Stephen's lack of a claim on the English crown – indeed, he was one of the barons who had sworn to support Matilda as heir. He was duly crowned.

Matilda, meanwhile, was in Anjou, the French county belonging to her sec-

Two years later, in 1066, Edward died and Harold was proclaimed King of England. William denounced Harold for having broken his supposed oath and mustered for war, recruiting men from France, Flanders and Brittany as well as Normandy. William was pipped to the invasion post by King Harald of Norway, who had his own slender claim to the throne, and who was backed by Harold's estranged brother Tostig. Both Harald and Tostig were killed at the Battle of Stamford Bridge. The victory weakened Harold's English army, playing in William's favour, as he was then landing in Sussex. Harold hurried south but was defeated and killed at the Battle of Hastings. Unwilling to accept a foreign conqueror, the English nobles proclaimed a royal cousin, Edgar, to be the new king. But William had the only functional army in England and rapidly imposed his will. He was crowned King of England in Westminster Abbey on Christmas Day 1066.

To further secure his grip on England, William began the construction of castles throughout the land. The Tower of London and Windsor

ond husband Geoffrey Le Bel ("the Handsome"). For the English, this marriage was part of the problem, as Geoffrey had come into conflict with Normandy – then still part of the Anglo-Norman kingdom established by Matilda's grandfather, William the Conqueror. Lacking support in England, Matilda failed to press her claim to the throne until 1139. In that year, however, her husband attacked Normandy while her half-brother Robert of Gloucester launched a rebellion in England and her uncle, King David of Scotland, invaded from the north.

Against the odds, Stephen fought back impressively until, in 1141, he was captured by Robert of Gloucester's forces at Lincoln, and imprisoned by Matilda. She still didn't have control of the country, however. Stephen's wife (also called Matilda, confusingly enough) managed to continue the campaign during his captivity. And when Matilda marched on London to finally get herself crowned, in June 1141, London rose up against her, and she was forced to flee. For many years, neither party had the upper hand. Meanwhile, as the *Anglo-Saxon Chronicle* put it, "there was nothing but disturbance and wickedness and robbery" for the ordinary people. Yet by 1147, the actual fighting was at least dying down. Many barons had departed for Palestine, on the Second Crusade, while Matilda herself retreated to Normandy, which her husband had successfully conquered. Finally, in 1153, powerful clergymen – whom Stephen had angered and alienated – forced the warring rivals to make a final peace. Stephen would remain king until his death, but Matilda and Geoffrey's son would inherit the throne. In 1154, therefore, after Stephen fell sick at Dover and died, Matilda's son duly succeeded as Henry II. His redoubtable wife, Eleanor of Aquitaine, would shape the course of English history even more than Matilda had done.

Castle are his best-known foundations, and his lead was then followed by the Norman knights and barons who took over some ninety percent of the English lands after the Battle of Hastings. William then reduced the powers of the shires, the earls and the Church, in each case centralizing power into the hands of the monarch. Turning next to taxation, William ordered his clerks to assess every village and manor in England. The work began in 1085 and was completed within the year. The final register became known as the Domesday Book because – as with God's book, to be used on doomsday – nothing written in it could be altered and everything was recorded.

Meanwhile, William had fallen out with Philip, the new king of France. He besieged, captured and burned the border town of Mantes, west of Paris; then his horse trod on a hot cinder and threw William off. The king, who had grown fat, suffered an internal abdominal injury that soon proved fatal. He was buried in Caen, and his sons promptly began a murderous feud over their inheritance.

William III and Mary II (1650–1702 and 1662–94)

It is often said that it was religion that brought William III and Mary II to the throne of Britain. But there was a lot more to it than that. Their reign was to establish many of the precedents and conventions that make up Britain's unwritten constitution to this day.

Mary was born on 30 April 1662, the elder daughter of James, Duke of York, younger brother of Charles II. In 1669 James converted to Catholicism, but Charles ordered that Mary and her sister Anne be brought up as Protestants. When she was fifteen, Mary was told she had to marry William of Orange, ruler of the Netherlands. She burst into tears on hearing the news.

At 27, William was twelve years older than his bride. He was Prince of Orange, a small Protestant state entirely surrounded by Catholic France. William's family had extensive lands in the Netherlands and often held the position of Stadtholder there, a sort of elected prince. William's mother had been Mary, sister of Charles II of Britain. The marriage thus linked the two most senior branches of the British royal family in a Protestant union.

Charles II died in 1685 and James of York became James II. James rapidly made himself unpopular and in June 1688 a group of leading politicians sent an invitation to William asking him to come to England to right the wrongs inflicted by James. William landed at Brixham, far from James in London. He advanced cautiously to gauge the mood of the country but need not have worried. James's army changed sides and leading figures rushed to declare their support for William. James fled to France and William summoned parliament to discuss what should happen next.

The political wrangling lasted for months. In the end the throne was offered jointly to William and Mary, but on condition that they agreed to the Bill of Rights. This key constitutional document stated that laws and taxes had to be agreed jointly by parliament and the monarch, that all citizens could petition parliament, that elections had to be free and fair, that MPs could not be punished for what they said or how they voted in parliament, and generally restricted the freedom of the monarch to act without parliamentary approval. The constitutional settlement has become known as the Glorious Revolution.

Within two years, two serious uprisings supporting the exiled James II took place. In Scotland the popular and talented Viscount Dundee led a rebellion that swept the highlands, but ended after his death at the Battle of Killiecrankie. In Ireland James himself landed to command the rebel forces. William also went to Ireland, and defeated James at the Battle of the Boyne on 1 July 1690. The Irish uprising continued for more than a year, but the Boyne had been decisive.

Britain had meanwhile joined the Grand Alliance against France and William was absent for extended periods as he led armies campaigning against Louis XIV. During his absences, Britain was ruled by Mary who continued their joint policies. The Bank of England was established in 1694 to organize the money supply and raise loans for the government. It proved to be a key move and laid the foundations for Britain's later dominance of the European banking and finance system.

In December 1694 Mary contracted smallpox and died after a short illness. William was devastated, went into deep mourning and refused to remarry. The heir to the throne was Anne, sister of Mary and Protestant daughter of King James II. However the succession problem raised its head again when the only surviving child of Princess Anne, William Duke of Gloucester, died childless in July 1700. The most obvious heir was James II's son, also James, but he was a Catholic and many worried he might have grudges to settle. Next in line was Sophia, a granddaughter of King James I of Britain. Sophia was married to Ernst of Brunswick and was already seventy years old. She did, however, have several legitimate adult children of whom the oldest was George of Hanover. The English parliament passed the Act of Settlement in 1701 which named Sophia and her heirs as the successors to Anne. The Irish parliament followed suit, but the Scottish parliament did not.

William was still only 52, but in February 1702 his horse stumbled on a molehill and threw the king to the ground. He broke his collarbone and then a bout of pneumonia led to his death two months later. Anne became Queen of Britain, but Orange was grabbed by France. A junior branch of the Orange dynasty remained influential in the Netherlands: the present monarch of the Netherlands is descended from them.

4

Pomp and ceremonies

It's often argued that the royal family justify the vast amount of money it costs to keep them because they do their bit for tourism. Whether or not this is true, there's no doubt that significant royal events – coronations, weddings and funerals – are watched by audiences of billions across the globe. While the arcane ritual and ceremony is no longer intended to reinforce the royals' absolute power and divine status, the world clearly still loves to gawp at ermine, sparkling jewels, sceptres, orbs and peculiar hats – especially when they're being shown off in spectacular ancient buildings.

Coronations

In 1838, amid preparations for Victoria's coronation, Earl Fitzwilliam complained that "coronations were fit only for barbarous ages, or semi-barbarous ages; for periods when crowns were won and lost by unruly violence and ferocious contests". The survival of the English coronation ceremony, once hereditary monarchy had been established and the line of succession agreed upon, is puzzling. It has proved remarkably resistant to any monarchical, religious and political upheaval: babies, boys, consorts and queen regnants, whether Catholic or Protestant (and/or foreign and/or illegitimate), have all been crowned according to more or less the same ritual.

While Spain abolished its coronation ceremony and regalia in the fourteenth century, British kings and queens clung on to the piece of theatre staged in Westminster Abbey, with its centuries-old words and props (swords, sceptre, orb, crown and holy oil). At its heart, the ceremony is supposedly a magical one: becoming a monarch is a consecration in which a body becomes sacred. At the coronation of Elizabeth II, in 1953, as Archbishop Geoffrey prepared to anoint the young queen, a silk canopy was held up to hide her from view.. "Bless and sanctify thy chosen servant Elizabeth," he said, "who by our office and ministry is now to be anointed with this oil, and consecrated Queen". It is the anointing, not the crowning, which symbolizes the physical transformation, and this solemn moment was considered too powerful, and too private, to be broadcast to the nation in 1953.

Rulers have always marked their election with an accession rite. But it wasn't until the eighth century that the church became involved, and bishops began to anoint rulers in imitation of the Old Testament kings David and Solomon. Consequently, kings have often wondered about what exactly is happening to them during their coronation. "What does the sacrament of coronation make me?" pondered Charlemagne, the Holy Roman Emperor, in 800. Henry II was convinced that he had been endowed with magical powers at his coronation, believing that when he "laid his hands on the sick" he cured them of scrofula (a disease also known as the King's Evil); the belief that the king's touch could cure skin disease was common in the Middle Ages. But Archbishop Thomas Becket insisted that being anointed king was simply a symbolic act, and that kings were not at all like priests.

Three hundred years later, when six-year-old Edward VI was crowned, Archbishop Thomas Cranmer explained that the "solemn rites of coronation have their ends and utility," but are not wholly necessary. "The oil, if added, is but a ceremony," he said. "If it be wanting, that king is yet a perfect monarch notwithstanding, and God's Anointed as well as if he was inoiled." And yet today's monarchs are still anointed with oil and the coronation rite looks remarkably like its medieval prototype. When Prince Charles is crowned Charles III he will swear an oath and be anointed, invested with the regalia and crowned with St Edward's crown. When Queen Mary, George V's wife, was crowned, newspapers reported that it was "as if she had undergone some marvellous transformation".

Will Charles think the same? The English coronation is for many a spine-tingling spectacle and the irrational idea that something transformative happens – and that it is still needed as an act of legitimation – has proved hard to shift. "Presume not that I am the thing I was," Shakespeare's newly crowned Henry V warns Falstaff, his former partner-in-revelry.

Coronation customs and etiquette

Before Elizabeth II was crowned, the then Dean of Westminster wrote that "the girding with the Sword, the clothing with the Royal Robe, the presentation of the Orb with the Cross, the Ring, and the two Sceptres ... with the culminating act of Coronation, are charged with spiritual meaning and intent which have remained constant for the past twelve hundred years, no matter how greatly outward circumstances have changed." The coronation ritual, which has developed over centuries, is successful partly because it retains the illusion of tradition. While the form of the ceremony has remained surprisingly constant, its meaning has not. "Kings are like gods," asserted James I; Elizabeth II could never make such a claim.

The order and Latin words of the English ritual began to be written down in Anglo-Saxon times. It went through three major revisions before reaching its final version at the end of the fourteenth century, which is now preserved in the *Liber Regalis* (the Book of Kings) – a huge, leather-bound illuminated vellum manuscript kept on display at Westminster Abbey. It is, in practice, one of the oldest prompt books around.

EDWARD THE CONFESSOR

Edward the Confessor (so-called due to his famous piety) ruled England from 1042 until the Norman conquest in 1066. He built the original Westminster Abbey to be a royal mausoleum, two centuries before it was renovated and expanded by Henry III in 1245. In 1161, after some years of petitioning the Church, the white-haired Anglo-Saxon king with a fondness for hunting was finally canonized. From then on, a set of regalia believed to have belonged to "the most sainted King Edward" became holy relics, to be used at the coronations of all subsequent English monarchs. Which they were, until they were melted down by Oliver Cromwell in 1649.

It was Henry III who really fuelled the cult of St Edward and, expediently, the notion of sacred kingship. During Henry's reign, Edward's body was translated to his final resting place, in a chapel in Westminster Abbey, east of the sanctuary. It is in this Chapel of the Shrine of St Edward the Confessor that newly crowned kings and queens divest themselves of the regalia, and hand it back symbolically to St Edward. Edward's marriage, to Edith, was childless, but whether or not he was celibate is a matter of debate among historians. Interestingly, this erstwhile patron saint of England – he was ultimately ousted by St George (see p.249) – remains the patron saint of difficult marriages for the Catholic Church.

The rite was translated into English for the first time in 1603, for James I's coronation, and substantially revised in 1689 for the coronation of William III and Mary II. Then the royal couple had to swear that they were indeed *below* the law, and that they would "maintain the Protestant Reformed Religion Established by Law". The coronation oath is the only element of the ritual to have undergone significant changes, and this is because it articulates the constitutional powers – and, crucially, the limitations – of a British monarch. As such, the oath can come back to haunt monarchs: Richard II and Charles I were both found guilty of reneging on their coronation promises, and Henry VIII tried to revise his oath some twenty years after he was crowned, to bring it in line with his newfound supremacy.

Westminster Abbey is now known as the coronation church but, before the reign of Henry III, kings could be crowned anywhere. In 973, King Edgar was crowned in Bath, for example. William the Conqueror was the first king known to be crowned in Westminster Abbey, on Christmas Day in 1066. In times when a monarch faced the real possibility of being deposed, a new king's coronation would follow hot on the heels of the old king's funeral - usually within three months. Nevertheless, the Abbey needed to be prepared, decorated and transformed into an appropriately grand stage for the occasion – and it still is today. A big raised dais called the Theatre, with steps leading up to it, is built at the transept beyond the choir, and covered in red carpet. The throne is positioned in the middle, facing the altar. King Edward's Chair (used for the anointing and crowning) is placed on a lower part of the dais, before the altar. Another chair for the monarch to use, called the Chair of Estate, is set up on the south side of the altar. Up near the dais, boxes are created for the rest of the royal family to sit in. Just before the ceremony, the regalia is collected from the Jewel House in the Tower of London, transported to the Abbey, and laid on the altar.

The ceremony then follows a very particular, prescribed order, opening with a curious hangover from the times of elective monarchy.

The recognition

The monarch makes his or her progress up the nave to the stage, with the bishops and peers bearing certain items of the regalia. The Archbishop of Canterbury then shows the monarch the four sides of the Abbey, beginning at the east, then the south, west and north. At each side, he stops and addresses the audience. "Sirs, I here present unto you [the name of the monarch in question], your undoubted King [Queen]," he announces, before asking "Wherefore all you who are come this day to do your hom-

THE CORONATION CHAIR

In 1274, Edward I became the first king to be crowned in Westminster Abbey, following its redesign by Henry III as a church to be used specifically for coronations. Towards the end of the thirteenth century, Edward ordered the construction of the Coronation Chair, also known as King Edward's Chair, which is said to have been used for the anointing and crowning of all subsequent monarchs. Edward built this chair to hold the Stone of Scone (also known as the Stone of Destiny), which he had seized from the Scots in 1296 and which Scottish kings apparently used for their inauguration rituals. This controversial symbol of England's relationship with Scotland used to be in prominent display in the Abbey.

The Coronation Chair, from an etching of 1845.

In 1653 Oliver Cromwell moved the chair to Westminster Hall and sat on it for his investiture as Protector. In the eighteenth and nineteenth centuries Westminster schoolboys etched their names into the chair's carved wooden frame and, in the twentieth century, the chair was partly blown up by a bomb in a handbag, placed by a suffragette.

The Stone was stolen back by a group of Scottish nationalist students on Christmas Day 1950, driven back up to Scotland, and placed into the safekeeping of Arbroath Abbey. However, the Church of Scotland returned it to Westminster Abbey, where it remained for decades. The oblong sandstone block was finally given back to Scotland in 1996 by Tony Blair. It is now in Edinburgh Castle, but will return temporarily to England, on loan, for the next coronation.

age and service; are you willing to do the same?" The people hopefully reply by crying "God Save [said monarch]!"

The oath

This is the king or queen's contract with parliament, and with the populace – and it is important that it precedes the anointing. The oath recognizes that the monarch is anointed because he or she has made certain promises to the people, and not because it is simply his or her irrefutable right to become an anointed monarch. The oath follows a question and answer format and, of course, must reflect all the countries and territories of which he or she is head – and their laws. Elizabeth II was asked the following mouthful of a question: "Do you solemnly promise and swear to govern the peoples of Great Britain, Ireland, Canada, Australia, New Zealand, the Union of South Africa, of your possessions, and other territories to them belonging or appertaining, and of your Empire of India, according to their respective laws and customs?"

The anointing
The monarch sits in King Edward's Chair, and a canopy is held up by four Knights of the Garter so that he or she is hidden. The Archbishop of Canterbury anoints the monarch in the form of a cross with holy oil (made according to a secret recipe of orange, rose, cinnamon, musk and ambergris oils) on the palms of both hands, the breast and head. The choir sing "Zadok the Priest", first sung in 973 and now sung to the stirring tune Handel wrote for George II's coronation in 1727. Monarchs used to also be anointed on their shoulders and elbows, and before the Reformation they were anointed twice on their heads, the second time with "chrism", an especially sacred oil reserved for the anointing of bishops.

The investiture
The anointed monarch is then reclothed, first in the *colobium sindonis*, a loose linen garment, and then the *supertunica* (or *dalmatica*), made from cloth of gold, is placed on top. He or she is then presented with the regalia – spurs, sword of state and armills (golden bracelets) – before being draped in yet more ceremonial livery – a stole and gold cloth robe. Then there's more receiving of regalia – the orb, the coronation ring (worn on the wedding finger), the sceptre with the cross (into the right hand) and rod with the dove (into the left hand). The monarch returns some of these, but retains the sceptre and rod.

The crowning
Finally, the monarch is crowned with St Edward's Crown. As the Archbishop places the crown on the head, all the princes and princesses, peers and peeresses put on their coronets and caps, and everyone shouts "God Save the King!" (or Queen). Trumpets sound and guns fire.

The enthronement
The monarch is lifted into the throne and all the bishops and peers pay homage. The coronation ends with the monarch taking communion,

before withdrawing to St Edward's Chapel. There, he or she takes off St Edward's Crown, puts on their state crown and recesses back through the Abbey, wearing a purple velvet robe and clutching the sceptre and the orb. The congregation sings the National Anthem.

Coronation paraphernalia: the regalia and robes

A British sovereign cannot be crowned without a crown (or two). And neither would the coronation be complete without the coronation ring, spurs, bracelets, sceptre, orb and priestly robes.

Many objects make up the regalia, and each has a specific role to play in this most theatrical of rituals. As well as being highly symbolic, each piece is, of course, hugely valuable. When Charles I lost his head in 1649, many of the royal gold, silver and bejewelled objects were melted down (and the gemstones sold) and turned into coins, on Cromwell's orders. With the restoration of Charles II in 1660, an entirely new set of regalia was commissioned for his coronation, costing over £12,000. Some gold from the medieval crown of Edward the Confessor was, apparently, saved and reworked into a new St Edward's Crown – and this is the crown used today. Charles II's regalia is now held along with the rest of the crown jewels in the Tower of London. Some medieval items survive: the gold anointing spoon, used to spoon out the holy oil, dates from the twelfth century and three swords "with scabbards of cloth of gold" also survived the Republic.

British royals are the only ones in Europe to still risk bringing out their crown jewels for coronations. Most of the key props are carried as part of the procession into the Abbey by peers (who's holding what in the coronation procession is an important indicator of household rank and favour) before being placed on the altar, along with the Bible, paten and chalice. The main pieces to look out for, in order of appearance, are these:

The Sword of State Five swords are used in the coronation ceremony: this one is carried before the monarch throughout.

Curtana This blunted sword is also known as both the Sword of Mercy and Edward the Confessor's Sword. Its blade is cut off short and square, supposedly symbolic of the quality of the mercy of the sovereign. In the ceremony it is carried in between the **Sword of Spiritual Justice** (symbolic of the Crown's relationship to the Church) and the **Sword of Temporal Justice** (symbolic of the Crown's relationship to the state).

The anonymous *Coronation Portrait* shows Queen Elizabeth I in her full coronation splendour, her hair down, dressed in the cloth of gold (previously worn by Mary I) and carrying her orb and sceptre.

The Jewelled Sword of Offering Traditionally presented to the monarch after the anointing, this sword has sometimes taken the place of the (significantly heavier) Sword of State.

The Ampulla This gold flask, in the form of an eagle, contains the holy oil used for the anointing. Both the ampulla and the coronation spoon are positioned on the altar.

The Colobium Sindonis A simple white linen tunic or dress worn by the monarch, once he or she has been anointed.

The Supertunica or Close Pall A long, wide-sleeved gold coat, and the second item of clothing with which the monarch is dressed following the anointing.

The Spurs Symbolizing chivalry, the spurs are now presented to the monarch by the Lord Great Chamberlain, rather than actually put on.

The Armills or Bracelets Symbols of sincerity and wisdom, these gold bracelets are put on the monarch's wrists by the Archbishop of Canterbury as "pledges of that bond which unites you with your peoples". New bracelets were presented to Elizabeth II in 1953 by members of the Commonwealth.

The Robe Royal or Pall A large and sumptuous open mantle or cloak, this is also referred to as the Imperial Robe and the Robe of Righteousness. It supposedly bestows "knowledge and wisdom … majesty and … power from on high".

The Orb with the Cross The golden sphere with the bands of jewels and topped by a cross is placed into the right hand of the monarch momentarily, and then picked up and carried in the left hand for the recess. It represents Christ's power over the world.

THE LONG AND THE SHORT OF ROYAL REIGNS

If you discount James Stuart, the Old Pretender, who spent 64 years claiming the thrones of England and Scotland but no years at all actually sitting on them, Queen Victoria is Britain's longest-serving monarch. She presided over unprecedented change. In the very year that she came to the throne, 1837, Daguerre invented photography, Darwin finished writing up his *Beagle* voyage, and Cooke and Wheatstone patented their electric telegraph. By the time she died, on 22 January 1901, after 63 years and 216 days on the throne, her country was covered in railways (not to mention photographs, telegraphs and telephones), and Britain had acquired a global Empire.

Until recently, Victoria's nearest rivals for longevity were George III, who kept going, despite poor mental health, for 59 years and 247 days, and James VI and I, who ruled Scotland for 57 years and 246 days (though in England he only managed a touch over 22 years). Now, however, second place goes to Elizabeth II, who at the time of writing was approaching her sixty-year jubilee. Assuming she – and the monarchy – survives, she will surpass Victoria's record on 10 September 2015.

Elizabeth has some way to go, however, before she achieves a world record. She has to watch out for multi-billionaire Bhumibol Adulyadej, aka Rama IX

The Ring A sapphire and ruby ring, worn on the fourth finger of the left hand, this symbolizes "kingly dignity" and is a "seal of faith".

The Sceptre with the Cross A long, gold and bejewelled rod fashioned in 1661, in the twentieth century this was set with the First Star of Africa, the larger of the two diamonds cut from the huge Cullinan Diamond given to Edward VII by South Africa in 1907. Held by the right hand, it is an "ensign of kingly power and justice".

The Sceptre (or Rod) with the Dove A long, gold rod, also from 1661, which is delivered into the left hand and represents "equity and mercy".

St Edward's Crown Only once the monarch has been invested with the regalia above can he or she be crowned with St Edward's Crown. Modelled on the medieval crown that supposedly belonged to Edward the Confessor, the current St Edward's Crown was made for Charles II in 1661. Golden, hooped, topped by a cross and studded with jewels, it weighs an impressive 2.23 kilograms and is, understandably, not worn for long.

The Imperial State Crown This is the crown worn by the monarch as he or she leaves the Abbey, dressed in a purple velvet robe and carrying

of Thailand, who is still going strong at over 65 years. It seems unlikely that she'll ever catch Bernhard VII, Prince of the German micro-state of Lippe; known as "Bellicosus", or "the Warlike", Bernhard is currently acknowledged as the European record-holder, with an 81-year reign stretching across most of the fifteenth century. The all-out global champion, however, is Ngwenyama Sobhuza II of Swaziland: he reigned from 1899, when the British were fighting the Boers in South Africa, to 1982, when they were grappling with the Argentinians in the Falklands.

The title of shortest-reigning English monarch is a tricky one to award. The strongest candidates, arguably, don't count, as they were never crowned. The top five uncrowned monarchs are Lady Jane Grey, the "Nine Day Queen" of 1553; Sweyn "Forkbeard", who managed forty days around Christmas 1013; Edgar II, who teetered on the throne for a couple of months in 1066; the boy prince Edward V, who vanished into the darkness of the Tower of London some time in 1483; and Matilda, who came out on top for a brief spell, in 1141, but is usually discounted in favour of her rival, Stephen. The title, then, should probably go to Edmund II, "Ironside", who just about got himself crowned in April 1016, while the Danes were laying siege to London. Unfortunately, he was dead by November.

the sceptre with the cross in the right hand, and the orb in the left. The current imperial state crown was made for the coronation of George VI in 1937. It contains 2868 diamonds, 273 pearls, 17 sapphires, 11 emeralds and 5 rubies, as well as the Second Star of Africa, the smaller of the two huge diamonds cut from the Cullinan.

Some paraphernalia has been lost over the centuries. Linen gloves used to be given to the monarch following the anointing of the hands, supposedly to preserve the oil's sanctifying powers. A coif or ecclesiastical cap used to be put on the monarch's head following its anointing and it was not to be removed for a whole eight days. There was also a comb used to smooth the monarch's hair prior to the anointing. It was found, in the inventory of the regalia made in 1649, to be "worth nothing".

Memorable coronations: a timeline

787 The earliest reference to a king-making ritual in England is that of King Offa's son, Ecgferth, who was, according to the *Anglo-Saxon Chronicle*, "hallowed to king" – possibly meaning that he was anointed with oil.

973 The first full account of an English coronation describes Edgar I's splendidly liturgical ceremony in Bath Abbey on Whit Sunday 973. While Saxon kings had long enjoyed some form of inauguration rite (outside, and with a helmet instead of a crown), Edgar's solemn ritual was carefully devised by his Archbishop of Canterbury, St Dunstan. It firmly established the idea of sacred kingship and set the precedent for the English coronation for the next thousand years.

1066 On Christmas Day 1066, William the Conqueror was crowned in Westminster Abbey, the first coronation to take place in the newly con-secrated church built by Edward the Confessor. When the congregation was asked if they would accept the Norman as their king, the cheers of acclamation were so thunderous that the troops standing guard outside, fearing a riot, set fire to neighbouring houses. Many fled the Abbey but William refused to leave and was crowned amid the chaos.

1274 Edward I and his wife, Eleanor of Castile, were both crowned on 19 August 1274, making their coronation the first ever of a king and his consort – and the first to take place in the Abbey following its redesign as a coronation church by Henry III. The popular young couple celebrated for a further 14 days, hosting feasts that got through a total of 60 oxen, 60 swine, 40 pigs and 3000 capons.

1399 Henry IV, who had deposed Richard II, was determined to stress his legitimacy and divine status during his coronation. He lay down before the altar on a cloth of gold and was anointed with oil that had supposedly been delivered to St Thomas Becket by the Virgin Mary (and which apparently prompted all the lice to scurry out of his hair). He was then carried aloft to his throne.

1547 Henry VIII's only son, Edward VI, was crowned when he was nine years old by the Protestant reformer Archbishop Thomas Cranmer. In his coronation sermon Cranmer famously declared that "the solemn rites of coronation have their ends and utility; yet neither direct force or necessity ... the oil, if added, is but a ceremony".

1533 Anne Boleyn was already six months pregnant with Elizabeth when she was crowned on 1 June, and her ostentatious ceremony was nothing if not controversial. The procession route was lined with banners decorated with the intertwined initials H and A, prompting some of the dissenting crowd to laugh scornfully ("Ha ha!"). Anne was also crowned with St Edward's Crown – a privilege reserved for kings, not female consorts. She was the last of Henry's wives to be granted a coronation.

1553 On 1 October, England's first queen regnant, Mary I, was crowned. She was anointed and invested with the regalia just like a king, according to lengthy Catholic rites. After seven hours, Mary emerged from the Abbey, clutching the sceptre in one hand and, in the other, the golden orb which she "twirled and turned".

1626 Charles I turned up for his coronation on 2 February dressed in white satin, earning him the nickname "The White King". For a man who believed in ritual, this sumptuous and orderly coronation was not without its worrying omens: an awkward silence followed Charles's presentation as king and, during the service, there was a short, sharp earthquake. Charles's French Catholic wife, Henrietta Maria, refused to attend the Protestant ceremony.

1689 William III and Mary II enjoyed a joint coronation on 13 February. They were anointed and crowned as two monarchs in one ceremony. Following the unpopular reign of the Catholic James II (who was still alive), the royal pair had to concede that they were definitely below the law: this evident curtailing of royal power, articulated in the coronation, ensured the survival of this medieval ritual and, indeed, of the British monarchy.

1761 Many of the congregation present at George III's coronation on 22 September could not hear the long-winded sermon, so they took the opportunity to tuck into their picnics. The ensuing clattering of knives and forks and the clinking of glasses was so preposterous that everyone in the Abbey burst out laughing.

1821 George IV's coronation was a great theatrical spectacle which cost the king and country £238,000. His estranged wife, Caroline of Brunswick (see p.151), whom he hated, was refused entry to the Abbey,

The British public had no need to panic: this leaflet ensured no one would forget to tune in their wireless at the right time.

despite legally being Queen of England. This coronation was so outrageously extravagant that the traditional banquet in Westminster Hall was never held again. In 1831, George's brother, William IV, had to be talked into having a coronation at all and he spent comparatively so little money that it became known as "the penny coronation".

1937 George VI (aka Albert, Duke of York) was crowned, with his queen consort Elizabeth Bowes-Lyon, on 12 May – the day originally set for the coronation of George's older brother Edward VIII, who had abdicated after less than a year on the throne. Bertie's diary documents all the things that went wrong. The Dean of Westminster couldn't find the wording of the oath and got the *colobium sindonis* inside out. The Lord Great Chamberlain was too frail to dress the king in his robes, so Bertie dressed himself, before one of the bishops stood on his train. "Horror of horrors!" Bertie wrote. With Europe standing on the brink of war, this coronation attempted to shore up national confidence with imperial pageantry. The Koh-i-Noor and Cullinan diamonds glittered in the crowns and Elizabeth's purple velvet train was embroidered with emblems of the ten countries belonging to the Empire.

Jubilees

Jubilees may seem as traditional as coronations, royal weddings or state funerals, but they're really a nineteenth-century invention. Even the word jubilee is a concoction – or at least a borrowing. Catholic "jubilee" years were invented by Pope Boniface VIII in 1300 when he decided to boost local tourism (and church coffers) by declaring that the sins of pilgrims visiting Rome could be especially thoroughly washed away that particular year. He'd taken the idea from the Bible's Book of Leviticus, which declared that every fiftieth year should be a year of liberty, when slaves should be released and land handed over to, ahem, the priesthood.

The Victorians did manage to dig up some snippets of medieval jubilee tradition. Henry III apparently released a few prisoners and recalled a few exiles for his fifty years, in 1265, and there were modest festivities for Edward III in 1377 – though His Majesty was by then almost dead, and in any case discouraged celebrations on the grounds that it was a time of "Wars … Pestilence, Murrain of Beasts and failure of the Fruits of the Earth".

It was under George III that the first big jubilee party was thrown. For this "spontaneous effusion of love" on 25 October 1809, incessant peals of church bells were rung by teams of ringers, houses were bedecked with evergreen garlands, and triumphal arches were set up across the streets. The Baltic squadrons enjoyed a grand naval fête and, according to one snarky account, "what few soldiers there were left in the kingdom were paraded". (Britain was not having the best of times in the Napoleonic wars.) Deserters had special reason to celebrate: they were universally pardoned. Debtors, too, were released from gaol in their scores, and Russian, Danish and Dutch prisoners of war were set free, all in the Biblical tradition.

Victoria's jubilees

By the time Victoria notched up fifty years on the throne, in 1887, expectations of royal spectacle were vastly inflated from George's day. Victoria treated fifty European kings and princes to dinner: "the King of Denmark

Crowds in Trafalgar Square, London, celebrating Victoria's diamond jubliee in 1897.

ROAST OX, PLUM PUDDING, STRONG BEER

At George III's golden jubilee, roast ox and plum pudding were the favoured dishes of feasting. The queen herself attended an ox-roasting before the royal family went on to a fireworks party at Frogmore (which was, unfortunately, a very damp squib). Vast quantities of strong beer were drunk in mugs specially made so as to hold a little *over* a pint: the country was determined to forget its wartime woes. As one versifier for the occasion put it, "When tossed upon the sea of life/By adverse fortune's gale, sir/You unconcerned may view the strife/Well lined with Burton ale, sir."

took me in," she confided to her diary, "and Willy of Greece sat on my other side." The next day, she processed through London in an open carriage to Westminster Abbey, with Indian cavalrymen trotting around her and crowds cheering all the way. Some had come long distances to see the show: Cook's tour company had even offered two-day package excursions for northerners wanting to attend the festivities.

Not everyone was enthusiastic. Victoria herself believed that "ostentatious pomp" was "utterly incompatible and unsuitable to the present day", and her ministers had to persuade her to agree to the celebrations on the grounds that it would impress an image of Britain's military strength upon foreign powers. Her government also took the opportunity to arrange a sting on the Irish republican movement. The public was told that police had foiled a Guy Fawkes-style "Jubilee Plot" to assassinate the Queen by blowing up Westminster Abbey during the Service of Thanksgiving. The public was not told, however, that it had been orchestrated by a British double agent working for the prime minister, Lord Salisbury, and was designed to discredit the Irish nationalist leader Charles Parnell.

Outspoken anti-monarchists were rounded up and imprisoned before the jubilee, as a precaution, and there were violent clashes between radicals and royalists at Oldham Edge, where a celebratory beacon had been lit. At Walton-on-the-Naze, in Essex, malcontents dressed an elderly man in drag, and paraded him along in an old cart drawn by eight donkeys. A radical newspaper, meanwhile, published an alternative national anthem: "Lord help our precious Queen/Noble but rather mean/Lord help the Queen/Keep Queen VicToryous/From work laborious/Let snobs uproarious/Slaver the Queen".

Still, Victoria and the monarchy survived, and the queen celebrated a diamond jubilee ten years later, in 1897. By this time, she was getting old – and recovering her popularity. On her return to Buckingham Palace, she was cheered by her people all the way along the six-mile procession route. It was, she wrote, "quite deafening and every face seemed to be filled with real joy". She confessed herself to be "much moved and gratified".

Durbars and empire in India

The grandest of all British jubilees – arguably the grandest state ceremonials ever held – were the three *durbars* of India. The word, taken from the Mughal word for court, was designed to fit the British into an established precedent of foreign overlordship within India. The first Durbar, of 1877, proclaimed Queen Victoria as Empress of India, a title Disraeli had procured for her as a form of flattery. Victoria didn't attend, but her viceroy, Lord Lytton, presided as 1200 civil servants, 14,000 troops and 75 Indian rajas and maharajas fawned and paraded at the huge "imperial assemblage" outside Delhi.

Unfortunately for British propaganda purposes, this jamboree was held during India's worst famine – created by a failed monsoon but exacerbated by British policies, including continuing grain exports to Britain and parsimonious relief efforts. As the empire polished its buttons in Delhi, some eight million Indians died. The effect was to mobilize Indian nationalism.

The 1903 Delhi Durbar, held for the coronation of Edward VII and his wife Alexandra, was still more sumptuous, even if the monarch, again, did not attend. The tent city was served by its own light railway, post office, court and police force. Lord Curzon, the viceroy, arrived on an elephant, while his wife dazzled in a now-legendary Parisian gold-thread dress embroidered with peacock feathers and embossed with iridescent beetle wings. Indian kings and princes came to pay homage in their scores, and to join in the endless programme of balls, tiger shoots, concerts, exhibitions and military reviews.

The last Durbar, of 1911, was for the coronation of George V. George actually attended in person, thus becoming the first British king to visit India. His pavilion alone covered 85 acres, and lesser encampments spread out from it in strict hierarchical order across 25 square miles of land – land that, George announced, would become his new imperial capital. He and Queen Mary sat on solid silver thrones weighing over half a ton each, while artillery gave a 101-gun salute, and Indian princes, generals and flunkies did obeisance before him.

Propaganda footage of the 1903 Durbar is supposed to have ignited India's taste for cinema, but it was the documentary film of the 1911 Durbar that became a massive international hit. Shot in innovative

Pomp and ceremony at the 1903 Delhi Durbar (with the British monarch notably absent again).

Kinemacolor, it was watched all over the world: "Nothing so soul-stirring, so varied or so beautiful has ever been seen," gushed London's *Evening News.* Certainly, nothing so staggering was ever seen again. By the time of the next British coronation, George VI's in 1937, the Indian National Congress was voting to boycott any Durbar. And after that came war, independence and the end of empire.

Silver and gold: Elizabeth's jubilees

The summer of 1977 was dubbed the Summer of Hate in Britain. Punk was all the rage. It was also the summer of Elizabeth II's 25-year silver jubilee, which was designed to reinforce royal traditions. Echoing Victoria, the Queen lit a bonfire beacon at Windsor on 6 June; other beacons were then ignited across the country in a fiery chain. The next day she drove in the golden State Coach (emphasizing the monarchy's glorious antiquity) to a service at St Paul's attended by heads of state and prime ministers from around the world (emphasizing the monarchy's supposed centrality in the globe's grand councils). On 9 June, Elizabeth took a boat along the River Thames from Greenwich to Lambeth, echoing Elizabeth I's barge pageants.

People look back on the silver jubilee largely as a genuine, old-fashioned community celebration these days. (Few remember the dissenters, though the story of how the BBC banned the Sex Pistols' republican punk anthem "God Save the Queen" – rhymed with "fascist regime" – is a great pop music tale, along with the fact that the song made it to number one.) Half a billion peopled ogled on television as the Queen processed down the Mall in her coach, and uncounted millions of Britons made their own flags and costumes and cakes, setting up their own, locally organized street parties.

The golden jubilee of 2002 was very different. Modernity and populism were the keynotes. The "Party at the Palace" on 3 June featured Brian May (formerly of the band Queen) playing the national anthem as an electric guitar solo on Buckingham Palace's roof, followed by 2.5 tons of fireworks; the event pulled in 200 million TV viewers. The Jubilee Parade down the Mall on the following day featured not Indian cavalrymen but massed, multi-ethnic Notting Hill Carnivallers. "Jubilee Chicken" was invented for people to make at home and press releases gushed about the 160,000 cups of tea pressed into the hands of grateful subjects at a succession of royal garden parties. (Another statistic, the £4 million policing bill, was explained away as having been met out of normal "national event" funding.) Wooing the crowd shamelessly, Prince Charles began his speech "Your Majesty ... Mummy..." This was a celebration designed by PR and Marketing for Windsor, plc.

Weddings

Victoria and Albert

Before Queen Victoria married Prince Albert of Saxe-Coburg-Gotha, on 10 February 1840, wedding dresses tended to be blue, or sometimes black, according to taste. Victoria, boldly, chose to wear white. It showed off the sheen of her dress's satin, with its trimmings of delicate orange flowers (she had more orange flowers in her nosegay and more still on her wreath), and it was the perfect colour for her four-yard-long lace flounce – which had been created by 200 English ladies working continuously over a period of almost nine months.

PRINCE ARTHUR AND KATHERINE OF ARAGON

Katherine of Aragon was sixteen years old when she sailed to England to marry Prince Arthur, son of the founder of the Tudor dynasty, Henry VII. The match was a major coup for England: Spain was an important Catholic power and this marriage broadcast to the rest of Europe that the Tudors were, after all, legitimate. Katherine also came with a huge dowry.

The young couple married in St Paul's Cathedral in November 1501. Katherine wore a big-hooped, Spanish-style gown in white satin, with a white silk veil. Arthur, too, was dressed in white satin. Arthur's younger brother, the dashing Prince Henry, led Katherine to the church and handed her to her groom. The couple exchanged their vows on the cathedral porch, standing on a little stage covered in red cloth. Katherine promised to be "bonair and buxom in bed and at board". The wedding reception was held at Baynard's Castle, and no expense was spared. For two weeks the guests ate and drank, danced in masques and tilted in the yard.

For the wedding night, the royal bedchamber was prepared according to strict regulations. The bed was sprinkled with holy water. Katherine was brought in by her ladies-in-waiting and laid in the bed, undressed but veiled. Arthur came in, escorted by his men. Musicians played softly. A bishop blessed the bed, and then everyone left Katherine and Arthur alone.

The next morning Arthur apparently boasted that he had "been this night in the middest of Spain". But whether or not Arthur and Katherine ever did consummate their marriage (Arthur died in April 1502) will never be known. Katherine, of course, famously insisted that she was still a virgin. But this brief marriage between two teenagers overturned English religion and monarchy a few years later when Henry VIII chose to marry his brother's widow.

The lace pattern was afterwards destroyed, so it could not be copied, but the colour of the dress became the new standard. Afterwards, almost all English brides would crave a "white wedding". Yet Victoria originally opted for white so that she could better be seen by the crowds. This was a wedding about show. It was even decided to change the timing from the usual evening slot to the afternoon, so that the masses could witness it. They duly appeared, Victoria noting in her diary that she "never saw such crowds as there were in the Park, and they cheered most enthusiastically."

Inside the Chapel Royal at St James's Palace, there was quite a press too, as chairs for guests had been put into every antechamber, as well as the chapel itself. There was hardly even room for the dress's eighteen-foot

JAMES II AND ANNE HYDE

In 1656, James, Duke of York, the unfortunate younger brother of the exiled king, Charles II, fell in love with Anne Hyde, his sister's plain but strong-minded Maid of Honour. As the romance developed, James began to plead with Anne to marry him. She held out for a year until, in November 1659, she agreed to a "contract" of marriage and to enter into what you might call conjugal relations.

By May 1660, Charles II was back on the throne, and James decided to make an indisputably honest woman of his betrothed. This was a problem. Anne was a gentleman's daughter, but she was an inconceivable partner for the king's own brother – no woman of non-noble blood would marry a potential future king again until Catherine Middleton, 350 years later.

James described how everyone from his brother down to his own servants opposed the marriage "with a violent zeal". Anne's father said he'd rather she was James's whore than his wife. James went through with it nonetheless. He married a heavily pregnant Anne on 3 September 1660, in a private ceremony held at around midnight in the chapel of Anne's father's house. Late evening, small-scale royal weddings were not unusual before the nineteenth century, but this was almost furtive: there were just four witnesses, including the chaplain and Anne's maid.

The romantic nature of the marriage didn't stop James taking mistresses, in the Stuart fashion. The diarist Samuel Pepys observed how, at one evening party, James "did eye my wife mightily". James's many lovers were apparently no more beautiful than his wife, however. The Bishop of Salisbury, Gilbert

train – and this was actually too short, at least for the twelve bridesmaids who failed to all get a secure hold of it. (The bridesmaids, incidentally, were not the daughters of spotlessly virtuous mothers, as Albert had demanded; this request was considered impossible to meet.)

After promising to love, honour and *obey* her husband – a controversial vow from a reigning queen marrying a poor German princeling – Victoria returned to Buckingham Palace. The newlyweds did not appear on the balcony (that "tradition" was only established at Victoria's daughter's wedding, when the queen felt sorry for the crowds outside who had been denied a sight of the princess), but they did exchange rings in private, and promised never to keep secrets from each other. Then came the grand banquet, which featured a cake that was nine feet in diameter and weighed 300 pounds, and was topped by a figure of Britannia presiding over the happy couple, with cherubs disporting themselves at their feet.

Burnet, claimed that King Charles drily told him that they must have been given to his brother by priests, as a penance. It was said of one mistress that nobody knew what James saw in her, because all she had to offer was her wit, and he was too stupid to understand it. James and Anne's first child, Charles, died before reaching his first birthday. Pepys wrote, cynically, that the child's questionable legitimacy meant that this would "please everybody; and I hear that the Duke and his Lady themselves are not much troubled at it". No one then could know that Charles II would die without heirs and that James and Anne's subsequent children, Mary and Anne, would both eventually sit on the throne as queens of England.

Anne Hyde, as painted by Sir Peter Lely.

The couple set off that same day for their three-day honeymoon in… Windsor Castle. The first night was apparently not spoiled by Victoria's headache: in her diary, she called it "a gratifying and bewildering experience". For all the showmanship, this was a marriage almost unique in royal history: it was inspired and underpinned by passion and great love.

Elizabeth Bowes-Lyon and "Bertie"

The 1923 marriage of Elizabeth Bowes-Lyon (the future Queen Mother) to Albert, Duke of York (the future George VI, though he didn't know it at the time), is often said to have been the first royal wedding of the high-glamour, mass-media age. In fact, the newly renamed "Windsor" family had already started rebranding itself, aware of the need to expunge the memory of hundreds of thousands having died in the trenches in the name of king and country.

This wasn't, for instance, actually the first royal wedding to take place in Westminster Abbey, as is often said. "Princess Pat", granddaughter of Queen Victoria, got married there in 1919. It was supposedly more suitable for the wedding of a "junior" royal than the Chapel Royal, in St James's. Princess Pat was also the first to marry a commoner (albeit one who was the third son of an Earl).

Hers was a grand show: the excitement of the crowds, blushed *The Times*'s correspondent, was "almost embarrassing". The unwashed masses were mortifyingly excitable again at the 1922 wedding of George V's daughter, Princess Mary, which also had Westminster Abbey as its venue. Some eager royalists even slept outside overnight to guarantee a good spot – another tradition born – and the archbishop's car struggled to get through the crowds.

The choice of venue may not have been original, then, but the wedding of Princess Elizabeth Bowes-Lyon did set a few other precedents. Elizabeth chose a high-fashion wedding dress: she went for ivory chiffon moiré in a very contemporary sack-shaped style, topping it with an odd lacy veil-cum-headpiece affair and a simple ermine cloak. Modern royal brides also copy Elizabeth's famous laying of her bouquet on the grave of the Unknown Warrior in the Abbey. This was praised as a great gesture of heartfelt spontaneity at the time, though it was in fact carefully modelled on the much-applauded action of Princess Mary the year before: Mary had handed her bouquet to an officer who had then laid it on the Cenotaph.

Elizabeth's decision to bump back to Buckingham Palace in the so-called Glass Coach (it's not wholly made of glass, disappointingly) is another regular feature of modern royal weddings, as is the gracious prancing on the balcony of Buckingham Palace for the cameras and the crowds. There's plentiful newsreel footage of Elizabeth's balcony scene, but unlike more recent royal weddings there was no kiss. There was also no live broadcast. The BBC asked permission to air the service on the wireless, but it was forbidden by the Chapter of Westminster Abbey. Undesirables, it was feared, might listen, "perhaps even some of them sitting in public houses, with their hats on". Some things really have changed.

Diana and Charles

"Sow your wild oats," Charles's uncle, Lord Mountbatten, advised him, and then, when ready, get hold of "a suitable, attractive and sweet-charactered girl before she has met anyone else she might fall for". Charles

AUGUSTA AND FREDERICK

Sixteen-year-old Augusta of Saxe-Gotha clearly found her wedding terrifying. She had been picked as a suitably German, Protestant bride for Frederick, Prince of Wales, by his father George II. She had arrived in the country – and had met her betrothed – only days before the ceremony, and barely knew any English. (Her parents had assured her that England, after twenty years of living under Hanoverian rule, had learned to speak German, so there was no need to study the language.)

In April 1736, England was in an uproar with "monstrous preparations" for the royal wedding, as one lady put it. Handel had written an extravagantly jaunty anthem, using the Biblical text "thy wife shall be as the fruitful vine". The Chapel Royal in St James's Palace, then the traditional venue for royal weddings, had been decked out with gold velvet hangings, roses and lanterns (admittedly, it was a somewhat hasty makeover: they'd only just cleared up after Easter). Augusta was presented with a stunning silver wedding dress, bedecked with diamonds and topped with an ermine-trimmed robe of crimson velvet.

On 27 April, the crowds gathered outside; inside, poor Augusta was struggling. She entwined herself in the skirts of her future mother-in-law, Queen Caroline, begging her not to leave her side, and Frederick had to yell into her ear to get her to repeat marriage vows she could not properly understand. She was so nervous, according to one account, that she was actually sick on the skirt to which she so tightly clung, even as she received George II's blessing. That night, her sister-in-law dressed her in her nuptial nightgown, and she waited in bed for her husband in his gold brocade gown. Later, the entire court came to pay its respects to the wedded and bedded royal couple.

As with so many royal brides, Augusta eventually found her feet. She learned to speak better English than her in-laws, and championed British fashions and fabrics to great effect. She bore nine children. The first, a daughter, was born in secret; Frederick having smuggled Augusta out of Hampton Court in the night to avoid her being forced to give birth under the watchful eyes of her parents-in-law (as was traditional). The last, another daughter, was born after Frederick's death, in 1766. Their second child, a son, became George III.

took his advice. His more public flirtations, as a young man with a vast income and no particular job, included actresses, models, a Belgian princess and a smattering of English aristocrats. He even had a relationship with Mountbatten's own granddaughter, Amanda Knatchbull; she refused his proposal of marriage.

One of the princely girlfriends was a Lady Sarah Spencer, but any chance of a deeper relationship collapsed after she told reporters she'd had "thousands" of boyfriends and anorexia. Charles moved on to her sister, Diana, a surprisingly naïve kindergarten helper who was quickly dubbed "Shy Di" by the British press. Diana seemed to fit Mountbatten's formula perfectly. Supposedly her uncle even offered assurances concerning her virginity. It looked perfect on paper, though Amanda Knatchbull's brother, Norton, advised Charles against pursuing a marriage which had no basis in love.

Charles himself let his lack of feelings slip in a joint TV interview with his fiancée, given after their engagement was announced in February 1981. Charles professed himself "amazed that she's been brave enough to take me on". Were they in love, probed the interviewer? Looking mortified, and shooting a prim look from under her concealing fringe, Diana replied "Of course". With an oddly superior smirk, Charles added, "Whatever 'in love' means." It later emerged that Diana knew, even then, that her husband was still involved – in at the very least an emotional way – with Camilla, the wife of Andrew Parker Bowles (who himself had once been the boyfriend of Princess Anne).

Public and private warning signs were brushed aside, however, and the wedding was set for 29 July 1981. It was widely touted as a fairy-tale event. St Paul's was chosen over Westminster Abbey because it could seat an astonishing 2600 guests: necessary space considering that all the kings, queens and heads of state of Europe were invited. Outside, 600,000 of the uninvited masses gathered, while roughly a thousand times as many again watched on television. In America, 60 million citizens of the US republic got up early to make sure they didn't miss it.

Diana arrived at the cathedral with the silk tulle of her 25-foot train filling the Glass Coach. On the steps, her designer had to fuss and primp it back into shape. Then, festooned in ivory silk taffeta, and veiled in lace hand-embroidered with 10,000 mother-of-pearl sequins (which didn't quite obscure her heavy waterproof mascara), she started processing down the aisle, with Clarke's regal Trumpet Voluntary ringing out. At that point, she later admitted, she considered turning around. Charles had confessed the previous evening that he did not love her.

Diana got to the altar, however, where she managed to muddle Charles's first two names, calling him "Philip Charles Arthur George". After returning to Buckingham Palace, with a headache induced by her tiara, Diana appeared on the balcony with her husband in now-traditional style. The newlyweds were greeted by rowdy chants demanding a kiss. No royal couple had ever even embraced at a formal public event before and it's claimed that Charles initially refused to get involved in what he called a "caper". (Or so press sources claimed, though it is very hard to see who, either on the balcony or off it, could possibly have overheard what he was saying.) Some say Prince Andrew, or Diana herself, encouraged him. Others that he asked the Queen's permission. Either way, Charles and Diana gave each other the called-for kiss.

Photographs appear to show her swooping up to him, with a swan-like uncurling of her body. In fact, they both turned to each other for the famous kiss, which was pretty perfunctory. With hindsight, it looks like a Judas kiss from him, and a piece of characteristic crowd-pleasing showmanship from her. As Diana later admitted, "there were three of us in this marriage" – and it quickly broke down under the pressure, ending in divorce in 1996.

Costume

The monarch's clothing is far more than a straightforward display of wealth and status. Not necessarily fashionable, royal costume has always been symbolic, working above all to maintain the institution rather than set new trends. There have been some exceptions, of course, with a few royal style leaders catching the public imagination – but whether audacious or conservative, royal costume is always full of meaning.

Tudor trends

The Tudors, and in particular Henry VIII and Elizabeth I, rejoiced in the power of display to enforce royal authority. Textiles were hugely expensive in the sixteenth century, decorated with gold and silver and valuable dyes, and clothes were crucial signifiers of wealth, taste and importance. Both monarchs were keen proponents of sumptuary laws, placing restrictions on what their subjects could own, consume and, in particular, wear. Henry decorated himself as flamboyantly as he adorned his palaces, evoking kingly magnificence in everything from large hats to bulky codpieces. Elizabeth, who used costume to nurture her cult, passed statutes that attempted, among other things, to ban the lower orders from wearing long cloaks and big ruffs. She herself wore colossal farthingales, ruffs and headdresses, brimming with the same allegorical imagery as her portraits (see p.220). Her sense of theatre was renowned, and while she preferred white (purity) and black (strength), these base colours would be embedded with jewels and heavily embroidered with complex symbols, including sea monsters, cobwebs, eyes and ears.

THE ORDER OF THE GARTER

One of the most overtly symbolic pieces of royal costume is the garter, the emblem of the Royal Order of the Garter, founded by Edward III in 1348. The garter is still Britain's highest order of chivalry with only twenty-four knights at any one time, each of whom has been chosen by the sovereign, alongside a handful of knights from the royal family. St George is the patron saint of the Order (as he is of England) and every summer there is a procession of knights and a special service at St George's Chapel, Windsor. Those selected tend to be figures who have either held high public office or who made a significant contribution to national live, but it also includes people who have served the monarch in a personal capacity.

The reasons the garter itself became the Order's emblem are obscure – as is the root of its motto, *Honi Soit Qui Mal Y Pense* (evil to him who evil thinks) – but this buckled ribbon of blue velvet, worn under the left knee by men and on the left upper arm by women, remains a profound totem of royal entitlement. Henry VIII was invariably painted with the garter tied around his sturdy calves, and most formal portraits up to the nineteenth century show the sparkling garter fastened to a royal limb. Other Order accoutrements are almost as potent – it's believed that Charles I wore his Order sash to his execution, and both Charles II, a wily manipulator milking its symbolism, and George II, a fan of uniform in all its forms, frequently donned their Garter robes.

The Windsor Uniform

Though the dandy George IV is well remembered for his fashion sense, it was his father, George III, who designed one of the most important royal costumes. Not a soldier himself – his grandfather, George II, was the last monarch to lead troops into battle – but recognizing the political power of military regalia, in the 1770s he designed the "Windsor Uniform". This ensemble of blue, red and gold was favoured not only by the king but also, in modified form, by his queen, children and court, creating a recognizable uniform that stood outside fashion and signified, above all, unassailable rank. Various versions of the Windsor Uniform have been worn over the years by royals, including Queen Victoria. The "full-dress" version, with gold trimmings, is no longer seen, but the "undress" version, which consists of a dark blue jacket with red collar and cuffs, is still occasionally worn by male members of the family: Prince Charles usually wears it when out hunting and both he and Prince Philip sometimes adopt it in place of a dinner jacket when in residence at Windsor.

Tartan

The royal family has a curious relationship with tartan, once identified exclusively with Highland clans. After the defeat of Bonnie Prince Charlie at Culloden, the cloth – associated with the Jacobites – was forbidden for anyone but government troops, and by the time the ban was lifted in the 1870s tartan was rarely seen. A conciliatory visit from George IV to Edinburgh in 1822, however, when David Wilkie painted the king looking rather dashing in kilt and bonnet, prompted a sudden upsurge in interest in things Scottish. Victoria and Albert's Scotland obsession led them to build a Scots Baronial castle, Balmoral, in 1855, kitting it out in their own tartan designs; "Balmoral" (red and black on grey) is still worn exclusively by royalty. Various designs have been produced for individual royals over the years, but tartan's days as a required royal costume may be numbered: Prince William has yet to don a kilt, even at Balmoral, where traditionally every royal is expected to tog up in Scottish garb.

Fashion leaders

The Tudor era saw two great peacocks, Elizabeth and Henry, define the look of a century, while the dandyish tastes of George IV – friend of that great arbiter of male attire, Beau Brummel – determined Regency fashions in not only clothing but also decorative arts and architecture. Victoria, for her part, shrouded herself in widow's black for forty years and helped generate the cult of death and mourning that swept the country during her reign. Her fashion-loving son, Edward VII, was another trendsetter: his style was widely copied, even in later years when his increased girth obliged him to leave the bottom button of his waistcoat undone.

Apart from the debonair Edward VIII and glamorous Princess Margaret – and look what happened to them – subsequent royals have tended to seem almost oblivious to fashion, though the press has valiantly forced the mantle of "style icon" onto outsiders like Princess Michael, Princess Diana and Catherine Middleton. In recent years, however, while official royal costume has remained largely conservative, there have been rumblings in the ranks. Kate Middleton's wedding dress, while not overtly radical, was designed by the house of East End maverick Alexander McQueen; that, along with William's resistance to wearing a kilt, implies a break with tradition that's congruent with the carefully constructed image of a new generation of "modern" royals.

Funerals

When a king (or a queen) was, in the words of James I, a "little god", a royal funeral could be as ritualized and spectacular as a coronation. The monarch's entrails and bowels would be removed, the belly stuffed with spices, and the body embalmed and wrapped. Palace walls would be draped in black cloth and a lifelike, life-size painted wooden effigy, richly robed, with a crown on its head and a sceptre and orb in its hands, would stand in for the dead monarch, and accompany the coffin in the long, ordered and solemn procession to the interment. Only at the end of the service would all the symbols of majesty be taken away and returned to God. But the reign of the successor had already begun. Ever since Henry III died in 1272, while his son Edward was abroad and England endured four kingless days between one sovereign and the next, the new king is considered to have acceded at the very moment of his predecessor's death: hence the proclamation "The King is dead! Long live the King!"

Mary II

Mary II was not a mere queen consort, the wife of a king, but a queen regnant. After the deposing of her father, the stubbornly Catholic James II, she ruled in her own right alongside her husband, William III, from 1689. She ruled well, by most accounts, but briefly, falling victim to the viral scourge of the age, smallpox, and dying on 28 December 1694. She was widely mourned. Bishops preached from Proverbs 31: "Many daughters have done virtuously, but thou excellest them all", thus rebutting the Jacobite accusation that she had dishonoured her own father by sitting on what was rightfully his throne. Her body was embalmed (though it was so cold that year that arguably it wasn't necessary – even the Thames froze over) and lay in state in Whitehall's Banqueting House for all to see and honour. Mary's written request that there should not be "any extraordinary expense" for her funeral was conveniently mislaid, so £50,000 was lavished on the proprieties, which vastly outstripped even the usual sumptuous spending on royal funerals (discounting that of the executed Charles I, who was allotted a beggarly £400).

A huge funeral coach was constructed in time for her funeral, on 5 March, and court composer Henry Purcell was commissioned to write music, which he did in the most sublimely solemn style. Court and populace alike turned out to view the cortege in all its finery. (No doubt the gentry "came laggering all along even tired with the length of the way and weight of their clothes", as one observer wrote of a previous royal funeral, that of James I's wife, Anne.)

Even MPs and lords came in full force, which was highly unusual: normally parliament was dissolved on the death of the sovereign. Because William continued to reign as joint sovereign, however, parliament was still sitting. Another novelty was that Mary was interred with her crown and sceptre, the symbols of her office, but without the usual warlike accoutrements of gauntlets, spurs, horse and battleaxe. These had featured in the funerals of Mary I (and, minus the gauntlet and spurs, Elizabeth I) but, curiously, by her namesake's time they were no longer considered appropriate for a female sovereign.

Princess Diana

A million people travelled to central London to witness the funeral, on 6 September 1997, of Diana Princess of Wales – more, even, than had attended her wedding procession. Shocked crowds gathered in an almost ominous silence – a hush that was utterly strange for such a large number of people pressed together in the very centre of one of Europe's busiest cities.

As the gun carriage carrying Diana's coffin trundled heavily from Kensington Palace to Westminster Abbey, it was followed, at a slow walking pace, by her former husband, her children, her brother and five hundred representatives of the charities she had publicly supported. Anxious discussions between the Palace and the Blair government had gone over all the issues and concerns. Prince William was said to be too angry with the media to accept any need for a public show. Advisors were reportedly terrified that if Prince Charles appeared on foot without his sons, but with Earl Spencer, it would be a disaster – he might even be in danger.

In the event, most of the watchers simply stood and stared. Some clapped, angrily. A few wept. Many threw flowers. One man repeatedly shrieked "My Princess!", in distress. The service in Westminster Abbey was marked by two radical departures from the usual stately protocols. First, Earl Spencer, Diana's brother, gave an astonishing address which both attacked the press and made covert swipes at the royal family – he pledged that her "blood family" would bring up her children so that their souls would be "not simply immersed by duty and tradition but can sing

The gates of Buckingham Palace in the days following Diana Spencer's death.

openly as you planned". He was clapped, even by those sitting inside the cathedral. Funeral orations are not generally applauded. Did this suggest it all seemed like a show? Or was this angry approval?

Then Elton John played and sang an old pop song of his own composition, with new lyrics written for the occasion by his songwriting partner; a song about the media stature and early death of one celebrity, Marilyn Monroe, became one about another, Diana. The very inappropriateness of it seemed oddly fitting. "A country lost without your soul," crooned Elton John, will "miss the wings of your compassion more than you'll ever know." Arguably, they would miss the kind of royal who could bring a pop star into Westminster Abbey just as much.

5

Royal controversies

Even in the Middle Ages, when a monarch behaving badly was par for the course, there were one or two characters who stood out from the pack for sheer viciousness, megalomania and skulduggery. Come the late seventeenth century, when power had shifted irrevocably from monarch to parliament, royal rumpuses tended to focus on more banal activities such as financial incompetence, sexual hypocrisy and dodgy politics. Below, in alphabetical order, are fifteen of the most undignified of royal episodes when the monarchy were embroiled in controversy or scandal.

Caroline of Brunswick: 1768–1821

It was the original Charles and Di scandal: he was the Prince of Wales with a taste for older mistresses; she was the politically chosen virginal bride who developed a penchant for foreign fancy-men. They couldn't stand each other and their marriage ended in legal wrangles and public scandal.

"Prinny", later George IV, was a high-spending, heavy-drinking playboy. Caroline was a blowsy, clumsy, ill-washed and ill-mannered princess from the German micro-state of Brunswick. She was picked in order to provide the prince with political connections, an heir and the wherewithal to pay off his debts.

Legend has it that on her arrival in England in 1795, George took one look at Caroline and asked for a glass of brandy. Caroline remarked, for her part, that the "very fat" prince was "not nearly as handsome as his

THE QUEEN'S TRIAL IN THE HOUSE OF LORDS.

A packed house. Queen Caroline's morals are put on trial in the House of Lords.

portrait". Despite his disgust and her contempt (she reported that on their wedding night he fell asleep, drunk, in the fireplace), they managed to conceive a daughter, but separated soon after. "We have unfortunately been obliged to acknowledge to each other," George wrote to her, "that we cannot find happiness in our union."

Instead, they sought happiness in lovers. George set up an inquiry into her behaviour, which uncovered rumours of a pregnancy and serious flirtations with men and women alike – but no proof of infidelity. But not long after George became regent, in 1811, following the final collapse of his father's mental health, a deal was struck by which Caroline agreed to live quietly abroad.

She went, but not quietly. In Italy, she held outrageous parties, and once drove through Genoa in a shell-shaped carriage while dressed in a revealing pink gauze bodice and pink, feather-adorned headdress. She also took lovers, notably her servant Bartolomeo Pergami. George set his spies on her again and, after he became king in 1820, brought his evidence to trial in the House of Lords, seeking divorce.

The plan backfired. George was already unpopular, and Caroline presented herself as a backer of liberal causes – a People's Princess, you might say. When it became known that George had secretly (and illegally) married his Catholic mistress, Maria Fitzherbert, the year before he wed Caroline, she became the Wronged Wife, too. Caroline quipped that she had only ever committed adultery "with Mrs Fitzherbert's husband". Jane Austen expressed a common sentiment when she wrote, "Poor woman, I shall support her as long as I can, because she *is* a Woman and because I hate her Husband."

The bill in the House of Lords that was supposed to dissolve their marriage became a public trial that descended into vulgar farce, with dubious Italian witnesses describing what they'd seen through keyholes or in Caroline's chamberpot. As the writer Leigh Hunt wrote to fellow poet and republican radical Percy Bysshe Shelley, "The whole thing will be one of the greatest pushes given to the declining royalty that the age has seen". It's arguable that George only survived the scandal because his divorce bill was quietly dropped and because Caroline made a grotesque exhibition of herself at his coronation in July 1821. Screaming abuse, she repeatedly tried to force her way inside Westminster Abbey, from which she had been barred, and was turned away at bayonet point.

With suspicious rapidity, Caroline fell ill and died the following month. As her body was escorted home, outraged Londoners turned out in force to protest against George. The echoes of Diana's death, again, are dimly discernible – although in Diana's case the military escort did not open fire on the crowds.

Catholic controversies

You could be a Jew or a Muslim, a Buddhist or an atheist, but you couldn't be King of England and a Catholic. That's the implication of the 1701 Act of Settlement. What it specifically states is that anyone who "shall hold communion with the see or Church of Rome, or should profess the popish religion, or marry a papist" should be banned from the throne.

Today, this seems like outrageous discrimination and the current government looks set to do away with it, but the Act is the product of a long, historical wrangle with Rome. The story begins with Henry VIII's establishment of his own "Anglican" Church, and gathers force with his daughter "Bloody" Mary's persecution of Protestants and the fear of Catholic insurrection under Elizabeth and James I. Guy Fawkes and his co-conspirators, who wanted to blow up the Houses of Parliament, were Catholic terrorists. But the constitutional question only really erupted in the reign of Charles II, when it was discovered that the king's brother and heir, James II, had secretly become a Catholic. (Charles only converted on his deathbed.) And Catholicism, England's political theorists liked to imagine, equated with Continental-style absolute monarchy – not with the liberties won by the English parliament over their king. Paranoia about Catholics had been widespread for some time (Catholics were blamed for the Great Fire of London in 1666) and a raft of anti-Catholic legislation was introduced.

When James II's son was born, in 1688, parliament finally revolted, inviting James II's Protestant daughter and son-in-law, William and Mary, to take power in his stead. James II fled and, to prevent his heirs claiming the throne in the future, and to guarantee a Protestant succession, the Act of Settlement was passed. Astonishingly, the Act has remained in force for over three hundred years. The Queen's cousin, Prince Michael of Kent, lost his place in the line of succession by marrying a Catholic in 1978. Lord Nicholas Windsor did the same by converting to Rome in 2001. In 2008, Autumn Kelly converted from Catholicism shortly before her marriage to the Queen's grandson, Peter Phillips – presumably so as not to jeopardize his claim.

It seemed crazy, and, in 2009, Liberal Democrat MP Evan Harris tried to bring a Private Member's Bill against this "anti-Catholic discrimination". Prime Minister Gordon Brown also made moves to change the Act, but all plans were dropped amid worries about looking too Popish, especially in Northern Irish Unionist eyes – and especially as Tony Blair had (finally) done the honest thing upon leaving office, and openly converted to Catholicism.

The Tory/Lib-Dem coalition government has now, it seems, grasped the nettle. As well as abolishing male primogeniture (see p.6), it plans to end *some* of the discrimination against Catholics. Marrying a Catholic will no longer bar you from the succession, however being a Catholic still will. This is because the Church of England has been the official, "established" Church ever since Henry VIII became its "Supreme Governor", a role still held by the sovereign. If you allow Catholic kings (or queens) – the argument presumably goes – you would then have to jettison the good old C of E as the official Church.

But once you start changing discriminatory laws, where should you stop? Female children will no longer be passed over in favour of male ones but what about children born outside of marriage? The monarch can now marry someone of any faith but what would happen if the heir to the throne was gay and in a long-term relationship? Would they be allowed a civil partnership? And, anyway, isn't it entirely absurd that anyone at all should, by virtue of their birth, inherit the throne and an official place at the head of the UK's "democracy"? As soon as you start to tinker with the rules and regulations, shrouded as they are in pomp and tradition, the whole edifice starts to unravel. But when it comes to monarchy, no government dares risk looking too secularist, modern or republican. Not now, at least. Not yet.

Diana: England's rose

Diana, Princess of Wales, told the world in her now legendary 1995 BBC television interview that she wanted to be "a queen of people's hearts". This was more than a job application, it was a dig at the royal family. Elizabeth II has long and successfully embodied traditional British values of service, stiff-lipped stoicism and cool conservatism. But coolness is close to chilliness, and stiffness to rigidity, and the royal family seemed to be constantly treading on the wrong side of the line – or, whenever they tried to warm it up a bit, they ended up looking absurd.

Diana did it differently. As she told her interviewer, Martin Bashir, this was "because I don't go by a rule book, because I lead from the heart,

Saint Diana? The Princess of Wales visits an AIDS hospice in Toronto, Canada.

ROYAL CONSPIRACY THEORIES

When the British Empire was at its height, to accuse the royal family of being behind a mega-conspiracy to rule the world would not have been entirely unreasonable. Even today, some remain suspicious. Despite all the enquiries concluding otherwise, allegations are still made that the Windsors orchestrated the accidental death of Princess Diana (see p.23), and some go further.

A stalwart of the American conspiracist political fringe, Lyndon LaRouche, has said that the royal family is the sinister force behind a host of international agencies and mega-corporations, from the UK's Department for International Development (a front for the old imperial concerns, apparently) to the World Wildlife Fund. In his role as President Emeritus of the WWF, the Duke of Edinburgh – sorry, "the Doge of London" – is apparently determined to impose environmental fascism, even to the extent of planning game-animal-style "culls" of humans. In 1988, the German news agency DPA quoted the duke as joking that "In the event that I am reincarnated, I would like to return as a deadly virus, in order to contribute something to solve overpopulation."

Conspiracists heard not a throwaway gaffe but a confession. The duke "leads the world in orchestration of ethnic conflict and terrorism", it was alleged, and even ran the Rwandan genocide. They spoke with fear of his environmental youth groups – not the teenagers collecting outdoor skills as part of the Duke of Edinburgh's Award but WWF's vicious youth "Pandas", in their distinctively fascistic black-and-white shirts. It was also claimed that the duke was the unofficial leader of a multi-trillion-dollar-wielding "Club of the Isles", an informal and highly secretive association of corporate and blue-blooded interests.

Prolific conspiracy author, TV presenter, ex-footballer and self-proclaimed Messiah David Icke has claimed that the real issue is not blue blood, but lizard blood. The Windsors, he has said, are shape-shifting alien reptiles. (He hasn't fully explained why aliens choose to follow terrestrial divisions of species along mammal/reptile lines.) Using their ability to shapeshift (as well as the relatively conventional practice of inter-marriage), the reptilians have worked their bloodline (or, more specifically, their "reptilian-mammalian DNA combination") into everything from the all-powerful Illuminati to powerful families such as the Bushes, the Rockefellers, the Rothschilds – and the Windsors. A supportive eyewitness has even claimed to have seen an extra membrane momentarily flicking across Queen Elizabeth's eyes. You'll never see that in the official portraits.

not the head". She was positioning herself as the modern against the traditional, the instinctive against the obedient, the ordinary against the high-powered. Ministers get on with the mucky business of governing, but modern-day queens, like presidents, need to stand for the aspirations and self-definitions of the people: they need to be screens onto which our dreams are projected. Diana spotted a new, emotive niche in the British self-image and filled it perfectly. She wove her miseries – lack of education, bulimia, an unloving and unfaithful husband, conflict with the in-laws, depression, unfulfilling affairs – into a story of suffering womanhood, of vulnerability and sensitivity.

Her insecurity was certainly something with which many women clearly identified, or at least sympathized. As her brother, Earl Spencer, pronounced in his incisive funeral oration, "the world sensed this part of her character and cherished her for her vulnerability whilst admiring her for her honesty." Diana reinforced her image with sincerely meant but also carefully chosen dips into charity work. She got close to patients with AIDS, lepers and the homeless, and campaigned on hyper-emotive issues such as sick children and use of landmines. She used the power of her image to great effect – she undoubtedly had an impact on perception of HIV/AIDS and the landmines campaign – and the effect rebounded on her image.

Somehow, the self-confessed "thick as a plank" aristocrat with an international jet-setting lifestyle and a string of dubious high-society boyfriends was becoming more than a star: she was in the next sphere up, the heavenly one. Death, no doubt, crystallized her saint-like or martyr-like status, especially given that many people believed she had been murdered or, at the least, thought that she had been hounded to her death by a cruel and heartless combination of the media and the royal family.

Earl Spencer went on to say that "You stand tall enough as a human being of unique qualities not to need to be seen as a saint", but he knew even then that the real Diana, after her death, would be dwarfed by the legend. All prominent women suffer by comparison to previous paragons of femininity, but Diana seemed to absorb the echoes she made. She was a new Marilyn Monroe, for some, with her flaws and temptations, her affairs and her sex appeal – Elton John was certainly saying as much when he got Bernie Taupin to adapt his Marilyn song for Diana's funeral. Diana was an Eva Perón for others, with her glitzy dresses and jewels offsetting an apparently radical social agenda (OK, Diana was no revolutionary, but she did occasionally hug the homeless).

Like Evita and like Marilyn, Diana had the blonde hair and the glamour and the controversy, and like them both, she died young. Behind and above these echoes, however, was a deeper cultural memory. Britain had abandoned veneration of the Virgin Mary when it embraced Protestantism, but Diana revived the old yearnings. She was the virgin bride, the suffering mother, bridge between ordinary people and the kingly, the icon of feminine beauty whose compassion drew people to her.

She was a new Mary. Elton John suggested this, astonishingly enough, when, in Bernie Taupin's words, he called her "the grace that placed itself where lives were torn apart". Grace is a divine quality as well as something that gets you noticed at parties. Calling Diana "England's rose" was very telling, too. Throughout the Middle Ages and well beyond, roses were the symbol of feminine sexuality: perfumed, sensual but surrounded by thorns. They were also the flower of Mary, as Queen of Heaven: "Now you belong to heaven," Elton sang, "And the stars spell out your name."

The duke and the actress

Dorothea (known as Dora) Jordan was one of the most successful actresses of the late Georgian era. Renowned for comedy, she was especially admired for "breeches" roles (acting male parts), which allowed her to display her famously shapely legs. Brought up in Dublin, she learnt her craft in the provinces before taking London by storm in 1785 at the age of 24 – the Prince of Wales was impressed enough to see her Viola in *Twelfth Night* twice. Never short of male admirers, she moved in with lawyer Richard Ford when he promised to marry her. He never did but she still had three children by him, two of whom survived. Despite the demands of motherhood, she was now one of the biggest stars of the London stage; painters fell over themselves to depict her, and her image became widely known via the fashionable print shops of London.

It's not known exactly when Dora first caught the eye of Prince William, Duke of Clarence, but by the middle of 1791 he was pursuing her in earnest. The third of King George III's sons, he may not have been quite as dissolute as his eldest brother, the Prince of Wales, but he was doing his best to catch up. He was a notorious frequenter of whorehouses, and when staying at his out-of-town house in fashionable Richmond had a London prostitute, Polly Finch, to keep him company. William turned to Dora Jordan when his overtures to Elizabeth Sheridan, wife of the playwright and MP Richard Brinsley Sheridan, were getting him nowhere. The Fords, as Dora and Richard Ford were known, were his neighbours in Richmond so it was natural that their paths should cross. She – initially at least – rebuffed the duke's advances, but when it became clear that Ford was never going to marry her, she gave in.

The scandal that ensued made her and the duke the butt of the satirists, who had no intention of sparing them. Though always known as Mrs Jordan, there never was (nor ever would be) a husband; her stage name derived from the river, and indicated her "crossing" from Ireland to England. Unfortunately, a "jordan" was also a slang expression for a chamber pot. The most vicious of the Gillray caricatures, entitled "Lubbers Hole, alias The Crack'd Jordan", shows the duke's upper body disappearing through a suggestively shaped crack in a giant chamber pot which is supported by a pair of female legs.

Despite the opprobrium, the relationship prospered and so did her career. Of course, the duke would never have been allowed to marry Dora, but after a few years they were living as man and wife, largely accepted by the royal family. The strait-laced king, in one of his moments of sanity, even supplied a royal home, Bushy House near Richmond, for the couple. They moved there in 1797 and it remained their family home for some fifteen years. There was certainly plenty of family to fill it up with. As well as the three daughters she already had, and the duke's own illegitimate son, the couple had a further ten children, seven of whom were born at Bushy. The couple were devoted parents and the duke found himself in the kind of lively, loving environment that had been absent from his own childhood. All his children bore the surname Fitzclarence.

One problem that didn't disappear, however, was that Dora had a job and he didn't. Although the duke had spent time in the navy as a young man and the country was at war, the government refused to allow him to go to sea, even though three of his brothers had seen active service in the army. The general consensus was that, though sometimes capable of being charming, he wasn't capable of much else, and he had to make do with an honorary promotion to Vice-Admiral. But there were always improvements to be made to the house, which he threw himself into with enthusiasm. Unfortunately, like his brothers, he was hopelessly bad at managing his finances and this was the rock on which his relationship with Dora ran aground. Debts kept piling up, which meant that she was obliged to keep acting and to take on regular tours of the provinces. It wasn't enough and, in any case, the duke (or his advisors) suddenly grew sensitive about his reputation and forbade her from performing in London.

In 1811 the pair separated. William had met a young heiress, Catherine Tylney-Long, who might just be a prospective bride. In the end he settled for Princess Adelaide of Saxe-Meiningen, marrying her in 1818 a week after they first met. There was now something of an imperative to produce a legitimate child, since the Prince of Wales's heir, Princess Charlotte, had died the year before. Adelaide did succeed in getting pregnant five times but none of the children survived more than a day.

As for Dora, she received a pay-off from the duke of around £4000 per annum but – according to the terms of the settlement – had to give up half of it when she returned to the stage. A further blow came in the shape of a son-in-law who ran up so many debts in Dora's name that she was forced to leave the country to avoid arrest. She died at Saint-Cloud near Paris in 1816, attended by a companion. In a gesture of affection (or to assuage his conscience) William, when he became king in 1830, commissioned Francis Chantrey to make a sculpture of his former lover nursing two of their children. Its intended destination was Westminster Abbey but the appalled Dean refused to accept it, and it languished in the artist's studio for many years, finally ending up in Buckingham Palace – an ironic reversal of fortune that Dora would probably have appreciated.

Edward, Wallis and the abdication crisis

The list of the shamed kings, the ones who didn't die on the throne, is not long. Edward II was deposed by his wife and her lover in 1327. Richard II was overthrown by a rival in 1399. Henry VI went insane, and was put aside by a cousin in 1461. Charles I was executed by parliament and replaced by a kingless Commonwealth in 1649. James II was thrust from power by an alliance of bishops, noblemen and his own daughter in 1688. Only Edward VIII, or so the story goes, went of his own accord.

In truth, he was forced out, too. In December 1936, Edward – who was known to friends and family as David – made it clear that he would marry his lover, the American socialite Wallis Simpson. The establishment regarded her as an unacceptable future queen. Part of the problem was that the couple mixed in louche and high-living social circles. A Special Branch police report noted that the couple's friends included Lady Emerald Cunard, who was "reputed to be a drug addict" and was the mother of Nancy Cunard, a lady "who is very partial to coloured men". Officers also discovered – or concocted – that Simpson was having a simultaneous affair with a "very charming adventurer" and "excellent dancer", the car salesman Guy Trundle. Her charming playboy friend, the Woolworth millionaire Jimmy Donahue, was said to have a party trick in which he would put his penis on the plate at a dinner party and ask the waiter to cut his meat very fine.

The Church of England was against the marriage, chiefly because Wallis was a divorcée – and she would become one twice over as the

No laughing matter: The Duke and Duchess of Windsor hobnobbing with *der Führer* in 1937.

crisis deepened. (In the 1930s, clergymen would still speak out against divorce.) Worse, her husband was still living and, worse still, her divorce had been granted by an American court and was not recognized under English law. This would make a marriage to Edward bigamous. The Archbishop of Canterbury, Cosmo Lang – a "shadowy, hovering presence", according to the embittered Edward – fulminated pompously that the king's "craving for private happiness" was "inconsistent with the Christian principles of marriage". The archbishop's chaplain, Alan Campbell Don, even repeated rumours that Simpson had some kind of sexual hold over Edward, possibly as his dominatrix. Popular whispers – passed on to Edward's mother, Queen Mary – suggested that she had picked up dark sexual arts in a Shanghai brothel. These "dark arts" are often said to have included oral sex.

Parliament wasn't much happier about the relationship. Prime Minister Stanley Baldwin argued that the British public would hardly take to a "Queen Wally". More worrying was the fact that the relatively puritanical imperial dominions were strenuously opposed to the marriage. If it took place, might it lead to the collapse of the Empire?

There was also the issue of the couple's fascist tendencies. To a government which was vacillating over how to deal with Hitler, this was a major problem. Wallis seemed to be actively entwined with the cause. She was close to Diana Mitford and her husband, the British fascist leader Oswald Mosley, and the FBI was even told that she had conducted an affair with the Nazi Joachim von Ribbentrop. Certainly, Wallis and Edward visited Hitler in 1937, and during World War II, Simpson was said to have actually passed military secrets to the German government. These allegations may have been smears. Nevertheless, an FBI report, which was only released under the Freedom of Information Act in 2003, claimed that the British government knew all about the couple's "obnoxious" pro-Nazi sympathies in 1936, and this knowledge lay behind its forcing of the crisis.

In a matter of days, Stanley Baldwin engineered a situation in which the king had to choose between his marriage and his throne. As the former Liberal prime minister David Lloyd George put it, the king was "hounded from the throne by that arch humbug Baldwin". Yet few in parliament were against it. When prominent Conservative Winston Churchill tried to argue in the House of Commons that the manoeuvres were unconstitutional, his voice was drowned by shouts and jeers. On 10 December 1936, Edward signed the Instrument of Abdication, with his brother and successor, George, by his side. His abdication was confirmed by a special act of parliament the following day, when the king also broadcast to the nation. "I have found it impossible to carry the heavy burden of responsibility," he famously said, "and to discharge my duties as King as I would wish to do, without the help and support of the woman I love." Sceptics felt that Edward never had much desire or ability to discharge those duties anyway, but some supporters were moved by the apparent romance of the relationship. Edward was putting his heart first, which seemed terribly modern of him.

Edward VII's royal flings

Edward VII's life was shaped by an affair with an actress. She was Nellie Clifden, and she had been smuggled into his encampment by fellow officers while he was touring with the army in Ireland in 1861. On his return to England, apparently with Nellie still in tow, his furious mother, Victoria, sent Prince Albert to remonstrate with their son, who she already considered a slow-witted gadabout, ill-suited to be heir to the throne. After making the visit, however, Prince Albert's poor health worsened dramatically and he was dead within a fortnight.

Victoria believed her son's immorality had effectively killed her beloved husband, and she resolved to detest him. "I never can, or shall, look at him," she wrote, "without a shudder." She also decided to deny her son any meaningful role in state affairs as long as she lived, and kept to her decision almost to the end. Given that Victoria reigned until 1901, this kept the Prince of Wales in a state of irresponsible unemployment for a dangerously long time. He was 59 when he finally ascended the throne.

While he waited, Albert Edward, Prince of Wales – or "Bertie", as he was known before his coronation – devoted himself to pleasure. He dressed in the height of fashion – he set the fashions – travelled, partied, hunted, played cards, went to the races and the theatre, and ate, smoked and drank heavily. In 1863, at the age of 21, he was married off to the affable and attractive Princess Alexandra of Denmark, but it made little difference to his behaviour. The Prince of Wales philandered insatiably with what was dubbed a "troop of fine ladies", though "regiment" would be nearer the mark. One was Lady Jeanette Churchill, later the mother of Winston. Another, Harriet Mordaunt, dragged him into a divorce case, which could have ruined him – though in the event she was committed to an asylum, where she would stay for 36 years.

Bertie's first truly celebrated mistress was the actress Lillie Langtry, to whom he was purposely introduced at a supper party in 1877. The affair was common knowledge: he insisted she be invited to weekend country house parties, and kissed her on the dancefloor at Maxim's in Paris. Paris was the scene of plentiful other affairs. He conducted a liaison there with the soprano Hortense Schneider (though he had to share her with other European royals – Schneider was nicknamed *Le Passage des Princes*). French detectives trailed about after him, detailing the "long afternoons" spent in hotels and apartments and mansions with his "intimate friends":

the Comtesse Edmond de Pourtalès, the Baronne Alphonse de Rothschild, the Comtesse de Boutourline, the Princesse de Sagan, the Russian beauty Madame Kauchine, the widow Signoret, a Miss Chamberlayne and a "Dame Verneuil" on the second floor at 39 rue Lafayette.

Bertie was also a regular at the Moulin Rouge, where he would apparently be greeted with shouts of "'allo Wales". He was feted by the legendary (and legendarily extravagant) Paris-based courtesan Cora Pearl, who dressed herself up for him in a string of pearls and a sprig of parsley. At the fashionable Maison Dorée restaurant, another famous prostitute, Giulia Beneni, notoriously turned her back on him – while lifting her skirts and protesting that she'd been advised to "show him my best side".

Bertie's particular love, however, was the legendary brothel Le Chabanais, where he had his own room with his coat of arms, a splendidly decorated bathtub that would be filled with champagne (and girls), and a specially designed padded chair that could assist and accommodate various positions, apparently including those involving oral sex, and more than one partner.

In the 1880s, Bertie was part of the scandalous Marlborough House Set, presided over by Daisy Greville, Lady Brooke. To the press, she was "the babbling Brooke", as she was notoriously indiscreet; to Bertie, she was his "own adored little Daisy wife". Her parties, some of them many days long, with special trains laid on from London, facilitated sexual shenanigans: the stable yard bell would be specially rung at dawn to enable wanderers to discreetly return to their own beds.

Such behaviour – and other scandals involving cheating at cards, and his attempt to get hold of an incriminating letter written by Lady Brooke to another of her lovers – hardly improved his reputation with his mother. "The monarchy almost is in danger," Victoria wrote, "if he is lowered and despised." No one could write it openly in an English newspaper, but the *New York Times* observed "the growing conviction that 'royalty' is a burden to the British taxpayer for which he fails to receive any equivalent".

Astonishingly, Bertie's wife, Queen Alexandra, tolerated his affairs until the end. In February 1898, Bertie met Agnes Keyser, who he kept as a discreet mistress until his death in 1910; he seems to have genuinely loved her. In the same month, he also took up with the lively society beauty and serial adulterer Alice Keppel (whose great-granddaughter is Camilla, Duchess of Cornwall), bringing her to parties and events almost as an official consort. The saintly Alexandra did find this trying, though she admitted that at least Keppel was good for "keeping her husband entertained and, therefore, good-tempered".

It's not really surprising that an idle and not particularly bright young man with unimaginable wealth and social access should become a playboy. What is more revealing is that Bertie pursued his lifestyle in the middle of an era that has become known for prudishness. It was the next generations, arguably, that were the strait-laced ones: Bertie's grandson Edward VIII, for instance, insisted that Wallis Simpson be his wife, not his mistress. As Alice Keppel famously commented, "things were done better in my day".

George, Sophia, the Count, the Elephant and the Maypole

The young George of Hanover (1660–1727) probably never imagined that he would become King of England. As the grandson of James I's daughter, his claim seemed distant. He was more concerned with his family's Hanoverian territories, in Germany, and in 1682 he married his rich first cousin, Sophia Dorothea, to make sure of a decent income.

Sophia was beautiful, and produced two sons, but the marriage was disastrous. George took up with his mother's lady-in-waiting, Melusine von der Schulenburg, and had three daughters with her. Sophia, meanwhile, began a passionate romance with a Swedish mercenary nobleman, Count Phillip von Königsmark – who was promptly murdered by either George or his father (or, some say, by his father's jealous mistress, who had herself been abandoned by the dashing count).

In 1694, George's marriage to Sophia Dorothea was dissolved and his wife was imprisoned in her manor house, Schloss Ahlden. She remained there until her death, thirty years later. George, meanwhile, prospered. The death of Queen Anne's son made him the nearest Protestant claimant to the throne of the newly United Kingdom. He arrived in England in 1714,

CONCUBINES' BALL

George I's Coronation, in 1714, was attended by not just his own mistress, Melusine von der Schulenburg, Duchess of Kendal, but by former mistresses of Charles II (Louise de Kérouaille, Duchess of Portsmouth), James II (Catherine Sedley, Countess of Dorchester) and William III (Elizabeth Hamilton, Countess of Orkney). As Lady Dorchester said to her fellow guests, "who would have thought that we three whores should find ourselves together here".

bringing with him two women who were not his wife: the tall, slender Melusine von der Schulenburg and the rotund Sophia von Kielmansegge, his father's illegitimate daughter. Both were assumed to be his mistresses (Sophia was not), and they were quickly dubbed "the Elephant and the Maypole". Officially, they were given more flattering titles: Duchess of Kendal and Countess of Darlington. Melusine was also given vast shares in the South Sea Company, and the patent for the Irish coinage.

George was ridiculed for the ugliness of his "mistresses". More dangerously, he was criticized for having abandoned and incarcerated his wife. There were also rumours that he had relations with his two Turkish grooms, Mustapha and Mehmet. None of this, nor his refusal to learn English, nor his reserved, serious manner, endeared him to his people. Yet still they preferred him to James Stuart, the "Old Pretender", the Catholic son of James II, and George duly passed on the throne to his son, who became George II – and never forgave his father for having imprisoned his mother.

George III, tyrant of the Americas

There's apparently no truth in the rumour that the British film *The Madness of George III* was retitled for the transatlantic market "The Madness of King George" on the grounds that Americans would otherwise wonder why they'd missed Parts I and II. Americans have always known George III as King George, because it was George's armies that fought against the rebel colonials in the War of Independence.

It was George's government that taxed America to pay for the military defence of the colony, giving birth to the historic 1750s slogan "no taxation without representation". It was George's government that taxed tea, giving rise to the Boston Tea Party of 16 December 1773. It was also George's government – though history often chooses to forget this – that attempted to protect the Indian lands west of the Appalachians from piecemeal encroachment by colonial settlers.

It was certainly George himself, rather than his prime ministers and his parliament, who was blamed, in the 1776 Declaration of Independence, for planning "absolute despotism". "The history of the present King of Great Britain," the founding fathers fumed, "is a history of repeated injuries and usurpations, all having in direct object the establishment of an absolute tyranny over these states." George was clearly not a tyrant in the ordinary sense, though he did choose to wield what constitutional power he had more actively than many of his more recent forebears. He couldn't

British General Cornwallis surrenders his sword to the American General Lincoln at Yorktown in 1781. George Washington, mounted on a white house, looks on.

rule directly, but he did shuffle his ministers to ensure reasonable compliance with his opinions. And he did push his government to win the American war – and pushed hard. But who would expect anything less?

When the war was effectively lost, at Yorktown in 1781, George was anything but tyrannical. As he wrote to John Adams, the United States' Minister Plenipotentiary to His Majesty, in June 1785: "I have done nothing in the late Contest, but what I thought myself indispensably bound to do, by the Duty which I owed to my People... I was the last to consent to the Separation, but the Separation having been made and having become inevitable, I have always said, as I say now, that I would be the first to meet the Friendship of the United States as an independent Power." The King wrote, he said, because he wanted Adams to believe him, and so "that it may be understood in America". Few Americans since have done so.

Henry VIII and the Pope

Henry did not set out to get rid of the Pope and turn England into a Protestant country. He was a good Catholic, and attached to Catholic doctrine and rituals. In 1521 he had been made Defender of the Faith

Rievaulx Abbey in Yorkshire, England. After Henry VIII's break with Rome many monastic centres were closed and their assets appropriated by the king.

by Pope Leo X, in recognition of his eloquent attack on the new young reformer, Martin Luther. Indeed, it could be said that it was precisely Henry's piety, and Christian conscience, that pushed him towards rejecting Rome and establishing the Church of England. The Pope, he claimed, should never have allowed him to marry his sister-in-law, Katherine of Aragon, and thereby commit the sin of incest. Henry believed his failure to father a (legitimate) son was God's way of punishing him.

But there was also another woman involved. In 1526, Henry met the vivacious and sophisticated but not particularly pretty Anne Boleyn. His marriage to Katherine was in trouble – she was now 42 and it was clear that there would be no more children. The poor woman had lost two baby sons, suffered three stillbirths and many miscarriages. Henry fell in love with Anne. He hated writing, but he sent her some seventeen love letters. And Anne steadfastly refused to sleep with Henry unless he married her. So Henry set about seeking an annulment.

In May 1527 Henry's marriage to Katherine went on trial, in secret, before Cardinal Wolsey and Cardinal Campeggio. What everyone imagined would take a few months took five years. Just as divorce proceedings began, Charles V, the Holy Roman Emperor, sacked Rome and took Pope Clement VII hostage. Charles was Katherine's nephew and supported her case. Clement, who also thought the case was weak, delayed. Henry became increasingly frustrated with both the Pope and his cardinal. In 1529, after

HENRY II AND THE TURBULENT PRIEST

Henry II had extraordinary energy but also a violent temper. The contemporary chronicler, Gerald of Wales, describes how "his eyes were grey, bloodshot and flashed in anger". One man who experienced the full force of his wrath was Thomas Becket. The two had started off as close friends. When Henry ascended the throne in 1154, he appointed Becket – then in the service of Theobald, Archbishop of Canterbury – his chancellor, and together they implemented many administrative and judicial reforms.

All of this changed in 1161 when Theobald died and Becket was made his successor, an appointment that angered many churchmen who thought him too worldly and too close to the king. Becket set out to prove that he was his own man and soon found himself in conflict with his former friend. Their antagonism reached a head over the issue of "criminous clerks". The king resented the fact that many clergy accused of capital offences were escaping justice by claiming the right to be tried in an ecclesiastical court. Henry wished to put an end to this but was resisted by the new archbishop who regarded the plan as an attack on the power of the Church.

When, in 1164, Henry forced the issue by demanding that bishops abide by the Constitutions of Clarendon – sixteen statements that put limits on ecclesiastical power – Becket wavered, eventually agreeing but then changing his mind. Henry was outraged and began a systematic persecution of the archbishop, seizing his property and making false accusations against him. The attacks continued even after Becket had fled England and taken up residence in France. He remained abroad for six years, returning in December 1170 to take issue once more with the king, this time over the coronation of Henry II's heir (also called Henry) which had taken place in June. Exasperated by what he saw as Becket's high-handed behaviour – among other things, he had excommunicated the bishops involved in the coronation – Henry II allegedly cried out: "Will no one rid me of this turbulent priest?" Taking this as their cue, four of his knights rode to Canterbury Cathedral where, in the middle of a service, they hacked the archbishop to death.

Becket's murder shocked the Christian world. His canonization was set in motion just over two years after his death and his tomb at Canterbury became one of the most important of all medieval pilgrimage sites. Henry did accept a degree of culpability and as penance he visited the tomb (walking barefoot for the last few miles) where he prostrated himself and was whipped by monks.

another aborted court hearing at Blackfriars, Wolsey's failure to ensure that the divorce should be decided in England and not in Rome lost him his job, and he was packed off to York.

At the same time, religious reform was sweeping through Europe, threatening the beliefs and practices of the Catholic Church. Instructed to compile evidence to support Henry's case for a divorce, university scholars came across medieval ideas about the divine right of kings versus the corrupt power of the papacy. In 1530, an Italian Carmelite called Giacomo Calco wrote a treatise which, for the first time, suggested that England could break with Rome. A series of parliamentary acts followed which denied papal authority and asserted royal power. This appealed greatly to Henry's pride, and his sense of a special relationship with his God. In 1531, Henry became "Supreme Head of the Church of England". In 1533, England was declared "an empire" – free from Rome and finally able to rush through the divorce (Anne was already pregnant by this time). The Act of Supremacy was passed in 1534, and in 1535 all members of the Church were made to swear the oath of supremacy. Those who didn't, like Henry's lord chancellor Sir Thomas More, were killed.

By the end of the 1530s, the Pope had excommunicated Henry. Following the break with Rome, Henry instituted doctrinal reforms, along with his formidable Lord Chancellor Thomas Cromwell and Archbishop Thomas Cranmer, which began to turn England into a Protestant realm. Meanwhile, it had all gone wrong with Anne Boleyn (see p.97) and Jane Seymour, Henry's next wife, had died. There was, at last, a legitimate male heir (Prince Edward) but England was a fearful and divided country. Those men and women who remained faithful to the Pope, and to the Roman Church that they knew and loved, either fled, kept low, or died. Henry's conscience, and his power struggle with the Pope, changed English monarchy, and then English religion, for ever.

Jacobite rebellions and the Union of Crowns

The Jacobite Rising of 1745 is traditionally regarded by less thoughtful Scots nationalists as the last, most despairingly heroic attempt to throw off the yoke of English rule. In truth, "The Forty-Five" was an abortive military coup led by the son of a deposed Catholic king living in exile in France. It was backed by the French, a few conservative Highland clans and the Tory–Catholic fringe in England.

The Duke of Cumberland (centre) directing the action at the Battle of Culloden, 1746. The battle, and the duke's bloody reprisals, marked the death knell of the Stuart claim to the throne.

It was the last in a sequence of inglorious failures. The Jacobite rebellions grew out of the longstanding conflict between Catholics and Protestants in Britain, and their mutual distaste for toleration of each others' heresies. This division was a direct cause of the Glorious Revolution of 1688, in which James II of England (VII of Scotland) was removed from the throne by the English parliament, which then invited his daughter, Mary II, and her Dutch husband William of Orange, to jointly wear the crown. Better a foreign but safely Protestant king like William, the parliamentary reasoning went, than a homebred one with a Catholic son like James.

That Catholic son was James Francis Edward Stuart, and he was brought up in exile in France. His supporters, notably the French king Louis XIV, knew him as James III and VIII; his critics (who included all but the most die-hard Tories and some but not all Catholics) called him the Old Pretender, meaning he'd claimed or "pretended" a right to the throne. He was the legitimate king, actually, if you go by blood; if you go by parliamentary vote, however, he wasn't. He was even less legitimate after the Scots and English parliaments passed their Acts of Union in 1706 and 1707. By those Acts, the Scots agreed to accept England's chosen heir to Queen Anne's throne, George of Hanover, in return for free trade, and the dual crown of England and Scotland, worn by every king (and queen) since James VI and I, became one crown of the newly "United Kingdom".

WELSH PRINCES

Gold mined in Wales has been used in royal wedding rings since the Queen Mother had one made for her wedding to George VI. There's a touch of Welsh gold in the British crown, too, as the heir to the British throne has been known as the Prince of Wales since at least the seventeenth century, and possibly as far back as 1301. As legend would have it, Edward I managed to pacify Wales – having invaded and conquered it – by promising a Welsh-born prince; he then revealed that his own son and heir, later Edward II, had been born at Caernarfon.

There were Welsh princes before the Edwards, of course, though the country barely ever existed as an independent, unified state. Much as in Anglo-Saxon England before the Conquest, it was made up of numerous, jostling micro-kingdoms. But the Welsh had their own language and identity, calling themselves *Cymry*, which means "people of one region". The first unifying prince, known as King of the Britons, was Gruffydd ap Llywelyn. After usurping the thrones of Powys and Gwynedd (both in the northern core of Wales), he set about conquering the lesser statelets until, by the 1050s, he was in control of the entire territory. Gruffydd was recognized as king of Wales by his English counterpart, Edward the Confessor, but his Welsh kingdom lasted only seven years: he died in 1063.

Regime change, of course, was looming across the border, and England's new Norman overlords guarded their Welsh borders tenaciously, establishing a group of semi-autonomous "Marcher Lordships" that penetrated deep into south Wales. A modest resurgence in native Welsh power came after the signing of Magna Carta in 1215, when one of King John's fractious barons, Llywelyn the Great (or Llywelyn I, as some like to call him), managed to get himself acknowledged by his fellow Welsh noblemen as Prince of Wales. Llywelyn's grandson, known (somewhat confusingly) as Llywelyn ap Gruffydd, was recognized under that same title by Henry III – but to get it he had to swear homage to Henry in the Treaty of Montgomery of 1267.

Within ten years, Henry had forced Llywelyn to swear full feudal fealty, accepting the English king as overlord. Ten years after that, in 1382, the tall and awesomely aggressive English king Edward I invaded, and it would be more than 600 years before Wales regained a measure of self-determination. This despite the best efforts of Owain Glyndŵr who, in 1400, proclaimed himself Prince of Wales and led a series of rebellions against the English. Greater autonomy finally arrived in 1999, bestowed by Tony Blair's government in the form of a National Assembly. Wales today remains "a country in its own right", according to the Welsh Assembly, but it still has no prince other than the UK's monarch: the current Prince of Wales, Charles, has no constitutional connection with the country whose name he bears.

This didn't stop James Stuart trying to claim the throne. His first attempt, in 1708, ended in his fleet being chased off the coast of Scotland and home to France. A marginally more impressive effort was made in the summer of 1715. "Jacobite" (from *Jacobus*, the Latin for James) armies were raised at Braemar, in the Scottish Highlands, in Cornwall, and in Northumberland, but after initial gains they were heavily defeated at the battles of Preston and Sheriffmuir. By February 1716 James was on a ship heading home to France.

James's son, Charles Edward Stuart (later nicknamed, according to taste and political outlook, the "Young Pretender" and "Bonnie Prince Charlie"), launched his own bid for the throne in 1745. He had French backing at first, but being easily as arrogant as his father – and not a fraction so charming – he soon alienated his hosts. When he actually arrived in Scotland, it was on the Outer Hebrides and with just seven men, most of them elderly. The clans rose up, somewhat unenthusiastically – only the MacDonalds and the Camerons troubled to turn out in any number. Still, much of the British army was away fighting the War of the Austrian Succession on the Continent, so the Jacobites – mostly made up of Highland Scots, despite promises of help from English Tories – won the first major battle at Prestonpans near Edinburgh before heading into England where they got as far south as Derby.

By this time, however, two major English forces were closing in, and London looked impregnable. The great Jacobite retreat began, therefore, on 6 December. It concluded on 16 April at Culloden, near Inverness, where government troops – including plenty of Scots – routed the Jacobite armies. The victorious forces were led by the Duke of Cumberland, George II's son, who became known as "Butcher" Cumberland for his ruthlessness. Like his father before him, Charles Edward fled to France, leaving his Scottish supporters to face a vicious government campaign of repression and retribution.

Charles Stuart left debts and enemies but no heirs: only the fiercest Jacobites called his younger brother King Henry IX of England. Even Henry never pressed the claim, preferring to pursue a long and distinguished career as a Catholic cardinal. As a priest, and a probable homosexual, he had no children, and died in 1807. So unless you count the descendants of James II's youngest sister, Henrietta Anne, who end with Franz Herzog von Bayern, today's self-proclaimed "Duke of Bavaria" (see p.7), the Stuart line was broken at Charles's death, and the Jacobite cause extinguished.

The many mistresses of Charles II

England's monarchs mostly seem pallid and lustless compared to, say, the kings of France or the sultans of Turkey. Louis XIV of France, for instance, had some twenty mistresses, including his own sister-in-law and at least one pair of sisters, while Turkish harems might house hundreds of women.

Charles II, however, is exceptional among England's kings. An affable but indolent man, he presided over a court devoted to pleasure, taking over a dozen mistresses and siring at least as many illegitimate children. He showered all with favour, titles and money, and scandalized contemporaries by letting his mistresses rule even beyond his bedchamber. As the scurrilous poet John Wilmot, Earl of Rochester put it in 1672, "his sceptre and his prick are of a length/And she may sway the one who plays with th'other". (Unfortunately for Rochester, he accidentally gave a copy of this poem to Charles himself, and was forced to flee the court.)

Charles's first truly significant other was Lucy Walter, a Welsh gentleman's daughter. The diarist John Evelyn described her as a "beautiful strumpet whom I had often seen at Paris", though it was in The Hague where she became Charles's lover – the young prince was living there while his father wrestled in vain with the parliament's armies. Other mistresses-in-exile followed, but Charles's most notorious concubine was Barbara Villiers, a fiery-tempered, self-seeking beauty with black, sensually arching eyebrows and a rich pout. After Charles's triumphant return to England, following the restoration of the monarchy, Villiers was appointed to be Queen Catherine's official Lady of the Bedchamber – much to the chagrin of the queen, the Portuguese princess Catherine of Braganza, who threatened to return home.

Barbara gave Charles five children, all of whom bore the name Fitzroy, meaning "king's son". By the late 1660s, however, the king was tiring of her temper, her infidelities and the political problems caused by her conversion to Catholicism. From 1667, he took up with actresses, first Moll Davis and then the infinitely more celebrated Nell Gwyn. She was the daughter of a brothel madam who had begun life selling oranges and probably much more besides to theatre patrons, and had risen to become one of the leading actresses of her time. She was famously as witty as she was pretty, and called the King "Charles the Third"; she had previously enjoyed two lovers of the same name.

For all her charms, Nell had to compete with another royal mistress: the aristocratic, clever and, inevitably, fiercely beautiful Louise de Kérouaille.

As a Catholic and a Frenchwoman (and probably a spy in both capacities), and as the recipient of vast sums of royal money, the duchess was popularly distrusted and disliked. Nell Gwyn became, by contrast, something of a public darling (she is supposed to have calmed an agitated Oxford mob in 1681 by instructing them to "be civil; I am the *Protestant* whore").

Gwyn had two sons by Charles, while de Kérouaille had one – Charles Lennox, Ist Duke of Richmond (a distant ancestor of both the wives of today's Prince Charles – which makes Prince William the first monarch since Charles II who could reasonably consider himself to be of the Stuart line). Catherine, Charles II's wife, never bore children – though she miscarried at least twice. On his death, in 1685, Charles was therefore succeeded by his brother, James II.

Piers Gaveston

Kings have always had their favourites and their mistresses but Piers Gaveston must have been one of the most adored ever, and the most threatening to the throne. Edward I, certainly, seems to have sensed danger when he banished Piers to France in February 1307, presumably to put him out of the reach of his son, Edward of Caernavon. The young prince gave his friend costly gifts as parting presents (five horses, sixteen tapestries, two green jousting outfits), and went with him as far as Dover – as far as he could go.

When the old king died, in July, Prince Edward, now Edward II, immediately summoned Gaveston, making him Earl of Cornwall, calling him "brother" and allotting him a vast income. Shockingly, when Edward went to France to fetch his fiancée, Isabella, he made Gaveston his regent. At Edward and Isabella's joint coronation in Westminster Abbey, Edward had Gaveston fix his spurs and carry his crown; Gaveston even wore the wedding jewels himself at the feast, and was so richly dressed "that he resembled the god Mars more than an ordinary mortal", as a chronicler put it. On the specially commissioned marriage tapestries Edward intertwined his coat of arms with Gaveston's, not with those of his wife.

None of this endeared Edward to the jealous barons at court. As for Gaveston, he was hated. The contemporary chronicle, *Life of Edward II*, says the favourite revelled in his primacy, lording it over his rivals "like a second king" and mocking them openly with nicknames such as "Burst Belly", "Whoreson" and "the Fiddler". Gaveston was thought to have acquired a strange, perhaps magical power over the king. Perhaps it was

DEPOSED, MURDERED, ABDICATED...

In the far-off days when chronology was king, history teachers would use a rhyme to help their pupils learn the roll-call of the kings and queens of England. "Willy, Willy, Harry, Stee", it began (with "Stee" standing in for Stephen, and no mention of Matilda, oddly), "Harry, Dick, John, Harry Three / Edward One Two Three, Dick Two / Henry Four Five Six, then who? / Edward Four Five, Dick the Bad (unreconstructed Shakespearean-style history, there) / Harrys twain, then Ned the Lad / Mary, Lizzie, James the Vain (a Scottish king got a poor press, inevitably) / Charlie, Charlie, James again / William and Mary, Anne O'Gloria / Four Georges, William and Victoria / Edward Seven and George Five / Edward, George and Liz – alive".

Another rhyme helped you remember the fates of Henry VIII's six wives: "Divorced, beheaded died", it went, continuing: "divorced, beheaded, survived." There was also a perennial interest in drawing up the list of those monarchs who were deposed or murdered, or who abdicated or otherwise forfeited their thrones in the non-conventional way (the usual way being by dying). Were you to make up a rhyme about it, it might go something like this: "Edward Two with a poker / Richard Two, Bolingbroker / Henry Six and Edward Five / Crouchback didn't want alive / Lady Jane the Nine-Day Wonder / Charlie One his head asunder / James the Second forced to flee (enter Mary and William Three) / Edward Eight did abdicate / Will Charles follow suit for Wills and Kate?"

love. Eventually, and perhaps inevitably, the barons objected. They threatened Edward with rebellion and, in 1312, had Gaveston abducted and murdered. Edward grieved with yet more costly gifts: legions of monks praying for his beloved's soul year-round, a fortune spent on candles and cloth of gold to bedeck his corpse.

Edward's reign post-Gaveston was disastrous. Catastrophic defeat in Scotland at the Battle of Bannockburn in 1314, and the effective loss of Wales, was followed by his own wife leaving him. She then invaded England from France with her lover, Mortimer, in 1326, forcing Edward's abdication. In October 1327, the king was murdered at Berkeley Castle, probably on Mortimer's orders. The legend is that a red-hot poker was thrust up his anus, though the story only surfaced several years after his death. As an act of revenge, it has a certain gruesome, vicious poetry, though in fact it's not clear whether or not Edward and Gaveston were lovers. Both had wives and children, and some historians have argued that theirs was a passionate friendship, or even that they were adoptive brothers or illegitimate half-brothers – anything but two men passionately, selfishly, foolishly in love.

Richard III: ultimate royal villain?

Richard III (1452–1485) has been damned by history as a usurper, tyrant and child-murderer. According to Sir Thomas More, writing thirty years after his death, he was not just "malicious, wrathful, envious", he was also "little of stature, ill featured of limbs, crook-backed, his left shoulder much higher than his right." More's Tudor contemporary, Polydore Vergil, added that Richard had "a short and sour countenance, which seemed to savour of mischief ... while he was thinking of any matter he did continually bite his nether lip as though that cruel nature of his did so rage against itself in that little carcass". Shakespeare, of course, turned Richard into a "lump of foul deformity" – and one of the greatest stage villains of all time.

Richard was born into the House of York, one of the two rival royal families in the so-called Wars of the Roses. His career in viciousness is said to have begun with the murder of Henry VI, the last king of the rival House of Lancaster, whom his elder brother Edward IV had defeated in battle. Richard is accused, too, of killing Henry's son, Edward of Lancaster: after the decisive Battle of Tewkesbury, in 1471, the young prince Edward was supposedly brought, captive, to face his father's usurper, and promptly murdered by a gang of nobles led by Richard.

With Henry VI and his son out of the way (and with Richard now married to Edward of Lancaster's former wife), the House of York seemed at last to have a firm grip on the country. Then, in April 1483, Edward IV died. His brother, Richard, was appointed Lord Protector as the king's son, now Edward V, was only twelve. Young Edward was living in Wales, and was hastily brought to London under the protection of three guardians, Richard Grey, Earl Rivers and Thomas Vaughan. Near Northampton, however, the escort was intercepted by Richard and arrested; all three would later be killed.

Edward V was hurried on to the Tower of London, ostensibly to keep him safe. He was soon joined there by his younger brother, Richard of Shrewsbury. Meanwhile, Richard moved quickly to neuter the boys' potential supporters – chiefly in the faction surrounding their influential mother, Elizabeth Woodville. On 13 June 1483, he accused Grey, Rivers and William Hastings (the latter a close ally of Edward IV) of treason and conspiracy. Hastings was taken to a courtyard and immediately beheaded; the others were imprisoned pending execution.

Nine days later, on 22 June, Edward V was declared illegitimate, on the grounds that his father had already been married when he wed Elizabeth

CLARENCE: THE JINXED DUKEDOM

Junior members of the royal family, especially younger sons, daughters and grandchildren, are usually given a title which allows them to wear their royal-related status on their sleeve. Some titles are created from scratch, others are recycled. Catherine Middleton, for instance, was made Duchess of Cambridge in 2011, reviving a title last bestowed in 1818.

A dukedom is the highest of all British ranks, but any junior royal could be forgiven for declining the title of Duke of Clarence. It was first created in 1362 for a third son of Edward III, taking its name from his estate at Clare, in Suffolk. He died without sons, and the title became extinct. Next, Henry IV bestowed the dukedom on his second son, Thomas of Lancaster, but he died command-ing the English defeat at the Battle of Baugé in 1421, and he too had no heir (though his illegitimate son, John the so-called Bastard of Clarence, fought at his side and even bore his father's body from the field).

The title was created for a third time for George Plantagenet by his older brother, Edward IV. This Duke of Clarence betrayed his brother, however, and in 1478 he was executed in the Tower of London – by being drowned in a butt of Malmsey, according to Shakespeare. The title was almost revived again when Lady Jane Grey, the so-called Nine-Day Queen, decided to make her husband Duke of Clarence at the time of her coronation, in 1553 (over his bitter protests – he wanted to be called king). Jane was soon displaced by Mary I, however, and her husband never got even his dukedom.

The jinxed title fared little better when it was revived in 1890 (as "Duke of Clarence and Avondale") for Albert Victor, the dissipated eldest grandson of Queen Victoria. Flu carried off the young rake two years later, and as if to finally besmirch the title, Albert was even accused (posthumously and entirely implausibly) of having been the notorious Victorian serial killer, Jack the Rip-per. In fact, the only Duke of Clarence that ever made good was William, third son of George III. He succeeded to the throne as William IV and, by doing so, forfeited the title. He thus shed the jinx, you might think, but no: William too died without a heir – though with eleven illegitimate children (see p.159).

Woodville. On 6 July, Richard was crowned king. The princes remained in the Tower, though for how long is uncertain: after that summer, they were never seen again (unless you count the moment when, in 1674, the skel-etons of two boys were found buried under a staircase). Richard was widely blamed for their deaths. Some say he also murdered his own brother, George Plantagenet, the ill-fated 1st Duke of Clarence (see box above).

Two years after his coronation, Richard was defeated at Bosworth Field by Henry Tudor, thus bringing an end to the House of York and the Plantagenet line. Henry claimed the throne by force, not hereditary right,

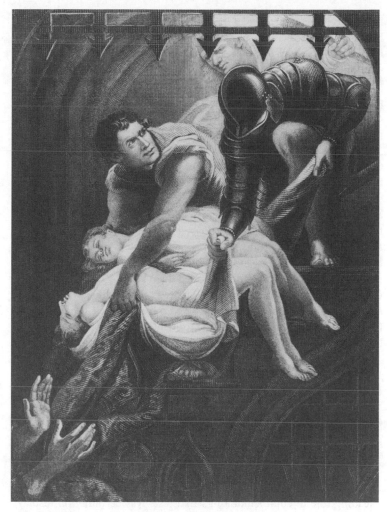

Disposing of the evidence. An engraving (based on a painting by James Northcote) showing the bodies of the two princes, allegedly murdered by Richard III, being hurriedly hidden away.

but it is crucial that the Tudors did descend from the House of Lancaster. To legitimize his cause, Henry (now Henry VII) married Edward IV's daughter, Elizabeth of York, but he also set about demonizing Richard III. The Tudor spin doctors – including Polydore Vergil, Thomas More and a certain William Shakespeare – did a superb hatchet job on Richard. It was so good, indeed, that it wasn't until 1768, when Horace Walpole published a celebrated defence of the maligned king, that anyone wondered how true the accusations were. Since Walpole, the historical argument has raged. Ricardians, who seek to reclaim their hero's reputation, have won some major points. The death of Henry VI probably can be blamed principally on Edward IV, as can the execution (which was authorized by parliament) of George, Duke of Clarence. Edward of Lancaster, probably died at the Battle of Tewkesbury, not after it. Richard's hunchback was probably a Tudor invention.

Richard does, however, seem to have been behind the deaths of Rivers, Grey and Hastings, as well as those of the Princes in the Tower. While there's no direct evidence that Richard killed the princes (and one conspiracy theory even suggests that Henry Tudor ordered their deaths so as to smear Richard), it seems likely that Thomas More was reporting the truth, a generation on, when he described how they died. Their jailer Miles Forest and "a big broad square strong knave" named John Dighton came into the Princes' chamber "and suddenly lapped them up among the clothes [and] so be-wrapped them and entangled them keeping down by force the feather bed and pillows hard unto their mouths, that within a while smored and stifled, their breath failing, they gave up to God their innocent souls into the joys of heaven, leaving to the tormentors their bodies dead in the bed" – and leaving the throne to Richard, their murderous uncle.

Royal Nazis and Nazi royals

On 13 January 2005, Prince Harry found himself on the front page of *The Sun* dressed in what looked like a Nazi desert uniform, and sporting what was, without doubt, a swastika armband. As the Board of Deputies of British Jews observed, this was in bad taste, "especially in the run-up to Holocaust Memorial Day ... which the royal family will be taking a leading role in commemorating". Bad taste was certainly on display: Harry was attending a fancy dress party at which the theme was "colonial and native".

The gaffe was at best insensitive, but as offensive behaviour goes, it falls a long way short of some of his relatives' actions. Although his grandfather, the Duke of Edinburgh, had an irreproachable war record, when his marriage to Queen Elizabeth was first proposed, there were objections to his German background – ironic given the family he was marrying into (see p.62). Philip's four sisters had all married German aristocrats, two of whom had become influential Nazis. His sister Cecilie's husband, for instance, was Georg Donatus, Grand Duke of Hesse. Husband and wife were both great-grandchildren of Queen Victoria and both had joined the Nazi Party in 1937. Worse was his sister Sophie's husband, Prince Christoph of Hesse-Cassel (another great-grandson of Queen Victoria), who joined the Nazi Party in 1930. Christoph rose to become a major in the Luftwaffe who actually flew fighters against Allied forces, and a colonel in the SS, who spent time on Himmler's staff and also, under Göring, ran the Forschungsamt, which spied on anti-Nazis. Sophie and Christoph named their son Karl Adolf – the middle name being in Hitler's honour. None of Prince Philip's sisters were invited to his wedding.

Worse still was Prince Charles Edward, the English-born Duke of Saxe-Coburg and Gotha (closely related to both Prince Philip and George VI). For fighting for the Germans in World War I, the duke was stripped of his British titles (see p.64). He then fell in with the Nazis, even turning up at the funeral of his first cousin George V wearing full uniform as an Obergruppenführer in the SA, complete with stormtrooper's helmet. As president of the German side of the far-right-leaning Anglo-German Fellowship – an organization which had been backed by Edward VIII, as Prince of Wales – he corralled various sympathetic English cousins and aristocratic contacts and tried to persuade them to help make peace with Hitler. In the war, he was president of the German Red Cross, and turned a blind eye to the state-organized mass murder of the disabled. Not, then, a relative that the royal family wanted to be reminded of.

There are other links with the Windsor family, however. Prince Michael of Kent married the daughter of the German Baron von Reibnitz, a member of the Nazi Party. As a close friend of Göring, the baron had joined the Party in 1931, and was made an honorary member of the SS, primarily so he could act as a spy for Göring. The file on him for the Nuremberg Trials was four inches thick, but he was eventually declared merely a *Mitlaufer* (fellow traveller) and no action taken against him. Prince Michael's father, George, Duke of Kent, the younger brother of George VI, was a pro-appeaser who died in a plane crash in 1942. Conspiracy theorists like to claim the accident was suspicious, largely by virtue of its proximity to where Nazi politician Rudolf Hess was then being held prisoner; they then try to link Prince George to Hess's attempted negotiations with the British government – presuming that George had a remarkable degree of influence in politics.

These days George VI is mainly lauded for triumphing over his stammer. It's less often mentioned that he intrigued against Churchill in the 1930s in a way that was entirely unconstitutional. (The controversial

ROYALS AND MASONS

If you read the more lurid conspiracist rantings on the internet, you can "learn" that the British royal family not only "controls parliament via Freemasonry" but uses hidden Masonic networks to send its tentacles throughout the world, teaming up with other sinister organizations, such as the World Wildlife Fund and the Duke of Edinburgh's Award (you thought it was an innocent scheme to get youngsters out on the hills? Think again: think Hitler Youth, with a Masonic twist).

It is true that many British royals have been Freemasons. Joining "the craft" was the done thing among the upper classes in the eighteenth century, and the Hanoverians were not immune to fashion. George III's father, Frederick, Prince of Wales, was a Freemason – in fact, it was partly his example that made Freemasonry so fashionable in England. George III himself never joined, but six of his seven sons did. His eldest son, George, who became Prince Regent and later George IV, was elected Grand Master, and Masonic architectural details were employed in the Royal Pavilion he had built in Brighton; rooms in the Pavilion were given over for use by Masons, too. George's seafaring brother, who became William IV, was Master of a Plymouth Lodge popular among army and navy officers. If all that seems sinister, consider that over a dozen US presidents, including most of the early ones (and George Washington) were also Freemasons.

Freemasonry waned in popularity in the nineteenth century, but it remained – and remains – popular in royal circles. Edward VII was elected Grand Master as Prince of Wales in 1874, and enjoyed a grand installation ceremony at the Royal Albert Hall. Queen Victoria and George V were patrons of various Masonic institutions, and Edward VIII and George VI were both Masons – George later becoming Grand Master. The Duke of Edinburgh was initiated in December 1953, six months after his wife's coronation.

The most active royal Freemasons, however, are the Kent brothers. Prince Edward, Duke of Kent, is Grand Master of the United Grand Lodge of England:

right-wing historian David Irving has even claimed that state records will eventually reveal that in 1940 he and his wife conspired to have Churchill overthrown and replaced with an appeaser.) It's not yet clear whether George VI was merely pro-appeasement, as many British politicians were, or whether he had more sinister allegiances.

It was George's brother and predecessor, Edward VIII, however, who is the real black-shirted sheep of the Windsor family. During the 1936 abdication crisis he was supported by the harder right element in British politics, and some believe that his mistress who precipitated the crisis,

top dog, in other words. The fact that he is also (or has been) President of the All England Club, the Football Association and the Lifeboat Institution, and is chancellor of two universities, suggests that his ability to lead an active Masonic life may be limited, however. Prince Edward's younger brother, the Right Worshipful Brother HRH Prince Michael of Kent, is Grand Master of the Grand Lodge of Mark Master Masons (which is big in Surrey) and the rather less grand-sounding Provincial Grand Master of the Provincial Grand Lodge of Middlesex. Prince Michael's onerous royal duties also leave him little time for day to day involvement, so his position is substantially an honorary and advisory one. He was up for being interviewed for the Masonic *MQ Magazine* in 2002, however, and described how "visiting groups of Masons around the country … being involved in policymaking and talking to senior Masons … all in all it has consumed quite a large part of my life".

In his interview, Prince Michael stressed the need for a new openness (balanced with privacy) and the importance of the craft's charity work. Masonic charities raised £20 million in the previous year, he said proudly – which if you divide it up among the 300,000 Masonic members of which he boasted, equates to an impressive £67 per Mason, per year. In 2007, Prince Michael attended a grand Masonic ceremony with 5000 other Masons at the Royal Albert Hall. Also present were the Duke of Kent and Camilla, Duchess of Cornwall – the latter in her capacity as president of the National Osteoporosis Society, receiving a cheque for £3 million raised by Masonic bike rides, dinners and other events.

There's little scandal to be dredged out of Freemasonry these days, though the *Daily Mail* tried to rake up some in 2008, when members of the royal household and the police protection units who protect the royal family announced they were setting up their own lodge. "Backstairs life is already complicated enough," an "insider" commented, "the last thing the household needs is a secret society." The palace wasn't too happy either, as the new lodge apparently wanted to use "Royal Household" in its name, and royal symbols in its regalia. "Buckingham Palace has not, and would not, endorse this sort of arrangement", a press spokesperson commented.

Wallis Simpson, was simultaneously having an affair with the German ambassador, Joachim von Ribbentrop. (She continued to communicate with him secretly as late as 1940, and may well have passed state secrets to him.) It's perfectly possible that the abdication was forced on Edward not because of Wallis's divorced status, but because she was leading Edward further towards fascism.

Hitler certainly thought Edward was on his side; Albert Speer quoted the Führer as having said that "If he had stayed, everything would have been different. His abdication was a severe loss for us." Hitler may have been overestimating Edward's power, but not his support. In October 1937, the newly demoted Duke of Windsor and his Duchess, Wallis, toured Germany in the teeth of British government disapproval. They were treated as if it was a state visit, wining and dining with Himmler, Hess and Ribbentrop. Later they met Hitler in his alpine eyrie in Berchtesgaden, greeting the Führer with a full Nazi salute – the official reason for the visit was to study "housing and working conditions". In later life, Edward disclosed that he "never thought Hitler was such a bad chap", and even in 1940, in exile in France, Edward was praising how Germany had "reordered" its society, and bragging that Britain had little chance of resisting German military might. Some believe he may have been in personal correspondence with Hitler (though if so, the papers have disappeared; it has been alleged that MI5 found and destroyed them, and rumours persist that he was cutting a deal with Göring in which he would be reinstated in the event that Germany won the war.) Certainly, the government thought Edward enough of a liability to pack the former king off to the Bahamas, where he was safely out of the way as governor, and could slowly pickle himself in alcohol and sunshine.

Seventy years later, in an interview with historian Jonathan Petropoulous, Prince Philip attempted to explain the appeal of Nazism: "There was a great improvement in things like trains running on time and building. There was a sense of hope after the depressing chaos of the Weimar Republic … a lot of enthusiasm for the Nazis at the time, the economy was good, we were anti-Communist and who knew what was going to happen to the regime?"

Swinging sister: Princess Margaret

"When there are two sisters and one is the Queen, who must be the source of honour and all that is good," Princess Margaret told the writer Gore Vidal, "the other must be … the evil sister." It would be very hard to consider Margaret as evil, not least because she never wielded any power, and precious little influence; she has certainly made a strong counterpoint to her sister, however. Where Queen Elizabeth II appeared reticent, duty-bound and loyal, Margaret was apparently sparkly, freewheeling – and disastrously inconstant. As their father said of them, Elizabeth was his pride, but Margaret was his joy.

Margaret was born in 1930, making her four years Elizabeth's junior. When she was six, life changed for both girls when their uncle, Edward

Princess Margaret and Antony Armstrong-Jones (Lord Snowdon), all dolled up in 1961, attending a performance of the Royal Ballet at London's Royal Opera House.

VIII, abdicated, and their father, the Duke of York, unexpectedly became king. Margaret, it is said, found it harder to come to terms with the fact that her sister was now heir to the throne than Elizabeth herself did. The princesses spent most of the war cosseted at Windsor Castle, where Margaret developed a reputation as a spoiled charmer all too able and willing to thrust Elizabeth out of the limelight.

After the war, and as the girls approached marriageable age, it was Margaret who was photographed in a bikini on the island of Capri, and Margaret who socialized with a racy aristocratic set, sporting a bohemian long cigarette holder and a much envied hourglass figure at parties and nightclubs. Then, in 1953, suspiciously close to the time of her sister's coronation, she announced to her family (perhaps with some satisfaction at the discomfort she was causing) that she was going to marry Peter Townsend, a former RAF fighter pilot fifteen years her senior who was recently divorced and had two children, and was at the time in charge of her mother's household.

There was an almighty fuss. Townsend had been Margaret's chaperone on a tour of southern Africa when she was sixteen (though the relationship seems to have begun much later, and only became public knowledge in the summer of 1953 when a journalist spotted Margaret picking a piece of lint off his jacket). Margaret was made to wait, while intense pressure was put on her to change her mind. The Church of England stated that the remarriage of a divorcee was out of the question, while Churchill's government indicated that she would have to renounce her place in the line of succession if the marriage went ahead.

Press speculation mounted until, on 31 October 1955, Margaret made a public statement, apparently drafting it with Townsend's help: "Mindful of the Church's teachings that Christian marriage is indissoluble, and conscious of my duty to the Commonwealth," she purred, "I have resolved to put these considerations before others." It made her look noble, but privately she and Townsend had run out of love.

In 1960, Margaret surprised again by getting engaged to a bohemian society photographer, Antony Armstrong-Jones. It was rumoured that Margaret had only agreed to marry him in a furious reaction to Townsend's marriage to a Belgian girl said to look just like her (and indeed there was a resemblance). Snowdon's status as a commoner, albeit one who had been to Eton and Cambridge, went down well with the public, and the Queen quickly made him Earl of Snowdon to regularize matters. (For all his bohemian pretensions, Snowdon took to his title, using it thereafter as his professional name.) Snowdon was still snubbed by royal society and royal servants, however. He didn't ease the situation. He later liked to tell a story about how, after his first visit to Balmoral, at which he wasn't invited shooting, he took lessons so as to come back next time and blast away better than the royals.

THE PHOTOGRAPHER, THE PAINTER, THE CABINET-MAKER

You might not envy his marriage, but at least Lord Snowdon had a proper job. He was a working photographer even before he took up with Princess Margaret, and kept up his profession right through their marriage. His critics say his work is superficial, and that without his royal contacts he'd never have become the lionized portraitist he is today, but still, he's one of the big names.

His children work, too – even though the proceeds from selling their mother's effects at Christie's, in 2006, ensured that they don't need to. (The sale netted £13.6 million, though some of that had to be given to charity after the Queen pointed out that a few of the effects had been given to Margaret in an official capacity.) David Armstrong-Jones, Viscount Linley, is a high-class cabinet-maker and interior designer whose furniture is bought by celebrities ,including the Queen, who gives it away to foreign dignitaries as official gifts. Linley has also been chairman of Christie's UK, which does like to stuff its boards with aristocrats. Lady Sarah Chatto is a moderately successful painter who, like her brother, has two children.

The newlyweds embraced their high profile. They let their wedding be televised, and enjoyed a six-week honeymoon cruise around the Caribbean on the royal yacht at (vast) public expense. They led a moneyed and fashionable set, and were touted as emblematic of the Swinging Sixties. The marriage, however, was troubled: both partners really were swinging – and both ways, in Snowdon's case. Margaret had relationships first with their daughter's godfather, then with nightclub pianist (and nephew of the prime minister) Robin Douglas-Home. Various scandal-mongers have tried to make the case that she also had flings with actors David Niven, Warren Beatty and Peter Sellers, the singer Mick Jagger and the irreverent Australian cricketer Keith Miller, among other celebrities.

It's hard to prove either way, and perhaps pointless; the point is that the marriage was falling apart. Snowdon maintained contacts with a fast-living, sexually experimental set, but the slide towards divorce really began when, in 1974, the 43-year-old Margaret took the 27-year-old Roddy Llewellyn to Mustique, in the Caribbean, where she had long maintained a house for parties and getaways, Les Jolies Eaux. Rumours of drug-taking and sex on the beach already swirled around the island, but when photos emerged of a bikini-clad Margaret cavorting on the sand with Llewellyn, they caused an outright scandal. As MPs demanded to know why taxpayers were funding this "royal parasite", Snowdon left her, and she divorced him in 1978 – the first royal to divorce in England since Henry VIII.

In the 1980s and 90s, as other royal marriages rose and spectacularly fell, Margaret's health deteriorated, and she withdrew almost completely from the public eye. She died in 2002, after a series of strokes and accidents, attracting little public comment.

6

The royals debate

A terrible anachronism? An affront to democracy? Or a beautiful institution that sums up all that is noble about British tradition and culture? There are as many opinions about the royal family as there are branches in its family tree. The worth of the royals has been debated for centuries – irrespective of the merits of any particular monarch – and arguments between monarchists and republicans look set to continue long in to the reigns of any future Charles III or William V.

Against the Crown: the republican cause today

The national anthem no longer plays at the beginning of films at the cinema, and few dinner parties begin by toasting the Queen. Historians don't always put the royal family at the centre of national history and identity. Parliament has chipped away at the royal powers over the last hundred years. In Australia, it looks as if the monarchy won't be acknowledged beyond the life of the current Queen. Is Britain on a long, slow, inevitable slide into republicanism?

History suggests not. The monarchy has survived phases of deep unpopularity – under the Regency, for instance, or during the scandals surrounding the widowed Victoria's relationship with John Brown. And the contemporary monarchy is in fact not that unpopular at all. An April 2011 poll found that only 13 percent of British people wanted it abolished. Admittedly, that was in the wake of the razzmatazz of the Wills and

Kate royal wedding. But at the very nadir of recent royal fortunes, in the aftermath of Princess Diana's death, the poll was not much different: just 19 percent of Britons, at the time, declared themselves republicans.

If republicans are a minority, they are an increasingly assertive one. The campaigning group Republic numbers some 14,000 supporters – and enjoyed a big swell in numbers after the 2011 royal wedding. Its belief is that the monarchy "embodies a spirit of ... dependence on others. It robs us of aspiration ... denies us the best democracy we could have." We enshrine legal duties of transparency and fairness in employment law, yet we make a mockery of all these efforts by allowing the inherited representative of an unimaginably rich family the right to cling to a position of extreme privilege. The American dream is that anyone could become president; the message enshrined by the British status quo is that everyone ought to stay in their allotted place. To further its cause, Republic organizes street parties, demonstrations and mounts legal challenges. It played a key role in persuading London's Metropolitan police to award compensation to a man who had been wrongfully arrested for carrying a republican placard on the day of the royal wedding.

There have been other independent but influential anti-royalist campaigners. The recently-deceased journalist Christopher Hitchens regularly furthered the republican cause with a mixture of contemptuous rationalism and inspired invective, condemning Prince Charles as a "morose, balding, New Age crank and licensed busybody that we flinch from". Peter Tatchell, the influential gay rights activist, has observed that "never in Queen Elizabeth II's 58-year reign has she ever acknowledged the existence of the LGBTI community ... the words "gay" and "lesbian" have never publicly passed her lips ... if she treated black or Asian people in the same way, she'd be denounced as a racist."

The Labour MP and historian Tristram Hunt has protested against the way Tories yoke the monarchy and national identity together, ignoring the alternative, rationalist, non-conformist tradition he himself admires: "from the anti-slavery movement to the anti-apartheid movement ... from the Political Register to the BBC," he wrote in *The Guardian*, "there is a national story unrepresented at the Queen Mother's funeral or the jubilee but more fundamental to British identity than any transient royal dynasty".

Neither Labour nor any of the other major political parties (other than the Green Party) have dared come out in favour of a republic. Not while the statistics remain as they are. Even the Welsh and Scottish nationalist parties, Plaid Cymru and the SNP, insist that they'd be happy to continue as independent states under the same old monarch – unless their people voted otherwise.

It is down to a few left-wing troublemakers to make empty protests in Westminster. In 1997, taking the (obligatory) Parliamentary Oath vowing loyalty to the Crown, MP Tony Benn began "As a committed republican, under protest, I take the oath required of me by law..." Dennis Skinner swore, naughtily, that he would "bear true and faithful allegiance to the Queen when she pays her income tax". Tony Banks MP visibly kept his fingers crossed.

More impressively, Martin McGuinness of the Irish Republican party Sinn Féin challenged the oath at the European Court of Human Rights in 1999. The court stated that it could be "reasonably viewed as an affirmation of loyalty to the constitutional principles", gently suggesting that Mr McGuinness shouldn't let himself get hung up on a few words.

However, it's worth reminding ourselves that there was a time when England got hung up on a lot more than a few words. It's instructive to look at what happened during the seventeenth-century period – deplorable for some, all too brief for others – in which England threw off its monarchy. No discussion of the tug-of-war between pro-royals and republicans should overlook the fact that England did away with kings only to bring them back.

Republicanism and all that

On 17 March 1649, the House of Commons passed an act stating that "the office of a King, in this nation ... is unnecessary, burthensome, and dangerous to the liberty, safety, and public interest of the people of this nation; and therefore ought to be abolished". This was not the view of the majority, but parliament had purged itself of dissenters in order to put the king on trial, and the radical minority remained in control. It had beheaded Charles I two months earlier, on 30 January, but many of the less extreme elements hoped that either Charles II, or even his illegitimate half-brother, could be crowned (with conditions, of course). Even among those who had fought against Charles, many could not reconcile their consciences to the killing of an anointed king.

The regicide may actually have fuelled the royalists' cause. The royalist spin doctors did such a good job of writing up Charles's death – facing the scaffold with dignity – that the man once seen as an irresponsible tyrant was quickly turned into a Christian martyr. Those who had signed his death warrant would forever have "bloody hands", as the poet Andrew Marvell put it.

An engraving from 1684 depicting the trial of Charles I (below centre). Charles refused to remove his hat, as he did not acknowledge the authority of the court.

The republican administration that followed struggled to live up to the charisma of sacred monarchy, in any case. It wasn't built on strong foundations. There had been no sustained republican movement in England prior to the English Civil War – it wasn't as if the country had been heading inevitably for revolution. Under the Tudors, there had been some quasi-republican murmurings by some writers, thinkers and counsellors who looked to the examples of ancient Rome, Venice and Holland, but this provided a way of checking absolutism, rather than amounting to a serious challenge to the very institution of monarchy. The word republic was used, but it meant simply the "commonwealth" or "state"; it did not describe a system of government incompatible with kings and queens until the late eighteenth century.

In the 1630s, however, as Charles I's relationship with parliament deteriorated, and as the country slid into a decade of bloody wars, radical MPs and army generals pushed the idea of a kingless state, and manoeuvred to put Charles, and the monarchy itself, on trial. In 1649, Britain was declared a "free state" – a *république*. The problem was agreeing on what exactly this free state should look like, and whether what parliament really wanted was a constitutional monarchy – a figurehead king with no real power.

One of the most important men in this new "free state", which fused England, Scotland and Ireland together, was Oliver Cromwell, a former farmer who was now second-in-command of the formidable New Model Army. As the architects of the state wrestled with defining the word "free", and as the Rump Parliament – the name referring to what remained of parliament after it had been purged of those who did not want the king tried for treason – became increasingly intransigent, Cromwell's influence grew. The spectre of monarchy raised its head again: twice Oliver Cromwell was offered the crown; twice he refused.

Cromwell died just a year later, in 1658. His corpse was clothed in a robe of state, his lifeless hands clutched a sceptre and an orb, and a crown hovered over his head on a little velvet cushion. As he lay dying, Cromwell named his son, Richard, as his heir. Within two years, "Queen Dick", as he was unfortunately known, had handed in his resignation and Charles II came back from the cold. While the Stuart restoration was not to last, the monarchy was back for good.

A republic with a crown

The "Glorious Revolution" of 1688 was a triumph for monarchy: the Catholic king James II (brother of the late Charles II) may have been deposed, but his Protestant daughter and her husband were crowned as

CROMWELL: A KING IN ALL BUT NAME

In 1649, the men in charge of building England's new republic tried to get rid of the word "king". But on 16 December 1653, Oliver Cromwell, a 52-year-old gentleman farmer from Huntingdon who had risen meteorically through the ranks of the New Model Army, was inaugurated as England's Lord Protector. It was a title synonymous with the institution of monarchy: England had last been a protectorate during the brief reign of Henry VIII's longed-for son, Edward VI.

Following the execution of Charles I, Cromwell had been away, subjugating first the Irish and then the Scots. He came home to a floundering commonwealth with a parliament in stalemate. The members of the Rump Parliament refused to put themselves up for re-election, so Cromwell, with the help of some of his soldiers, sent them packing and began to rule as Commander-in-Chief. As a new constitution for this military dictatorship was hammered out, it was decided that "supreme legislative authority" should, after all, reside "in one person". This person could not, it was agreed, be called a king, but Lord Protector was seen as acceptable. At the simple investiture ceremony, Cromwell dressed all in black.

By the following April, Cromwell had moved his wife, Elizabeth, and their children into Whitehall. They slept in the very rooms which Charles had been forced to abandon in 1642. A surveyor of works was employed to refurbish and redecorate the palace. And, every weekend, Cromwell left the city for the peace and expanse of Hampton Court. (He was, after all, a country boy.)

Lorenzo Palucci, the ambassador from Venice, commented that Cromwell "may be said to assume additional state and majesty daily, and lacks nothing of royalty but the name, which he is generally expected to assume when he wants to". Like Charles I, Cromwell levied illegal taxes; like Charles, Cromwell disbanded parliament at his will. And he set about closing pubs, theatres and brothels.

Parliament responded by offering Cromwell the crown, a seemingly paradoxical move intended to rein him in. The army was against it, but Cromwell

joint sovereigns. William III and Mary II did, however, have their royal prerogative severely curtailed, and the people's liberties (and taxes) were protected according to the Declaration of Rights. It was, in many ways, a crowned republic. However, as David Hume said of the Hanoverians, it may be "a magnificent idea of the British spirit and love of liberty" but actually "the power of the crown, by means of its large revenue, is rather upon the increase".

The stout British monarchy managed to weather the republican tidal wave that swept through Europe in the eighteenth and nineteenth centuries, toppling many of the continent's monarchs. In 1848, the Court Journal declared that "there can be no doubt of the Republic being the ideal of a human

only refused at the eleventh hour. Instead, he accepted a second inauguration as Lord Protector. On 26 June 1657, Cromwell appeared in Westminster Hall dressed in an ermine-lined robe of purple velvet and wielding a gold sceptre. Within eight years, England had re-created another absolute monarch.

government", but it went on to wonder what England "may gain under a republican form of government, that she may not gain under that which she [already] possesses".

That the monarchy was bankrupting the country, or that hereditary power was simply irrational, were never convincing enough arguments for the fledgling republican clubs in turn-of-the-century Britain to take off. Few radical voices could be heard among the clamour of the more conservative MPs who were also peers. And there were always other, more pressing and harmful matters to debate. More to the point, the British *liked* their royal family, and they watched on while, one by one, France, Austria, Russia, Italy and Portugal all shrugged off their kings.

For the Crown: monarchists today

For the most part, even ardent royalists don't attempt to claim that an empowered monarchy makes rational sense. As the great eighteenth-century radical Thomas Paine put it, a hereditary monarch is as absurd as a hereditary judge or mathematician. And a position which is inherited and inheritable, he further observed, is one which is dangerously unaccountable.

Even with a powerless monarchy, the arbitrary nature of who gets to sit on the throne is worryingly whimsical. Writer Simon Jenkins put it neatly when he observed in 2011 that if Prince William becomes king it will only be because he is "the elder son of the elder son of the elder daughter of a man who got the job because his elder brother married the wrong woman". And Jenkins is in *favour* of the monarchy. Plenty of supposed royalists are happy to accept Queen Elizabeth II because, broadly, they admire her, but may feel very differently when they're confronted with the real prospect of King Charles III and Queen Camilla. Yet the argument for skipping a generation to King William V is self-defeating: if you want to pick and choose your monarch according to taste, why not hold an election?

Elections, in fact, are what many convinced monarchists are most eager to avoid. We've got enough politicians running the country, they argue. Would you rather have President Blair? Or President Thatcher? Or how about a President Sarkozy? Actually, this rather misses the point: the French presumably did want Sarkozy, given that they elected him.

Monarchists like to claim that the royal family earns more than it costs, through tourism, though the figures on both sides are opaque and highly disputable (see p.200). They claim that the royal family does wonders for charity too, though again you could argue about the relative levels of input and output. In 2005, Prince Charles's former press officer, Mark Bolland, observed that "the Windsors are very good at working three days a week, five months of a year and making it look as though they work hard".

Monarchists are instinctive conservatives, however, with either a small or a big C. As the republican Will Self wrote in 2011, they tend to put their case like this: "See that noble oak over there? That's our system of government. What kind of foul oik are you to chop it down with your regicidal axe?" There is a point here. Longevity in a constitutional settlement is closely linked to consensus, and consensus is linked to stability. The oak is strong, and firm, and the monarchy supposedly guarantees stability. Even when governments are blown about in the winds of fashion, the Crown sits there, like a weight holding the whole thing down. Of course, when you look at it closely, British history isn't all that stable, but it is true that Britain hasn't had the same degree of wrangling over the constitution that many of its European neighbours with written constitutions have suffered. But then, neither has the US. And the US is, significantly, a republic.

Political debate and constitutional argument don't get the British public out on the streets and cheering, however. There's the fun and glamour and pageantry and kitsch of it all – and more profound emotional pulls too. There is a powerful shared sense that the royal family represents the nation, or at least its history, bearing all the old-fashioned values that many people still cherish (even if they don't actually adhere to them in practice).

In medieval times, the actual physical body of the sovereign was something only an elite few were ever close to, yet it stood for something its population could passionately believe in: the nation state. For many people, this feeling remains. The Queen may be the most undemocratic thing going, but she still somehow represents us. When the British cheer the Queen, you might say they're actually cheering themselves.

Powers and prerogatives: what the royals can actually do

If anyone thinks the modern monarch is a toothless figurehead, they clearly aren't aware of the extensive list of powers that come under the Royal Prerogative. These are the powers that belong to the Crown alone, not to parliament or the people, and there is an astonishing number of them. The Crown has the power to: make treaties, declare war and make peace; to command and deploy the armed forces; to initiate criminal prosecutions, pardon offenders and shorten sentences (under the beautifully named Royal Prerogative of Mercy); to summon, prorogue and dissolve parliament; to appoint ministers, judges and bishops; to confer honours and create peers; to never be sued; to intern or expel enemy aliens; to requisition ships in time of emergency; to print the Authorised version of the Bible; to own treasure, if discovered, as well as all the swans, sturgeons and whales in the kingdom.

For good measure, under the Crown's Personal Prerogative, the monarch has the power to appoint the prime minister and grant (or withold) royal assent to parliamentary bills. (The age-old power to dissolve parliaments was taken away in September 2011 by the Liberal Democrat-sponsored Fixed-Term Parliaments Act.)

These prerogatives cannot be questioned by the courts and can rarely be controlled by parliament. They cannot, in truth, be exercised by the individual reigning monarch, however. In practice, and by convention (and convention, in the UK, virtually is the law) the Queen appoints as prime minister the politician who leads the largest party. That lucky politician pretty much handles the rest, perhaps in consultation with his or her cabinet, and with at least a perfunctory nod to the wishes of parliament and party. A prime minister picks his or her own ministers and his peers, for instance, by the simple means of passing a list to the Queen.

HIGH TREASON – OFFENCES AGAINST MAJESTY

When Princess Diana revealed in her notorious 1995 BBC interview that she had conducted a long affair with James Hewitt, one *Daily Mirror* journalist (with tongue in cheek) tried to have Hewitt arrested. While this was just a headline-making stunt, according to the law, Hewitt could have been executed for treason.

The Treason Act, passed under Edward III in 1351, defined high treason as any of the following crimes: planning to murder the king, his wife or his heir; making war against the king inside the kingdom; counterfeiting the Great Seal or any English coin (partly because these bore an image of the king's head); killing the chancellor or various named justices; and "violating" the king's wife, his unmarried daughter or his heir's wife.

The Treason Act still stands on the statute book, though it is very rarely used – in 1981, for instance, a seventeen-year-old was convicted under the renewed Treason Act 1842 for firing blanks near the Queen. (He wasn't executed; he was given a five-year sentence and released after three.) And James Hewitt is safe, thanks to a 1695 statute which states that an indictment must be brought within three years of the offence. In fact he's doubly safe, since the 1998 Crime and Disorder Act abolished the death penalty for the crime.

The last person to be executed for treason was William Joyce, aka Lord Haw Haw, the Berlin-based voice of Nazi propaganda radio broadcasting in World War II. Despite not actually being a British subject – Joyce had lied about his Irish-American origins in order to get a British passport – it was argued that he owed loyalty to the sovereign of the country of his choice. He was hanged in Wandsworth Prison by the executioner Albert Pierrepoint.

Other executions for treason, in the preceding war, were equally controversial. Over a dozen Irish nationalists were shot by firing squad for participating in the 1916 Easter Rising; they were British subjects in the eyes of the law, though they would have denied it passionately. In the same year, Irish

(It used to be much the same way with judges, but the Blair government transferred the powers to a non-governmental public body.)

Even the celebrated Queen's Speech, or "Speech from the Throne", in which a government sets out its stall for the year ahead, is only read out aloud by the Queen. She doesn't play any part in writing it. This doesn't mean that the powers of the royal prerogative are meaningless, however. The fact that the government derives its authority in these areas of prerogative directly from the Crown, and not from parliament, means that a prime minister can, on occasion, act with astonishing personal freedom. Tony

nationalist Roger Casement was tried for buying German weapons for the rising. At his sensational (and sensationally unfair) trial, Casement's defence pleaded that the Treason Act specifically stated that the enemies which the traitor served had to be "in the king's realm", and that Casement was thus innocent, as his arms deals had taken place in Germany.

The judge, however, demanded that the original rolls of the Act should be looked at again, with a magnifying glass, and ruled that

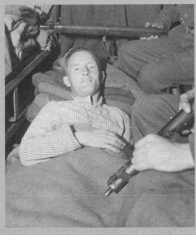

William Joyce, aka Lord Haw-Haw, under British guard, having been captured in Berlin.

a crucial comma lay in the middle of the phrase about giving the king's enemies "aid and comfort in his realm or elsewhere" (this allowed "or elsewhere" to apply generally to treason, not just to the specific giving of aid and comfort). Casement was duly hanged, as the saying goes, "on a comma".

If killing the king or casting doubt on his blood line are still crimes, one once-treasonable act is not. After his break with Rome, a nervous Henry VIII invented a new kind of treason. "If any Person," the statute read, should "slanderously and maliciously publish and pronounce ... that the King our Sovereign Lord should be Heretick, Schismatic, Tyrant, Infidel or Usurper of the Crown," then they too were guilty of treason, and liable to be executed. Fortunately for the writers of this book, Henry's "treasonable words" statute no longer stands.

Blair did as much when he declared war without parliamentary approval in 2003 (as did Neville Chamberlain, in 1939). Margaret Thatcher invoked the same powers when she outlawed union membership at the intelligence-gathering agency GCHQ in 1984. All in the name of the Crown.

The prime minister also has to watch her or his step, to a certain degree. The fact that it has been many years since the monarch, on his own authority, dismissed a prime minister (William IV in 1834), appointed one of her own choosing (Elizabeth II in 1963 – albeit on the advice of the outgoing PM) or refused royal assent to a parliamentary bill (Queen Anne in 1708) doesn't mean it couldn't happen again. Elizabeth II refused her consent to the Military Action Against Iraq (Parliamentary Approval) bill of 1999 – admittedly this was a special case as the government had asked her to refuse consent to the bill to prevent it getting a second reading. Of course, there's nothing to stop a future government passing an act to take away other royal powers – except the royal assent, that is.

Alongside the prerogative powers, the sovereign has enormous personal influence. The Queen has weekly meetings with the prime minister at which, as the great Victorian constitutional expert Walter Bagehot put it, she exercises "the right to be consulted, the right to encourage, and the right to warn". She also wields power by virtue of her public support and her extreme wealth – though this power is not exclusive to the monarchy, of course. Plenty of press barons, party donors and businesspeople can boast as much.

Monarchy and the nation: earning one's keep

Royal income and expenditure both reside within the public gaze, yet remain shrouded in more than a little mystery. The funding arrangements have a long and complicated history and protocol. Strange terms abound within bizarrely complicated arrangements. Mechanisms have existed whereby payments are made to the Queen that are then reimbursed, with no obvious rationale for the exchange. Both royalists and republicans tend to agree that, in this century at least, the monarchy has been pretty canny in managing its own financial affairs. They disagree strongly, of course, over whether this state of affairs is for the ultimate benefit of the nation.

The official figure – as declared by Buckingham Palace accounts – for the amount of money paid for the upkeep of the British royal family in the financial year 2009–2010 was £38.2 million. But this, as pressure groups

SUBJECT TO TAX?

Many people believe the royals only started paying income tax after the Queen announced in 1992 that she would start doing so, in a post-Diana-fallout PR move. In fact, both Queen Victoria and Edward VII had paid income tax on their personal Duchy of Lancaster earnings – before George V then put a stop to it. It was part of a deal he struck in the midst of a 1930s belt-tightening recession, whereby he volunteered a much-publicized ten percent reduction in the Civil List money (on which tax has never been paid) he received from parliament.

The 2012 settlement (see below) has many similarities. As well as sharing a recessionary backdrop with the 1930s, the new deal is also being presented as a rationalization – good for the country. The new Sovereign Support Grant is exempt from tax and the arrangement allows the royals a slightly greater degree of freedom over their financial affairs. Voluntary income tax will continue to be paid on Privy Purse income that it is not used for "official purposes".

There are several exemptions and kinks in royal tax rules – most of which relate to the family's status as public servants. The charitable way of looking at these would be to call them expenses of the job. More cynical souls might deem them unnecessary gratuities for the already over-privileged. Not only does the royal family have the massive perk of a choice of palaces to live in, "held in trust" for the nation, but the monarch pays no inheritance tax or death duties on the huge Balmoral castle and land. Despite the fact that it is privately owned (it falls outside the Crown Estate because it was not bought by a monarch: purchased by Prince Albert, not Queen Victoria), it is rather conveniently "owned" by trustees (one of whom is the holder of the Privy Purse). If that wasn't indemnity enough, the number one royal in the family gets an extra special get-out clause: "bequests from Sovereign to Sovereign are exempt" from inheritance tax. When the Queen Mother died, her will remained private (under the terms of an agreement so secret that most MPs were unaware of it) and no tax was paid on her personal estate, valued at an estimated £30–50 million, which included her art collection. The *Daily Mail* estimated the inheritance tax saving at nearly £20 million.

Republicans see the special status of royal affairs as glorified tax dodging: the family receive huge tax exemptions on luxurious properties, sprawling estates and valuable works of art. Royal supporters point to the unique duties and responsibilities that go with the monarchy, and the need for them to have "financial independence". The lesson to be learnt from history is that the issue of royal tax will always be topical: rules can – and do – get changed in line with the times and the preferences of the government (and monarch) of the day.

such as Republic point out, does not factor in many significant expenses – not least the huge security costs incurred by the Ministry of Defence and other departments in protecting Britain's poshest family.

The Civil List

Until 2012 the majority of royal expenses were paid via the Civil List. This royal allowance dates from 1697, and its unusual name derives from the fact that the sovereign was originally expected to contribute some of this gargantuan sum towards the costs of running the civil government. (The word "civil" was used simply to distinguish it from the military and naval expenses, which were funded by a separate, specific taxation.) The name is now an anachronism as, since 1830, it has had nothing to do with contributions towards government. It is a payment from parliament to cover the costs of the royal household. The Queen is the sole official beneficiary of the Civil List, although it's the list which ultimately pays for her consort Prince Philip and the running expenses of the immediate royal household: £13.7 million was granted in 2010.

Grants-in-aid

These are supplementary payments, made by government departments, which mainly cover travel costs and the upkeep of royal residences. In 2010, the Department of Culture, Media and Sport paid £11.9 million towards the maintenance of Buckingham Palace, St James's Palace, Clarence House, Marlborough House Mews, the residential and office areas of Kensington Palace, Windsor Castle, Hampton Court Mews and Paddocks, and The Queen's Gallery. The Department of Environment, Transport and the Regions (DETR) paid £6 million for official travel costs for engagements in England and Scotland, the majority of which was for air travel. A further grant-in-aid of £0.5 million was paid for "communications and information".

The Privy Purse and the royal estates

The peculiar-sounding Privy Purse is another ancient term with a nomenclature unhelpful in explaining what it refers to. It is income from the Duchy of Lancaster that the Queen can use for both personal and official spending. The Duchy of Lancaster is a large portfolio of land and property that the Queen does not technically own – just like Buckingham Palace, it is "held in trust" by the sovereign – but which she may profit from. In other words, it's not far off being a hereditary fiefdom; Duke of Lancaster is one of the Queen's many titles.

Prince Charles is the beneficiary of a similar setup: he receives income via proceeds (after voluntary tax) from the Duchy of Cornwall – another huge collection of estates and properties comprising around 54,521 hectares across 23 counties, mostly concentrated in the southwest of England. In 2010–2011, the prince's declared income from the Duchy was £17.8 million.

Neither of these are to be confused with the Crown Estate. While this is yet another set of handed-down properties – including Regent Street, Ascot Racecourse and "more than half of Britain's fore shore" – it does not generate any personal income for the royal family. It is run as a statutory corporation accountable to parliament: profits from the Crown Estate go to the treasury.

The Sovereign Support Grant

As of 2012, the Civil List and Grants-in-aid are no more, consolidated into the Sovereign Support Grant (which may well have been titled to sound a little like a means-tested benefit), kicking off at £31 million. In succeeding years it will be based upon 15% of the profits of the Crown Estate and is therefore expected to rise in line with the Estate's performance. (This percentage rate will be reviewed once every five years.)

Several commentators expect this to be a better deal for the monarchy – which has of late complained of a 19% reduction in public income – and at least provides the opportunity (via the activities of the Crown Estate and its prime urban holdings) of tracking the real economy and faring accordingly well or ill. In bad times and good, the people and the monarchy will be seen to be "all in it together" – or at least as close to it as super-wealthy, titled landowners receiving millions from the state ever could.

The B-listers

But what about the peripheral royals – those hangers-on frequently cited as a drain on the country's coffers? Recent practice has been to pay parliamentary annuities to the immediate family, as follows:

The Duke of York	**£249,000**
The Earl of Wessex	**£141,000**
The Princess Royal	**£228,000**
The Duke and Duchess of Gloucester	**£175,000**
The Duke and Duchess of Kent	**£236,000**
Princess Alexandra	**£225,000**

The treasury was then reimbursed out of the Queen's private income in the form of the Duchy of Lancaster's profits (often referred to as the Privy Purse). As with the Grants-in-Aid and the Privy Purse, however, the Sovereign Support Grant is taking over as the source of this finance.

The even wider family has to make its own way (with or without a little help from the Queen) but their own hereditary wealth and connections still give them a big helping hand. And their royal celebrity status provides quite a boost to income prospects and an "in" with parts of the establishment – notably the military and financial sectors. Aristocracy is, after all, about inherited wealth – and the power that comes with it.

Royal wealth: a grey economy

If royal income is a hot potato, royal wealth is a can of worms. It is almost impossible to put an actual figure on the royal coffers, owing to a lack of information. But in 2010, *Forbes* magazine estimated the Queen's private wealth at $450 million – sandwiched in the royal ranks between the oil-rich rulers Sultan Qaboos bin Said of Oman ($700 million) and Sheikh Sabah Al-Ahmad Al-Jaber Al Sabah of Kuwait. *Forbes* upped their estimate to $500 million in 2011.

Property complicates things. Among the many ancestral piles attached to the Crown, only Balmoral and Sandringham are actually owned personally by the Queen. (Strictly speaking, Balmoral is owned by trustees acting on the Queen's personal behalf.) But there are plenty of other royal properties which are neither private residences nor tourist attractions open to the public. The full picture of all royal property moves and transactions – including, for instance, the sale of Prince Andrew's Sunninghill Park house to Kazakh oligarch Timur Kulbayev for £3 million over its market value – is difficult to fathom. The palace has always denied any impropriety or evasion of taxes in relation to Sunninghill's sale. But the complex nature of the form in which this type of residential wealth is held or owned, the extent to which various properties are used for state duties, and the way in which the best professional tax and financial advice is deployed on the palace's behalf all remain highly controversial.

Dig even deeper and there are further peculiarities and omissions. The *Daily Mail* reported in February 2011 that the European Union has paid around £500,000 to the Queen and £100,000 to the Prince of Wales in the form of agricultural subsidies, but deemed disclosure of precise details about these to be an "invasion of privacy". It aptly illustrates the point that freedom of information rules routinely do not apply to many subjects relating to the monarchy and finance. The monarchy's vast wealth generates a lot of income, which could help pay for itself, but operates under a unique set of rules.

The royal family is still permitted to increase its wealth. The new funding system does not break with the old in allowing the royal family to profit from its assets: the treasury says this will be capped at 50% of the Sovereign Support Grant value, and that the size of the grant may be reduced if funds rapidly accumulate.

Value for money?

Discussions about the bang-per-buck of the royal family tend to hit a brick wall. Despite the efforts of a few economists, exactly how much they cost us relative to how much revenue they bring in (in terms of heritage tourism, for instance) remains bafflingly opaque. All sorts of royal financial information is unclear, deliberately hidden or simply unknowable. The BBC even kept schtum over the costs of its royal wedding coverage, despite the fact that the public-interest criteria of its charter would suggest that the information should be available.

In 2011 it was reported that the costs of the royal family amount to the equivalent of 51p per person in the UK – a fall from a recent high of 69p a

DUCHY ORIGINALS

The best-known royal enterprise is not the shadowy Crown Estate Corporation but Duchy Originals, a central strand of Prince Charles's enthusiasm for all things natural. The organic food arm of the Duchy of Cornwall estates produced its first biscuit in 1990 after Duchy Home Farm converted to organic farming – many years before the organic bandwagon started rolling. Nine years later it made its first profit. The brand then consolidated its position, successfully riding the UK's brief organic food wave before recessionary pressures in 2010 saw it report a loss.

Most of its produce is now made under licence by major food manufacturers (Walkers make their biscuits while Crabtree & Evelyn do their preserves) and retailed almost exclusively via Waitrose supermarkets in a partnership that has revived Duchy's fortunes and considerably expanded its range. Though one of their products – Duchy Herbals Detox Tincture – received a lot of flak from a leading academic expert on complementary medicine. Professor Edzard Ernst dismissed the food supplement, which combines artichoke and dandelion and promises to rid the body of toxins, as "quakery" based on "implausible, unproven and dangerous" notions. (Ernst's gripes, it must be said, are not just directed at Duchy Originals products, but at the homeopathic movement in general: he's as much of a homeopathy naysayer as Charles is a cheerleader.)

Several millions of the company's profits have made their way into the Prince's Charities Foundation, which has made donations to farmers and rural communities. Like many other business ventures of the current House of Windsor, the variable fortunes of Duchy Originals suggest there is no Steve Jobs or Alan Sugar in the royal ranks: commercial acumen certainly isn't their strong point. But many have applauded the prince for enthusiasm, the charitable outcomes and, above all else, the quality of the biscuits.

year per person. Republicans claim that, once other debits are taken into account, the costs of the monarchy are closer to £200 million per year. In support of this total, pressure group Republic cites missing revenue from the duchies of Cornwall and Lancaster (around £30 million), the cost to local councils for royal visits (a guesstimated £10 million) and – the elephant in the royal chambers – a whopping £100 million in security costs, which is subsumed within Home Office and Defence budgets.

Other, slightly more conservative estimates for the security costs of the royal family range between £30 and £50 million, though the actual sum remains impossible to gauge. But anecdotes about the costs of "protecting" this or that royal will always periodically flare up. Was it reasonable, for instance, for the state to pay round-the-clock security costs of £250,000 a year when Princess Eugenie studied at Newcastle University? Probably not: security at such a high level was withdrawn after the story hit the headlines. And should anyone other than her royal parents have really had to stump up for the refurbishment of a four-bedroom apartment at St James's Palace (another £250,000) for Eugenie's sister Beatrice while she studied for a degree at Goldsmith's College?

How about the costs of a Buckingham Palace garden party? *The Independent* in 2005 reported that the average guest (and there were 8000

Royal guards march outside Buckingham Palace: royal supporters argue that such displays earn the royals their keep in tourist revenue.

that year) ate an average of "14 cakes, sandwiches, scones and ice-creams", piling up to an annual food bill of £500,000. This all seems a bit much – though how many of us would refuse the invite if it came, or wish to deny the opportunity to hard-working public servants or charity workers?

Or what about the costs of heating all those multiple residences (see p.45)? This figure is now considered to be so high that the Queen technically qualifies as suffering from fuel poverty. How many residences and how many rooms does any family need – even a royal one?

Tourist attraction: the royals as heritage industry icons

If they can't persuade you of the constitutional value of the royal family, monarchists fall back on another supposed benefit: money. The royal family, it's argued, earn Britons far more than they cost them, because of all the tourists they attract. The official British tourist organization, VisitBritain, noisily champions this point of view. A typical press release in 2010 trumpeted that foreign tourists spent more than £500 million visiting attractions "associated with the history of the royal family". It added, somewhat fatuously, that 60% of foreign visitors surveyed expressed the desire to see places associated with the royal family – "and several others said they would send home a postcard of the Queen".

It's certainly true that the royals are worth something to British tourism, but how much that really amounts to is rarely interrogated closely. VisitBritain didn't trouble to reveal exactly what it meant by "associated with the history of the royal family". After all, how many castles or palaces in Britain are not? Nor was it explained to what extent having a living royal actually inhabiting a particular palace makes it any more attractive to visitors. The writer Henry James recounted a splendid and rather telling story about meeting a fellow tourist at Windsor Castle who was beside himself with excitement after spotting the Queen through a window (James thought it was a housemaid), and many modern-day tourists undoubtedly enjoy a similar frisson. Why else would there be such a fuss about whether the flag is flying above Buckingham Palace (to signify that the Queen is in residence)?

Sceptics, however, argue that if the royal palaces weren't in use they wouldn't so often be closed. And being run by a republic hasn't stopped the former French royal palaces of Versailles and the Louvre pulling in six million and eight million visitors, respectively, a year. Compare the 400,000 who made it to Buckingham Palace during its restricted opening

MONARCHY USA

For a nation whose very identity is founded on its pride in throwing off the yoke of the tyranny of King George, Americans show a surprising degree of interest in the present-day British royal family. At least, the ones who come to Britain do. Since the Victorian era, promotion of tourism in Britain – and in London and Scotland especially – has relied heavily on the royals. The royal family is, ultimately, part of America's heritage, too, even if it's a rejected one.

America's enduring appetite for Brit royals was revealed yet again when Prince William and his new bride visited the US after their wedding, in July 2011. The American press was all over them. At a particularly well-reported dinner in Los Angeles, they were served by waiting staff wearing bowler hats and Union flag-themed costumes; they rubbed gilded shoulders with stars such as Jennifer Lopez and Barbra Streisand. Of course, their status as all-purpose global celebrities was arguably as much the draw as their royal status, yet, as fellow dinner guest Stephen Fry observed, "If the grandson of the president of Italy arrived in Hollywood it wouldn't make half a paragraph". He added that "The best hotdog stall in town, Pinks, has even produced a Royal Frankfurter – two dogs in one bun – to greet their arrival."

season. And compare that, again, to the number of people who visited the history-stuffed but entirely royal-free Tower of London: two million. Even Windsor Castle is far less popular than Legoland Windsor.

The Windsors, for their part, do try to help out the tourist industry. They occasionally show up at specially organized tourist board events. In June 2003, for instance, the Queen admired a Lego version of herself at that neighbouring attraction while Prince Edward was packed off to a caravan park in the middle of Wales in order to boost Welsh tourism. And of course they also cooperate, to an extent, with the media circus, which in turn helps advertise "royal Britain" around the world. If you believe VisitBritain's figures, the 2011 royal wedding alone attracted four million extra visitors to the UK and earned the country £2 billion. That really sounds like a show worth putting on – until you learn from the Confederation of British Industry that the associated extra public holiday cost the economy £6 billion in lost productivity and overtime.

The *Hello!* monarchy: royals as soap celebrities

"We must not let in daylight upon magic," said the great Victorian constitutional expert, Walter Bagehot. Nowadays, we don't so much let in the daylight as blink at the flashbulbs: the British royals are all over the press, all over the world. There's little to distinguish the younger members of the family from any other celeb. They go to the same parties and nightclubs. They date and even marry each other – consider the union of Zara Phillips, daughter of Princess Anne, and the rugby player, "sports personality" and two-time drunk-driver Mike Tindall.

They appear in the same glossy magazines too. In 2008, Princess Anne's son, Peter Phillips, and his fiancée, Autumn Kelly, flogged photographs of their marriage at St George's Chapel in Windsor to *Hello!* magazine for a reported £500,000. The images included some of the Queen herself. One Labour MP, Ian Gibson, professed himself shocked: "She is the Queen," he said, "not a footballer's wife." But the difference was getting blurred. The same magazine has run photo features, with permission, on the families of Princess Margaret's son, Viscount Linley, and Prince Edward, among others. And don't even mention the cavortings with the press performed by the estranged Duchess of York – the royal family certainly tries not to.

Before she wearied of press harassment, Princess Diana thought the monarchy needed to open itself up to the media in order to survive. "You could equate it to a soap opera really," she told BBC interviewer Martin Bashir in 1995. "It goes on and on and on, and the story never changes." This was an insightful comment. The extraordinary thing about the royals is that, unlike most other celebrities, they never go out of fashion.

Diana went on to say, however, that: "People don't care any more. They've been so force-fed with marital problems, whatever, whatever, whatever, that they're fed up. I'm fed up of reading about it. I'm in it, so God knows what people out there must think." Her assessment of hearts and minds in this matter wasn't as good as all that. Almost twenty years on, the popular appetite for royal news is as voracious as ever.

Keeping up appearances? The royal household

Employing around 1200 staff, the Queen's household covers a large range of routine organizational functions: finance, communications, PR and administration, in addition to many more posts related to ceremonial and curatorial roles that reflect a monarchy with extensive property maintenance and public duties. The taxpayer funds some 38% of these posts. This means that 750 or so employees are supported by the Queen's own immense private financial resources.

At the time of writing, household vacancies existed for an Assistant Anniversaries Officer (to help deal with the sending of congratulations messages: £18,500 per year), a Security Coordinator (£23,500–£30,000), a Senior Metalwork Conservator (£30,000), a Travel and Logistics Officer (£26,000–£34,000) and a Senior Gardener (a miserly £15,750). On the royal website you can also find out more about such esoteric roles as footman, deputy yeoman of the royal cellars, liveried helper at the royal mews (one of an eyebrow-raising 26 staff working there – mostly with horses) and a Demi Chef de Partie in the royal kitchens, one of a team of 19. Earlier in the year, those with the right qualifications could also seek a post as Royal Pigeon Loft Manager or the £80,000-a-year role of Chief Helicopter Pilot, managing a team of six who ferry the royals round the country on those occasions when National Express just won't do. However, you may have to wait a long time to secure a role as either Keeper or Marker of the Royal Swans, with the current incumbents having enjoyed their roles continuously since 1993. Less salubrious positions at the palace include contract cleaning; in May 2011 *The Guardian* reported that cleaners subsist on a rate of £6.45 (just above the minimum wage, but well below the London living wage of £7.85).

There are two posts at the top of the heap. First and foremost is Keeper of the Privy Purse, responsible for the financial management of the household, currently held by Sir Alan Reid. Then there is the Queen's Private Secretary, Christopher Geidt. Her "eyes and ears", he is the conduit for communications between the Queen, the government and Commonwealth nations. Both are on higher salaries than the prime minister.

The big downstairs job is held by ex-RAF man Sir David Walker. Master of the Queen's Household, he keeps an eye on 250 employees looking after food, ceremonials, travel and housekeeping, and craftspeople such as gilders, French polishers and furniture restorers.

All the other royals have households of some sort, with Prince Charles running the largest. Funded via proceeds from the Duchy of Cornwall and still expanding, it has around 133 full-time staff and several irregular appointments, such as Royal Harpist (the current incumbent being Hannah Jones). Like many in the Queen's household – Royal Waterman, Astronomer Royal and Poet Laureate – this is an honorary role.

Judging by Prince Charles's Clarence House operation, the department to watch is Communications: managing public perceptions of royalty and its expenditure appears to be increasingly seen as key. Since royal expenditure will always attract scrutiny, managing press and public expectations about what precise details emerge – and how they do so – is likely to attract the best brains to the royal households. It's not as if governments and showbiz celebs find this sort of thing easy either.

THEY GET AROUND: ROYAL TRANSPORT COSTS

Air Miles Andy Former trade ambassador Prince Andrew hit press turbulence when it was revealed he had hired a private jet for a lightning three-day trade visit to Saudi Arabia. The cost was in the region of £150,000, with a similar sum quoted for another single trip to the Far East. The prince was accompanied by a valet, with a six-foot ironing board among his luggage.

Britannia sunk In its prime, it boasted a 300-strong crew. But the royal yacht *Britannia* was decommissioned in December 1997, prompting a public tear from the Queen's royal ducts. Its last mission was to ferry Prince Charles and Chris Patten (Hong Kong's last governor) away from Hong Kong following its handover back to China. John Major's Conservative government had pledged to replace the ship if they were re-elected. They weren't, and New Labour decided the timing for an upgrade (at an estimated cost of £60 million) was all wrong: the government was cutting back on defence spending and there had been several recent royal scandals and controversies. However, there is a slow-burn campaign for the yacht's reinstatement. Proponents cite economic grounds – that it's cheaper to own a big boat than hire one for trips or functions.

The Royal Train More or less any royal rail trip angers some republicans, which is hardly surprising when you consider that in 2011 a total of fourteen royal journeys cost the taxpayer £900,000. Prince Charles, the most frequent regal rail user, hit taxpayers with a princely £25,829 bill for a visit to the Eden Project. Mind you, in a year or two that will probably be the going rate for a peak-time return to Cornwall on Britain's notoriously overpriced railways.

Soaring helicopter costs The costs of helicopter training for aspiring airman Prince William came under criticism, although the Armed Forces Minister insisted that Wills's £162,000 worth of flying lessons were no more expensive than those of any other military trainee. Eyebrows were raised by a familiarization exercise (costing £8716) that consisted of piloting a Chinook helicopter to a friend's stag do. In another training exercise, he parked his chopper in Kate Middleton's garden.

"Was it a particularly heavy award?" So quipped the Environment Secretary in 2007 when Prince Charles picked up a Global Environmental Citizen Prize in New York. Instead of accepting it by video link, the prince and his entourage flew there, at a cost of £116,000. Apparently stung by the criticism, the prince cancelled his annual skiing holiday later in the year at Klosters, Switzerland, to reduce his carbon footprint.

A bicycle monarchy?

If we must have a monarchy with hereditary privileges, does it have to be so expensive? Queen Juliana of the Netherlands (1909–2004) was a keen cyclist and fond of appearing unannounced amongst her subjects. She was the inspiration behind the idea of the "bicycle monarchy": royalty that is inexpensive to run and closer to the people. Attractive though it sounds, the truth is that if there is a low-cost monarchy today, it is to be found in Spain and not the Netherlands. Holland has, in fact, one of the more expensive royal families in Europe.

The nearest to clarity on how much royals cost their countries is provided by the regular studies undertaken by Herman Matthijs of the Free University of Brussels. Matthijs regularly compiles the known spending of European countries' spending on their royals – though obviously, the significance of a total will vary according to a country's population. In terms of an outright spending total, the British monarchy emerges as the most expensive – costing around £40 million in 2009. However, if

Not everyone loves HRH: could the writing be on the wall for the Windsors in Australia?

THE ROYALS DEBATE: A bicycle monarchy?

HEAD OF STATE: CANADA AND AUSTRALIA

Outside the UK, fifteen countries, formerly of the British Empire, acknowledge Elizabeth II as their Queen. All of them, incidentally, refer to her as "the Second", though of course she's really their first queen by that name: Elizabeth I possessed only Ireland as an overseas colony, despite efforts on her behalf in North America. Most are tiny Caribbean or Pacific Island states, where having Britain as a nominal overlord might perhaps have its advantages. For St Lucia or the Solomon Islands it could be seen as useful to maintain a link with the UK, in terms of preserving an influence on the world stage.

For large, independent-minded, assertive states such as Australia and Canada, however, to have a foreign head of state seems anachronistic to many of her subjects. Technically speaking, however, the Queen isn't a foreign head of state: she is Queen of Australia and Queen of Canada quite independently of her sovereignty in Britain. (And in both countries, these days, she is represented by a locally born governor general who is appointed, in practice, by the local prime minister.)

It's a bizarre system, and controversial in both states. In 1975, the Australian governor general dismissed the Labour prime minister, Gough Whitlam, in the name of the authority of the Royal Prerogative, and appointed the opposition leader, Malcolm Fraser, to form a caretaker government pending new elections. (Fraser, admittedly, won them with a substantial majority.) In Canada, the governor general prorogued (suspended) parliament for over a month in 2008–09, to support the prime minister's efforts to stop a minority-led coalition government taking office. Such political manoeuvring would be harder without the institutional hierarchy of the British set-up.

Despite the twin scandals, and the debates they helped reignite, there are not enough republicans in either country to secure change. In Australia, polls still echo the results of the 1999 referendum, which persuaded only 45 percent of Australians that a president would be a better alternative – though many republicans voted no alongside monarchists because they didn't like the proposed alternative system either. In Canada, polls find the nation broadly split two ways on the question – with the exception of Québec, the former French province which has little loyalty to the "British" Queen. To jettison the Queen as head of state would require, by Canadian federal law, the agreement of every province. Québec could feasibly use this issue to make greater demands for its autonomy, or even to break away from the federation entirely.

In Australia, Elizabeth II has announced that she will only remain Queen as long as her Australian people want her. While this sounds like a magnanimous, gracious offer on Liz's part, it's irrelevant in practice: if Australians didn't want her, she quite simply wouldn't have any choice in the matter. Polls strongly suggest that upon her death Australia will cut the apron strings and relaunch itself as a republic. And who knows which other Commonwealth states might follow Australia's lead?

you take all the eight constitutional monarchies together (leaving aside Liechtenstein and Monaco) and divide royal budgets by population numbers, the picture is rosier. Factoring in Britain's large population puts it in the lower end of this European per capita league: around 66p per person.

Compare this to tiny Luxembourg, top of the per capita table: its Grand Duchy's spending of £7 million stings its 500,000 odd local taxpayers for over £14 each. The second costliest monarchy is Norway's King Harald and family at £4.76 per head. The Netherlands, Sweden and Belgium all come in between £1 and just over £2 (to keep things in perspective, the Netherlands spends £33.9 million on its royals). If we think the UK's 66p makes the British royals good value for money, we should remember that Spain pays a mere 12p per head. Nor do Matthijs' aggregates include security or maintenance of residences – neither of which comes cheap in Britain.

How do the royals compare, in value for money terms, with elected officials? Republic.org tells us that Austria and Germany's parliamentary figureheads appear respectably thrifty at £3.5 million and £21 million a piece. France's semi-presidential system is pricey – an estimated £90 million – though it's debatable whether that is a plus or a minus for the republican cause. (One could argue that presidential models are as close to a monarchy as a republic gets.) It is notable that all the countries with really expensive heads of state – the Netherlands, the UK and France – were once large colonial powers, which suggests that their decline in world status perhaps required some compensation in terms of grand appearances and pomp. Spain, the exception to this rule, had 38 years without a monarchy, courtesy of fascist leader General Franco – perhaps it lowered its taste for regal splendour.

Matthijs' figures on the monarchies are not the last word: he has noted that the eye-catchingly thrifty official aggregates for the Spanish are the least transparent, whereas the British and Dutch – the continent's most expensive monarchies – are the clearest. Matthijs does not include in his surveys Prince Hans-Adam II of Liechtenstein (who has a $3.5 billion fortune) nor Prince Albert of Monaco (who has a $1 billion hoard and a stake in Monte Carlo's casino). Both rulers have exceptional powers in their principalities and a serious say in day-to-day politics; both countries are notorious tax havens with relatively homogenous wealthy populations. So it is hardly surprising that the issue of their royal families' value for money does not arise.

Even so, the Council of Europe criticized the actions of Liechtenstein when the populace voted in favour of the Prince Hans-Adam's referen-

Prince Hans-Adam II of Liechtenstein: Europe's last absolutist monarch.

dum proposal to increase his powers. In a way Liechtenstein's status as Europe's only absolutist monarch is living proof, albeit on a small scale, that the seemingly inexorable trend towards dilution of a monarchy's political power can be reversed. A vestige of this kind of royal political privilege surfaced in the UK in 2011 when it was revealed Prince Charles is routinely privately consulted over legislation that might affect his private Duchy of Cornwall estates. For most members of parliament and the press, this came as a shock: they were unaware that he had an honorary right of veto, even if it has never – as far as anyone is aware – been used. In accordance with this right, ministers had sought clearance from the Prince of Wales for a dozen draft bills since 2005. Some constitutional experts dismissed the power as merely an archaic convention, given that the prince would hardly dare exercise his right of veto. Others pointed out that the right itself might influence government legislation in advance, especially given Charles is a known, repeat lobbyist.

That said, on the whole the British monarchy doesn't emerge too poorly from European comparisons. This may not be too lofty a yardstick when so little about royal financial affairs remains unknown. Freedom from unelected tyrants or hereditary blunderers has taken Europe centuries to achieve. Now we have won the right to *elect* the inappropriate and unqualified, rather than having them in charge because of who their mum or dad was. Perhaps the question should not necessarily be whether unelected monarchs really earn their keep (though the case for more transparency seems unarguable), but why countries don't consider investing in better and more extensive forms of democracy in which everybody gets a say and is properly informed about the issues.

7

Royal representations

Nowadays, we are mostly aware of the current royals through paparazzi snaps and official photos illustrating the ongoing royal soap opera – with Hollywood and TV stepping in to cover the more dramatic of their ancestors. Images of royalty were no less ubiquitous in the past, from profiles impressed on coins to full-length portraits exuding pomp and power, and even evocations in verse. This chapter highlights some of the most enduring royal representations, both sycophantic and satirical.

Portraiture

There are plenty of contemporary images of early medieval kings and queens. These are mostly funerary monuments, such as the tomb of Henry II and Eleanor of Aquitaine at Fontevraud (see p.102), or illustrations to religious texts or chronicles, for example Matthew Paris's *Historia Anglorum* (c.1253), in which Henry III is depicted placing a wedding ring on the finger of Eleanor of Provence. Portrait painting as such did not come into its own until the late Middle Ages and the Renaissance.

Richard II

The first English monarch to appreciate the power of painting to represent his royal majesty was Richard II. Cannily aware of his image – typically dressing in rich garments and holding court in spectacu-

TOP TEN ROYAL STATUES

1. **Alfred the Great** (c. 1395) Trinity Church Square, Southwark, London. Commonly believed to be the oldest outdoor statue in the capital. With his classical stance and drapery, Alfred doesn't look typically medieval, however, and some sources claim it was sculpted as late as the 1820s.

2. **Charles I** (1638) Trafalgar Square, London. The oldest statue in Trafalgar Square, by Hubert Le Sueur, and the first statue to render an English king on horseback – a ruse frequently employed in paintings of the pint-sized monarch, to make him appear taller.

3. **William III** (1736) Queen's Square, Bristol. Many statues of King Billy have been subject to abuse – the 1701 William in College Green, Dublin, in particular, faced numerous Jacobite indignities before being blown up in 1929. Not so, however, J.M. Rysbrack's vital equestrian bronze.

4. **George IV** (1828) The Royal Pavilion, Brighton. Based on Thomas Lawrence's "official" portrait of George, with Romantic curling hair and an imperious tilt of the chin, Francis Chantrey's statue garbs him in classical, waistline-flattering robes.

The Albert Memorial, a widow's grandiose homage to her dead spouse.

lar buildings draped with priceless tapestries – he also commissioned imposing portraits. The oversized image of Richard with crown, sceptre and orb (c.1390–95), now hanging in Westminster Abbey, was like an icon, standing in for the king in his absence. The resplendent Wilton Diptych (1395–99) shows Richard being presented to the Virgin Mary and Christ child by a trio of St John the Baptist and two English kings – St Edward the Confessor and St Edmund. Painted for Richard's own private devotions, like the Westminster painting, it reinforces the idea of the monarch as God's representative on Earth.

5. **Prince Albert Memorial** (1872) Kensington Gardens, London. The monument to end all monuments – a piece of high-Victorian Gothic pomp designed by George Gilbert Scott, bursting with elevated imagery and studded with jewels. Seated at the centre of the melee, a gilded figure of Albert quietly holds a catalogue for his Great Exhibition of 1851.

6. **Queen Victoria Memorial** (1911) Buckingham Palace, London. This clompy, 82ft-high, 2300-ton wedding cake of white marble, bronze and granite, has the seated queen gazing gloomily up the Mall. The space is shared with Charity (facing the palace) and Angels of Truth and Justice, and the whole extravaganza is surmounted by the gilded figure of Victory.

7. **Edward VII** (1914) Rotunda, Cheltenham. Standing atop a water fountain/ horse trough, this curious marble statue shows the king protectively holding hands with a ragged waif. Designed to illustrate his kindness to the poor, it also has the fashion-loving Edward dressed in a sporty Norfolk suit, a style he helped to popularize.

8. **Edward, Prince of Wales** (1922) New Promenade, Aberystwyth. The only known full-length statue of Edward VIII, erected here because he was chancellor of the university, this bronze likeness has fallen victim to a number of student pranks over the years. Covered in paint more than once, in 1976 its head was cut off and discovered nearby.

9. **George V** (1931) Coronation Memorial Park, Delhi. Originally standing in imperial splendour opposite Lutyens' India Gate, the 49ft statue was relocated to this desolate spot in the 1960s. The site of grand Durbars celebrating the Empire, the park was intended, post-Independence, to become a kind of graveyard for imperial statues, but George remains an oddly lonely figure.

10. **Innocent Victims** (2005) Harrods, London. Forego the official Diana memorial fountain in Hyde Park and nip into Harrods instead, where a bronze statue of Diana and Dodi shows the couple dancing beneath a huge seagull.

Tudor assertion

It was the Tudors, however, who truly exploited the potential of portraiture. Henry VII was the first king to have a coin made bearing a recognizable likeness of the monarch, in 1503. And although paintings were valued far less than tapestries – materials were cheaper, and painters seen as "craftsmen" rather than artists – under Henry VIII royal portraiture flourished. Portraits were used to preview prospective spouses, to spread propaganda (famously, an earlier picture of Plantagenet Richard

III was reworked to give him a fictional hunchback and an uglier face) and, above all, to create lasting images of a magnificent, all-powerful king. Court painter Hans Holbein's Whitehall mural of Henry VIII, alongside his wife Jane Seymour, and in front of his parents, is perhaps the definitive portrait, showing an oak-like king, swathed in opulent fabrics, staring challengingly out from a setting of lush brocades and rugs. Painted in 1537, the year Henry's long-awaited son Edward was born, it's riddled with phallic imagery, a defiant challenge to those who doubted the king's ability to father an heir. Fortunately, numerous copies were made, as the original perished in a fire in 1698.

In 1563, five years after coming to the throne, Elizabeth I – another monarch supremely aware of her image – decreed that no portrait was to be made of her without her consent. Unsurprising, then, that no official paintings show the queen as an old, or even ageing, woman; instead, her many portraits, such as the *Coronation Portrait* on p.127, rely on increasingly complex allegory to emphasize her virginity, femininity and power. The *Armada Portrait* (unknown artist, 1588) shows Elizabeth in typically elaborate costume, her hand resting on the Americas on a globe, the Armada being vanquished behind her; feminine imagery – pearls, bows, a carved mermaid – abounds. The *Ditchley Portrait* (Marcus Gheeraerts the Younger, 1590) depicts the queen as an almost celestial being, standing on a globe with England beneath her feet, the train and sleeves of her white-and-gold dress evoking angel's wings.

Stuart elegance

Charles I, a great collector and patron of the arts, is represented in the light, deft works of Van Dyck as a graceful, thoughtful figure, exuding quiet authority. Van Dyck's fashionably elegant style was much favoured by the English aristocracy, while a more robust alternative can be found in the work of his English contemporary William Dobson. The lesser-known artist John Weesop's grisly *Eyewitness Representation of the Execution of King Charles I* (1649) provides a suitably visceral corrective to the official portraits of the king. After Charles's death, his image – largely produced abroad – was displayed in secret, with royalists wearing his likeness in lockets or rings. Following the Restoration, court painter Sir Peter Lely continued to represent Charles II much as Van Dyck had portrayed his father, but John Michael Wright's vibrant, red-and-gold depiction of Charles II's coronation (1661) is quite different, packed with regal symbolism – from his resplendent parliamentary robes, crown, garter, sceptre and orb, to the tapestry behind him showing the Judgement of Solomon – a classic case of a royal portrait working hard to make a political point.

Hanoverian heft

While the monarchy lost much of its real power in the eighteenth century, portraiture in Britain – by native as well as foreign artists – continued to thrive. Not much could be done for the stolid features of George I, although Godfrey Kneller – a successful portrait painter since the time of Charles II –

James Gillray's caricature of the Prince of Wales (later George IV) as a bloated sybarite picking his teeth with a fork is relatively restrained by the artist's normal savage standards.

did his best. His son George II was no more prepossessing, but he did have the distinction of being the last British king to lead his army into battle, a fact commemorated in John Wooton's *George II at the Battle of Dettingen*. It was during George III's reign that homegrown artists really came into their own. Allan Ramsay's *George III* (1762) shows the king in shimmering coronation robes with an assured, relaxed stance: a new kind of portrait, for a new kind of ruler. Johann Zoffany placed George and his family in relatively informal, even domestic settings – idealized and supremely elegant, but still intimate and relaxed – while Gainsborough applied his light touch to emphasize their innate humanity. Meanwhile, satirists like James Gillray (see p.221 and box opposite) seized upon the same family's physical quirks with a savage lack of reverence – a particular source of distress to George IV, who envisaged himself as a proud, romantic figure despite his substantial girth. His official portraits, by Thomas Lawrence, depict a fashionable dandy with upswept hair and a haughty demeanour.

The modern age

Queen Victoria became an iconic figure thanks not only to painting, but also to newspaper sketches, engravings and the new art of photography. Much like Elizabeth I, Victoria used her gender to her advantage: in Sir George Hayter's *Queen Victoria* (1860), she cuts an imposing Britannia-like dash with her sceptre, crown and noble, heavenwards gaze; while in Franz Xaver Winterhalter's family portraits, for all her Garter regalia and grand accoutrements, the queen is clearly a loving wife and mother. Winterhalter also painted an erotic portrait of the young queen – hair tumbling, lips parted, shoulders bare – which she gave to Prince Albert as a birthday present. With their lustrous colours, these vibrant paintings couldn't be more different from the gloomy black-and-white photographs that captured the more dour, funereal image that Victoria adopted later in life.

As the variety of media in which we see our monarchs has mushroomed, so has the range of representations. Queen Elizabeth II has sat for countless portraits, some quite startling – most famously the harshly naturalistic portrait from Lucien Freud (2001), but also two oddly unsettling official paintings by Pietro Annigoni (1956 and 1969) portraying an isolated figure in empty, desolate landscapes. Several photographers, most memorably Cecil Beaton, Baron, Dorothy Wilding, Marcus Adams, Lord Snowdon and Lord Lichfield, have all created iconic shots. As family members, Snowdon and Lichfield produced images notable for their intimacy and informality. Such official respect was turned on its head in

SATIRE

In an era informed by the world and his wife's whip-smart viral spoofs, we may feel we invented satire, or that the monarchy has never been so open to ridicule: in fact the royals have often been fair game, and frequently to a far greater extent than today.

In the eighteenth century, when royal power had been dealt a drastic blow by the 1689 Bill of Rights (see p.118), Britain was known throughout Europe for its scabrous satire. Nobody – monarchs or bigwigs, socialites or street people – was immune. This was the great era of caricature, lorded over by figures like James Gillray, who created grotesque prints of George III – "Farmer George" – as dull, if affable, pretentious and mean, Queen Charlotte as grasping and short, and their son, soon to become George IV, as an overweight sybarite with no personal hygiene. George IV was also a favourite subject of illustrator George Cruikshank; so threatened were the palace by his drawings of the monarch as fat, drunk and dissolute that in 1820, during the trial of Queen Caroline for adultery, they paid the artist £100 to stop.

The magazine *Punch*, founded in 1841, paved the way for a series of satirical publications that used cartoons to poke fun at the establishment; relatively few of these directly targeted the royal family, however. The royals were pretty much left alone for more than a century, until the 1960s satire boom brought *Private Eye* onto the scene. Its biting covers, which marry news photos with transgressive captions, have featured the queen more than fifty times, and Prince Charles more than thirty, but few royals have received as much *Eye* cover-art contempt as Princess Margaret. In one early cover false captions show her husband, Anthony Armstrong-Jones, calling her a fat bitch, while in another – even more outrageously – she's portrayed as a stark naked Jane to Roddy Llewellyn's Tarzan.

The 1980s saw a wave of alternative comedians let rip, emerging from a recession, a silver jubilee and a royal wedding in quick succession. In 1981, artists Peter Fluck and Roger Law, who created comic models to illustrate print articles, presented a particularly ugly Charles and Di to a half-shocked, half-thrilled nation; three years later their TV puppet show *Spitting Image* added a CND-badge-wearing queen, a drunken Princess Margaret, a pig-like Sarah Ferguson and, perhaps most shocking of all, a Brummie, gin-soaked Queen Mum to the happy family.

More recently, photographer Alison Jackson has applied her trademark style to the royals – taking blurry paparazzi-style shots of lookalikes staged in incongruous or risqué situations – but these are more a commentary on celebrity than royalty. Will and Kate's marriage created a wealth of ironic memorabilia – from "Throne Up" sick bags to "knit-your-own royal wedding" manuals – but very little satirical art. Gillray would be turning in his grave.

1977 – the year of the Queen's silver jubilee – by Jamie Reid's record cover art for the Sex Pistols' single "God Save the Queen", which shows her eyes and mouth obliterated by brutal cut-out lettering.

Poet laureates

British monarchs had surrounded themselves with court poets since medieval times, but the first formal laureate was John Dryden, whose role as Poet Laureate, given to him by Charles II in 1668, involved being advocate and effectively PR man for the king. Dryden remained laureate – and Royal Historiographer – under James II but was dismissed twenty years later after refusing to swear allegiance to the Protestant King William. His successor, Thomas Shadwell (laureate 1689–92), started the tradition of writing (rather bad) poems for the monarch's birthday and for New Year; with the next postholder, Nahum Tate (1692–1715), the historiographer role withered away entirely. Tate did write odes celebrating, among other things, Queen Mary's birthday in 1694 (beautifully set to music by Henry Purcell) and the Act of Union in 1707, but as the eighteenth century progressed the role lost muscle. After 1790 the poet laureate was selected by the prime minister rather than the monarch, and under George IV the position officially became honorary.

William Wordsworth accepted the post in 1843 on the condition that he would not be required to write poetry in praise of the royal family, which, officially, has been the case for laureates ever since, though many have chosen to do so anyway. His successor Alfred, Lord Tennyson, who held the title for nearly fifty years (1850–92), is widely thought to have been the greatest laureate; since then most – however respected – have tended to be slammed for their royal output. Tennyson's successor Alfred Austin (laureate 1896–1913) will be remembered as one of the worst, though the lines attributed to him, about the Prince of Wales's illness – "Across the wires the electric message came,/He is no better, he is much the same" – are by an unknown parodist.

Even good poets have a hard time as laureates: Sir John Betjeman (laureate 1972–84), for example, with his hymn for the Queen's silver jubilee ("In days of disillusion, / However low we've been / To fire us and inspire us / God gave to us our Queen") and his wedding poem for Charles and Diana ("Blackbirds in city churchyards hail the dawn / Charles and Diana on your wedding morn..."). Ted Hughes (laureate 1984–98), who was famed for his unsentimental nature poems, took to the post with great enthusiasm. Among fine work written for the royals is the powerful "Rain-Charm for the Duchy", a typically mystical celebration of Devon's rivers which he adapted for Prince Harry's christening in 1984.

Andrew Motion hoped to modernize the role, writing poems for organizations from the TUC to the BBC, and an anti-war poem about Iraq; his eight royal poems include a much-derided rap for Prince William's 21st birthday ("Better stand back / Here's an age attack / But the second in line / Is dealing with it fine"). He was the first laureate not to keep the post for life and retired after ten years (1999–2009). Carol-Ann Duffy (2009–), the first female laureate, made it immediately clear she wouldn't write for royal occasions unless moved to, but then went on to write a free verse poem, "Rings", for the engagement of William and Kate Middleton. This, wisely, kept to more general images of rings rather than trying to rhyme their names.

Ceramics

As early as 1661, delftware potters were creating memorabilia for the coronation of Charles II: simple cups, plates and bowls bearing schematic portraits of the new king, their decorative nature was part of post-Puritan

The royal mug. Jubilees and weddings may bring out the crowds but they also bring out the worst in manufacturers of tourist tat.

WACKY ROYAL MEMORABILIA

Mugs, plates, biscuit tins, tea towels – since as far back as Charles II, royal memorabilia has been produced in increasingly frenzied quantities to commemorate births, deaths, coronations and weddings. Some is valuable, much is tacky, and some – just some – is a little bit wacky. Take underwear. Two years after Queen Victoria's capacious bloomers sold for thousands at auction in 2008, the story went around that a pair of big knickers supposedly left by Queen Elizabeth II on a plane in 1968 were also up for sale – the auction was postponed until after Prince William's wedding, however, and those right royal undergarments have yet to go under the hammer.

Dolls, too, a huge part of the official memorabilia industry, can be a wee bit odd. The two-foot-high 1953 dolls that warbled "God Save the Queen" if you wound a key in their stomachs, for example, or the necessarily shortlived Edward VIII in Highland dress – or even the new, oddly creepy, Danbury Mint porcelain doll of Diana as a toddler. That's not to mention the Steiff teddybear created to celebrate Diana's fiftieth birthday, complete with limpid eyes and a sapphire pendant. Often the more serious the memorabilia, the more startling: the Annus Horribilis mug, produced for Christmas 1992, for example, with its poem that opens "God save our Queen this Christmas time / From the fanatic's knife and bomb".

Since Victoria married Albert, royal wedding memorabilia has mushroomed into an enormous industry. The deluge that came around Charles and Diana's nuptials included a few offbeat items – among them the feminist "Don't Do It, Di!" badges – but in the flood of kitsch memorabilia surrounding Will and Kate's wedding, from sick bags to condoms, it was difficult to find anything that wasn't wacky. Even the Royal Mint commemorative engagement coin looked like a bad joke, depicting a lumpen duo that bore no resemblance to the engaged couple. Postmodern irony scaled new heights, however, when a printed mug from one "Guangdong Enterprises", which showed Kate with not William but Harry, became a viral hit – before it dawned on everyone that the "mistake" was intentional all along.

Restoration pomp. A century later, improved manufacturing methods under George III led to the mass production of printed earthenware souvenirs that ordinary people could afford; there were even souvenirs made to celebrate his return to health after his psychosis left him unable to rule.

Usually emblazoned with a portrait, most royal ceramics were patriotic. Unpopular figures, however, made for unpopular merchandise – mugs marking the 1820 coronation of George IV ("Britons rejoice, cheer up and sing, and drink this health. Long live the King") weren't a hit with a population who regarded the ex-Prince Regent as a feckless spendthrift; ceramics marking his death in 1830 proved far more saleable, as did those in support of his estranged wife Queen Caroline, whom he hated but the public loved.

During the reign of Queen Victoria, sentimental knick-knacks became all the rage and royal memorabilia really took off. British pottery firms such as Minton, Wedgwood, Spode and Doulton competed to produce moneyspinning souvenirs, creating a huge number for Victoria's gold and diamond jubilees. Manufacturers needed to be flexible: when Edward VIII stood down in 1936, the mugs made to commemorate his intended coronation were altered to mark the abdication instead.

Many commemorative ceramics are historically interesting but stylistically conservative. Not so, however, the designs of war artist Eric Ravilious. So desirable was the graphic he created for George VI's 1937 coronation mug that Wedgwood adapted it to mark the 1953 coronation of Queen Elizabeth II. A jubilant burst of fireworks over the royal coat of arms, with the date spelt out in flowing numerals, the 1953 mug is a mid-century modern masterpiece, its simple exuberance copied countless times since.

While royalist ceramics continue to be churned out, today even republicans can get in on the act. In the 1980s, Carlton Ware produced *Spitting Image* (see p.223) mugs and eggcups portraying the Windsors in stark white 3D caricature – even baby William, with a screwed up, bawling face and sticky-out ears – while in 2011 cartoonist Steve Bell designed a limited-edition "Unroyal Wedding" mug with caricatures of Kate Middleton, a horse, the prime minister David Cameron and his chancellor George Osborne, and the words: "Royal Thoroughbred, Member of the Servant Class, We're All In This Together... My Arse".

Coins and stamps

Royal imagery has remained remarkably consistent on British stamps and coins through the ages. Due perhaps to this, and their sheer ubiquity, they have captured the public imagination less than other royal memorabilia. Although special-issue stamps have been produced since George V's day, and special-issue coins since Victoria's – that's not counting the silver penny made to commemorate King Alfred's taking of London from the Danes in 886 – they tend to have little value. More intriguing perhaps are the commemorative stamps and coins produced overseas: the stamp from the Pacific island of Niue, for example, for William and Kate's wedding. A perforation separates the two figures; the prince's portion costs NZ$3.40 and Kate's just NZ$2.40.

Victorian innovations led to images of the monarch being disseminated on a previously unknown scale – not least on the Penny Black. Adopted in 1840, the world's first adhesive postage stamp showed an engraved profile of the young queen in classical, statue-like stillness, with a bare neck, loosely gathered hair, and wearing the state diadem, the diamond-encrusted crown made for the coronation of George IV. The colour of the stamps changed throughout Victoria's reign, but the image remained stoically constant, even as the real woman aged and physically changed.

The first postage stamps to show a photograph of the monarch were created for Queen Elizabeth II in 1952. Based on a Dorothy Wilding three-quarter photo, these portrayed the new queen as a vibrant and glamorous – and real – young woman. There were suggestions in the 1960s, when the socialist Tony Benn was the postmaster general, that the Queen's head should be removed from stamps; she, however, was not amused, and in 1967, sculptor Arnold Machin's classic design was adopted. This simple, less personal image remains on British stamps today, rendering a queen unchanged for nearly fifty years.

Coins, too, have shown only the most subtle of changes in the image of the Queen. From 1953 to 1967, her head, based on a design by sculptor Mary Gillick, was in the classic side-on pose, wearing a simple wreath headdress. In an updated version, adopted for decimalization – a more fluid Machin effigy, based on a Snowdon photograph – the floral wreath was replaced by a more regal tiara. This image remained until 1984, when the tiara was replaced by the state diadem.

Monarchs in the movies

From the silent *Les Amours d'Elisabeth, Reine d'Angleterre* (1912), which starred Sarah Bernhardt, to the Oscar-scooping triumph *The King's Speech*, the royals have always made great movie subjects. As ever, history, perpetually open to contesting accounts and reinterpretations, is stretched and contorted to fit particular artistic visions, but certain tropes remain constant: individual heroes making personal journeys, usually in lavish locations and always against the backdrop of epic events. Most enduring of all is the portrayal of the monarch, male or female, as a "real person" trapped by the constraints of their role, struggling between duty and free will.

Henry VIII, Elizabeth I and Queen Victoria have notched up the most screen time, with films invariably portraying Henry as bumptious, narcissistic and loud, Elizabeth unlucky in love and anxious about age-

SCREENING SHAKESPEARE'S HISTORY PLAYS

Commonly known as the "history plays", Shakespeare's ten plays about the English kings between 1399 and 1485 – *King John, Richard II, Henry IV Parts I and II, Henry V, Henry VI Parts I–III, Richard III* and the lesser known *Henry VIII* – had their first performances between 1592 and 1612. *Edward III* is a recent tentative addition to the canon which was only partly written by Shakespeare, while *Henry VIII* was co-authored with John Fletcher. *Edward III* to *Richard III* represents an unbroken run of eight English kings (nine if you include Henry Tudor's appearance at the end of *Richard III*), most of which covers a particularly bloody period of internecine warfare called the Wars of the Roses.

The earliest known movie adaptation is the 1899 British silent *King John*, starring Herbert Beerbohm Tree. The most popular have been *Henry V* – notably masterpieces from Laurence Oliver (1944; see p.231) and Kenneth Branagh (1989; see p.232) – and, by a long chalk, *Richard III*. Olivier created the archetypal hunchback king in 1955 (see p.231); forty years later, Ian McKellen reprised the role in an audacious reinterpretation that transplants the action to a fictional 1930s London.

Few of the other plays, however, have made it to the big screen. *Henry VI* and *Henry VIII* are nowhere to be seen, and *Richard II* has a poor show in the straight-to-video *Richard the Second* (2001). Neither has the *Henry IV* series seen its way to becoming a movie. The closest thing to it is Orson Welles' *Chimes at Midnight* (1966), based on Welles' own play *Five Kings*, which focuses on the character of Falstaff, played by Welles himself. Dialogue is drawn from *Richard II, Henry IV Parts I and II* and *Henry V*, along with *The Merry Wives of Windsor* (in which Falstaff also appears).

When it comes to TV, things are very different. Key among the many small-screen adaptations of the history plays is the BBC's high-profile and big-budget series *An Age of Kings* (1960), which presented eight plays – *Richard II, Henry IV Parts I and II, Henry V, Henry VI Parts I–III* and *Richard III* – across fifteen sixty- to ninety-minute episodes. It appears dated to modern audiences, but as a way of understanding the plays – and the complexity of the monarchy in that historical period – *An Age of Kings* still has a lot to offer. Packed with top-flight stage actors including Judi Dench (Princess Katharine), Robert Hardy (Henry V) and Paul Daneman (Richard III), the series also features a star turn from Sean Connery as Sir Henry Percy (Hotspur).

A couple of decades later, the history plays also appeared as part of the BBC Shakespeare Productions (1978–85), an ambitious project to put all of Shakespeare's plays onto the small screen. Many of these, while dated pieces of TV, feature iconic performances – Anthony Quayle reprising his stage triumph as Falstaff in the *Henry IV* cycle, for example, or the entire cast in *Richard II* (among them Derek Jacobi, John Gielgud and Wendy Hiller). *Henry VIII* and *Henry IV Part II* are arguably the most successful of the entire series.

ing, and Victoria imperious but devoted to her subjects and her beloved Albert. Anne Boleyn and Mary Queen of Scots also recur, though they are open to a broader range of interpretations. The Anglo-Saxons and Normans barely get a look in, the Plantagenets are represented by a few choice gems, and nobody quite knows what to do with the Stuarts. The Windsors, meanwhile, have provided a wealth of filmic fodder and, in recent years at least, a massive boost for the British film industry.

Some actors have come to shape popular views of specific monarchs. Mention Henry VIII and, even if we haven't seen the film we think of a rotund Charles Laughton, slapping his thighs and bellowing with laughter in *The Private Life of Henry VIII*. And Bette Davis's caustic Elizabeth I, who features in two films, is accepted as the definitive version, holding firm against strong renditions by Glenda Jackson and Cate Blanchett. The kings as written by Shakespeare, and portrayed on the screen by Laurence Olivier, remain entrenched in our consciousness, too – Richard III, the scheming hunchback; Henry V as a valiant, if troubled hero. To modern audiences, meanwhile, Helen Mirren will always be The Queen.

Given the shifting changes in attitudes to the monarchy, it's striking how little variety there has been in the movies. A few films play with the conventions, while others offer a cool look at the system – a movie might empathize with the monarch as a human being while damning the institution as rotten, particularly for women – but very few make it their business to rip the lid off. For that we must turn to the avant-garde, and filmmakers who are little concerned with winning massive audiences.

The Plantagenets

TOWER OF LONDON USA 1939, 76 min
Director Roland V. Lee **Cast** Basil Rathbone, Boris Karloff, Vincent Price

A real oddity. From Universal Studios, famed for the horror classics of the early 1930s – *Dracula, Frankenstein, The Mummy* – it's usually sold as a horror movie, and stars three giants of the genre; but it's also a historical drama, telling the Shakespearean story of Richard III, with Rathbone as the "crookback" compelled to get rid of Edward IV, his young nephews, his brother and Henry Tudor in his bid for the throne. The horror elements – Karloff as "Mord", the clubfooted executioner, some derring-do in dank dungeons and Rathbone's mad-eyed business with a dollhouse – give it a certain camp zest, and in 1962 it was remade by cult maestro Roger Corman with Vincent Price as Richard.

HENRY V UK 1944, 137 min
Director Laurence Olivier **Cast** Laurence Olivier, Renée Asherson, Robert Newton

Olivier's astonishing Shakespeare adaptation is in many ways more experimental than Kenneth Branagh's grittier version (see p.232). Following a naturalistic opening sequence that recreates a Globe theatre performance of the play in all its populist, tomato-throwing merriment, the camera sweeps us away from the confines of the stage to a dreamier world with stylized backdrops and lush colours. For cinema audiences nearing the end of a long and dreadful war, with British troops about to head into Normandy, Henry's rousing "Once More Unto the Breach" speech at Harfleur – not to mention the quieter meditations on the nature of monarchy, patriotism and duty ("few die well that die in battle") – would never have been more resonant.

RICHARD III UK 1955, 150 min
Director Laurence Olivier **Cast** Laurence Olivier, John Gielgud, Ralph Richardson, Claire Bloom

While it may not have quite the extraordinary emotional impact of *Henry V*, Olivier's second movie adaptation of a Shakespeare history play is enormously enjoyable. He relishes the role of the "deformed, unfinished" usurper in a royal house riven by vicious rivalries, and even the daft false nose and witchy wig can't detract from the power of his performance. Opening captions cheerfully state that much of the "history" is myth: rendering the last Plantagenet king as quite so evil, and Henry VII – who defeated Richard to finally establish Tudor rule – as quite so heroic, would have been a politic move for a playwright writing for the Tudor court.

THE LION IN WINTER UK 1968, 129 min
Director Anthony Harvey **Cast** Peter O'Toole, Katharine Hepburn, Anthony Hopkins

It's Christmas 1183, and the ageing King Henry II is gathering with his wife, Eleanor of Aquitaine – whom he has kept under house arrest for a decade – and his sons John, Geoffrey and Richard the Lionheart, each torn between a desire to inherit the throne and a rageful yearning for parental love. Added to the mix is Philip II of France – the son of Eleanor's first husband (Louis VII), and paramour of Richard – and young Alais, who is at once Philip's half-sister, Richard's betrothed, Eleanor's surrogate daughter and Henry's lover. Based on James Goldman's stage play, it's histrionic, rollicking good fun, full of perversity and snappy one-liners. While this Christmas from Hell never actually took place, the political machinations and infighting certainly did, and O'Toole's scenery-chomping performance may not be too far off the mark – the real Henry II was known to indulge in wild tantrums. Meanwhile, Hepburn's fiercely intelligent Eleanor is more than a match for the men around her – a rare and welcome portrayal of this fascinating figure.

Incidentally, O'Toole had already played a younger Henry II in the less watchable *Becket* (1964), which focuses on the events that led up to the murder of his friend Thomas Becket (Richard Burton), the Archbishop of Canterbury.

HENRY V UK 1989, 137 min
Director Kenneth Branagh **Cast** Kenneth Branagh, Paul Scofield, Ian Holm, Derek Jacobi, Emma Thompson

Branagh sticks closer to the text of Shakespeare's play than Olivier – while also plastering the proceedings with a visceral, bloody realism that filters the rousing patriotism through the dirty horrors of war (parallels with the battlefields of the Somme are not accidental). And his babyfaced Henry gives us a different angle on the young king proving himself as a hero – a perhaps more complex, and certainly less likeable, character than in the earlier film.

EDWARD II UK 1991, 90 min
Director Derek Jarman **Cast** Steven Waddington, Andrew Tiernan, Tilda Swinton

Loosely adapted from Christopher Marlowe's play, Jarman's postmodern masterpiece is a tour de force: at once knockabout travesty and impeccable high art, it retells the story of the doomed king entirely from his own intensely subjective point of view. Marlowe's play was unusual in overtly portraying Edward's homosexuality, but Jarman takes it to the extreme: the king's *amour fou* for nobleman Piers Gaveston becomes a tragedy more about cruel homophobia than medieval political intrigue or personal greed. Spitting vitriol, violence and savage beauty, it offers us the king as a sacrificial victim, difficult perhaps, and deeply flawed, but also at the mercy of crueller forces.

The Tudors

THE PRIVATE LIFE OF HENRY VIII UK 1933, 90 min
Director Alexander Korda **Cast** Charles Laughton, Elsa Lanchester, Merle Oberon

This opulent comedic and blithely ahistoric gallop through five of Henry's marriages (Katherine of Aragon, dismissed in the opening titles as being "respectable" and "of no particular interest", is ignored) – was the first British movie to break the US market in a big way. Charles Laughton – who enters the frame in classic Hans Holbein pose, complete with sturdy splayed legs – almost singlehandedly defined the image of Henry, booming with laughter and flinging capon bones over his shoulder. It's old-fashioned, for sure, and there are longueurs, but the comic scenes with his real-life wife Elsa Lanchester as the feisty Anne of Cleves are delightful.

THE PRIVATE LIVES OF ELIZABETH AND ESSEX UK 1939, 106 min
Director Michael Curtiz **Cast** Bette Davis, Errol Flynn, Olivia de Havilland

Although, as the title suggests, this is a romantic two-hander, and Flynn was at the peak of his star powers, this is above all Elizabeth I's story – and Bette Davis's film. A brittle mix of hauteur and humour, all twitches and nervous handwringing, Davis, face painted white and hair shaved, is suitably magisterial as a powerful woman entering her old age with trepidation. History, and in particular foreign policy, are played out as simple consequences of the ageing queen's sado-masochistic passion for the young Robert Devereux, thirty years her junior, while the lush Technicolor vision of the court is a sensual feast. Davis reprised her role in 1955 in the less compelling *The Virgin Queen*, which sweeps the action back fifteen years earlier to see a swashbuckling Raleigh (Richard Todd) and Bess Throckmorton (an unlikely Joan Collins) share the stage.

A MAN FOR ALL SEASONS UK 1966, 120 min
Director Fred Zinnemann **Cast** Paul Scofield, Wendy Hiller, Robert Shaw

The violently unstable Henry VIII (Robert Shaw), one moment a jovial bon vivant, the next a dimwitted infant screeching to get his own way, is a mere foil here for Sir Thomas More (a brilliantly wry, rueful performance from Scofield), whose tenacious belief in the word of the law will not permit him to support Henry's bid to divorce Katherine of Aragon. Thus the complex story of England's split from the Catholic Church is reduced to a straightforward – and, given the performances and the writing (it's based on Robert Bolt's popular play), not unsatisfying – morality tale, in which right is pitched against wrong with no grey areas whatsoever.

ANNE OF THE THOUSAND DAYS UK 1969, 145 min
Director Charles Jarrott **Cast** Genevieve Bujold, Richard Burton, Irene Papas, Anthony Quayle

Bujold and Burton give us Anne Boleyn and Henry VIII as they are commonly perceived – she strong, principled and loving, he spoilt, arrogant and charismatic. Burton adds a rough vulnerability to the role of the volatile king who wants what he can't have and always finds ways to convince himself that he is right, while Bujold offers a far more appealing Anne – though her status as a political player and active supporter of the Reformation are rather subsumed here in matters of the heart. It's a solid movie, however, clearly outlining the events that led up to the dissolution of the monasteries and the creation of the Church of England.

CARRY ON HENRY UK 1971, 89 min
Director Gerald Thomas **Cast** Sidney James, Kenneth Williams, Barbara Windsor

Or Anne of the Thousand Lays, as it was unofficially called, in a saucy dig at the po-faced sincerity of the prestige historical dramas made in

From left to right: Kenneth Williams as Thomas Cromwell, Sid James as Henry VIII and Terry Scott as Cardinal Wolsey ponder affairs of state in *Carry On Henry*.

the 1960s. James's coarse, riproaring Henry VIII provides a merry counterpoint to Burton's actorly rendition of two years earlier, and the film
barrels ahead with all the usual Carry On puns, in-jokes and bawdy
humour. ("Has she been chaste?" "All over Normandy!")

ELIZABETH UK 1998, 124 min
Director Shekhar Kapur **Cast** Cate Blanchett, Geoffrey Rush, Joseph
Fiennes

Bold casting – Australian newcomer Blanchett as the queen; Christopher
Ecclestone as the plotting nobleman Norfolk; John Gielgud as an evil
Pope – and Kapur's outsider's eye add an edge to this artistic vision of the
young Elizabeth I's life. Here is a brooding, Gothic court, dominated by
terror and subterfuge and defined by religious sectarianism. Blanchett
is outstanding as the uncertain young girl who learns the hard way she
must lose her humanity in order to survive; the final shot of her, ghost-
white and deathly still as the iconic "Virgin Queen", is as chilling as it is
revealing. Kapur's sequel, *Elizabeth: the Golden Age* (2007), a lacklustre
account of the queen's later reign and the defeat of the Spanish Armada,
is far less interesting.

THE OTHER BOLEYN GIRL UK 2003, 90 min
Director Philippa Lowthorpe **Cast** Jodhi May, Natascha McElhone, Jared
Harris

Adapted from the hugely popular (if historically dubious) novel by
Philippa Gregory, in which Anne Boleyn is driven by her power-hungry
rivalry with her sister, Mary (who had been a mistress of Henry VIII), this
BBC-produced film is quite different from the later Hollywood version.
Arty and offbeat, with its grainy, overexposed colours, reeling, handheld
camera and raw, improvised deliveries, it's a compelling but oddly distant portrayal of Anne, who, despite the to-camera confidences, remains
unknowable and self-deluded. Wild-eyed, angry, sadistic and perhaps a
little mad, this is not your usual Anne Boleyn.

THE OTHER BOLEYN GIRL USA 2008, 115 min
Director Justin Chadwick **Cast** Natalie Portman, Scarlett Johannsen,
Eric Bana

Tudor machinations and battles for survival translate into romantic
rivalry and sisterly catfights in this high-octane melodrama. Here, as in

Philippa Gregory's novel, but not in real life (or the earlier British movie; see above), Anne (Portman) is the older sister, Mary (Johannsen) the younger. Family dysfunction and a cold mother create this Machiavellian Anne, whose desperate desire for the throne transforms her into a hysterical, depraved harpy – by the end, Portman is playing her as a wicked witch, which is, of course, exactly what the real queen was accused of being. As a story about English royalty it's preposterous; as a pacy Hollywood soap, it's great fun.

The Stuarts

MARY OF SCOTLAND UK 1936, 123 min
Director John Ford **Cast** Katharine Hepburn, Fredric March, Florence Eldridge

John Ford, best known for his later Westerns, turns his eye towards Scottish history in this pacy retread of one of the great Tudor/Stuart power struggles. With its arch performances, it's dated, but far from dull, and offers a coherent take on two very different women and the impulses that drive them. Hepburn's Mary Stuart, an idealistic naïf with a fiery temper and high ideals, lacks the hardheaded political know-how of her Tudor rival, Elizabeth – an unusually unsympathetic Good Queen Bess from Eldridge – and it's this, even more than her romantic infatuation with Bothwell, that proves the Scottish queen's downfall.

MARY QUEEN OF SCOTS UK 1971, 126 min
Director Charles Jarrott **Cast** Vanessa Redgrave, Glenda Jackson, Trevor Howard

This time Redgrave (Mary) and Jackson (Elizabeth) fight it out as the two warring queens – the scene in which they secretly meet (of which there is no historical record) provides a dramatic fulcrum for the wider context of machinations within the English, Scottish and French courts. It's compelling to watch two great actors play two of the greatest female figures in British history, but the film does suffer in places from its own self-importance.

RESTORATION US 1995, 117 min
Director Michael Hoffman **Cast** Robert Downey Jr., Sam Neill, Meg Ryan

Based on Rose Tremain's novel, this offers a stunning recreation of the opulent seventeenth-century court, and Sam Neill makes a splendid

Charles II: wily, charming and with a boundless enthusiasm for the arts and science. He is a supporting player, however, in a morality tale centring on physician Robert Merivel (Downey Jr.), and the film goes rapidly downhill when Merivel leaves court.

TO KILL A KING UK 2003, 98 min
Director Mike Barker **Cast** Rupert Everett, Tim Roth, Dougray Scott

Few filmmakers have taken on the execution of Charles I and the establishment of the Commonwealth; unfortunately, this movie should perhaps not have bothered. Everett, however, gives us a convincing Charles I, at once imperious, self-righteous and steadfast; Roth, on the other hand, does little to shed light on the character of Cromwell.

The Hanoverians

SIXTY GLORIOUS YEARS UK 1938, 95 min
Director Herbert Wilcox **Cast** Anna Neagle, Anton Walbrook, C. Aubrey Smith

Retitled *Queen of Destiny* for the US market, this fascinating period piece makes a sumptuous vehicle for the British star Anna Neagle, capitalizing on the wildly successful *Victoria the Great* made with the same team a year earlier. Galloping through Victoria's reign from her marriage to her death, it's a work of slick propaganda, fiercely pro-monarchy and pro-empire. Neagle plays Victoria as high-handed yet devoted to her subjects – Walbrook, meanwhile, depicts Albert as a sensitive pacifist who was never totally accepted. It looks glorious, with real-life locations including Osborne House, Balmoral, Windsor and Buckingham Palace, but there's a whiff of anxious over-compensation about it all, patching up the cracks in a nation where the king had recently abdicated and war loomed on the horizon.

SARABAND FOR DEAD LOVERS UK 1948, 96 min
Director Basil Dearden **Cast** Stewart Granger, Joan Greenwood, Flora Robson, Peter Bull

Ealing Studios, best known for their deft, quirky comedies, took a risk with this costume drama and found themselves with a flop on their hands. It's not hard to see why: depicting the Hanoverian court at the moment when George I (a wonderfully unpleasant Peter Bull) was to become Britain's first Hanoverian monarch, it's a relentlessly gloomy film, sagging under

THE ROYALS ON TV

There have been countless mini-series about the royals, from both sides of the Atlantic, most of which play it pretty straight and are of interest to completists only. The following is a selection of the best. For an account of Shakespeare's history plays on TV, see p.229.

Royal Family BBC, 1969
Revealing the family at home, eating dinner, chatting and generally being "real people", this ahead-of-its-time reality doc caused a storm of interest upon release. The family soon came to regret this warts-and-all attempt to modernize their image, however, and made sure it was withdrawn within a year, never to be made available again.

Elizabeth R BBC, 1971, 8hr 43min
Six-part series in which Glenda Jackson gives her second Virgin Queen of the year – she also starred as Elizabeth in the big-screen *Mary, Queen of Scots* (see p.236). Widely praised for its historical accuracy, it has suffered a little over time, and comes across as rather too ploddingly earnest for modern audiences.

Edward and Mrs Simpson Thames TV, 1978, 5hr 50min
A huge hit in its native Britain, this exposé of one of the greatest royal scandals of the modern era – the abdication of Edward VIII – won rafts of BAFTAs for its no-holds-barred portrayal of the affair between the people's favourite Edward (Edward Fox) and the American divorcée (Cynthia Harris). It stands up well today, largely thanks to a smart script from Simon Raven.

The Lost Prince BBC/Talkback Thames, 2003, 1hr 19min
Written and directed by Steven Poliakoff, this is the tale of Prince John, the youngest son of George V, who was hidden away due to a developmental disorder and autism, and died of epilepsy aged thirteen in 1919. Though in *The King's Speech* (see p.241) Bertie refers to John's erasure from history as an example of parental cruelty, the series is relatively sympathetic toward King George V (Tom Hollander) and Mary (Miranda Richardson). The wider story is just as fascinating, outlining the devastating effect of World War I on the monarchies of Europe.

the weight of its suffocating production design. Oddly, though, its flaws are its strengths – ostensibly the story of George's wife, Sophia, and her doomed affair with Count Königsmark, it falls short as a romantic melodrama, but as a rendering of the oppressiveness of the House of Hanover, and the ugliness at its core, it packs a bold punch.

Henry VIII Granada Television, 2003, 4hr 10min
All credit to Ray Winstone that it's possible to get over his Hackney accent, – which is about as preposterous as Sid James's, in the same role (see p.234) – and come to believe in him as the Tudor king. Helena Bonham-Carter, too, gives us a credible Anne Boleyn: smart but not witchy, attached to Henry but not abject. A solid, if sometimes stodgy overview of Henry's life, starting with his failure to conceive a boy with Katherine of Aragon.

Elizabeth I Channel 4/HBO, 2006, 3hr 30min
With a multi-award-winning performance from Helen Mirren (who also won an Oscar for her big-screen role as Elizabeth II in *The Queen* that same year; see p.241), and deft direction by Tom Hooper, who went on to sweep the boards with *The King's Speech* (see p.241), this entertaining, punchy mini-series has impeccable credentials. It's a naturalistic, authentic vision of Elizabeth's reign in all its savagery, from brutal gynaecological examinations to bloody beheadings.

Monarchy: The Royal Family at Work BBC/RDF Media, 2007, 5hr 30min
This fly-on-the-wall documentary series caused a scandal when clips shown during a press view implied that the Queen had stormed out of a photographic shoot with Annie Leibovitz after being asked to remove her crown. The BBC had to offer a formal apology, BBC One controller Peter Fincham was forced to resign, and the series went on to give an uncontroversial PR account of sundry members of the royal family going about their business over the course of a year. A warts-and-all account it is not, but it does give an insight into the mighty behind-the-scenes machinery that goes into making it all work.

The Tudors Peace Arch/Reveille/Working Title/CBC, 2007, 31hr 55min
This four-part series was premised on the fact that Henry VIII had six wives and a burning desire to have a son, therefore he must have had a hell of a lot of sex. That's it really. There's an occasional nod to history, and Sam Neill as Cardinal Wolsey does his best to take it seriously, but this is essentially an historical soap opera – all heaving bosoms and quivering cod-pieces. Given all the connubial exercise, is it any wonder that Jonathan Rhys Meyers' Henry doesn't seem to get much fatter or, indeed, older by the end of the series?

THE MADNESS OF KING GEORGE UK 1994, 107 min
Director Nicholas Hytner **Cast** Nigel Hawthorne, Helen Mirren, Ian Holm

Adapted from his own stage play by Alan Bennett, this portrayal of George III's descent into and recovery from psychosis has a peculiarly English bent – infused with scatological humour, its amused affection

The Madness of King George: Nigel Hawthorne as the king enjoys a relatively sane moment with Helen Mirren as Queen Charlotte.

for the royals is underpinned by a conviction that they, and probably the entire system, is quite barmy. Interpreting George as an arrogant churl whose increasing disinhibition leads him from liberation to abject humil-iation, Hawthorne pulls off no mean feat by winning our sympathy for an unlikeable man; that the film was made at a time when the monarchy was in crisis, and Prince Charles's popularity was shaken – he and Diana were separated, and he had yet to marry Camilla – adds resonance.

MRS BROWN UK 1997, 105 min
Director John Madden **Cast** Judi Dench, Billy Connolly, Antony Sher

Despite a potentially fascinating story, about the close relationship between the mourning Queen Victoria and stableman John Brown – and despite its rave reception from critics and audiences – this is one of the drearier monarch movies. Dench's queen is peevish and remote, a harsh foil for Connolly's boorish Highlander, and their chemistry is minimal. Watching the shift of power from the virile, powerful alpha male to the woman – who by dint of her unassailable political power reduces him to a hysterical, overprotective wreck – holds some interest, but ultimately their love story is unconvincing, and the opportunity to reflect on gender dynamics, political realities and the role of the mon-archy is wasted.

YOUNG VICTORIA UK 2009, 105 min
Director Jean-Marc Vallée **Cast** Emily Blunt, Rupert Friend, Jim Broadbent, Miranda Richardson

A co-production between Martin Scorsese and Sarah Ferguson sounds an unlikely prospect, but this enjoyable, good-looking movie offers a refreshingly different take on the widow queen – Blunt plays the princess as a feisty, modern girl who longs both for independence ("even a palace can be a prison" she declaims, as her food is tasted for her, and adults hold her hand every time she goes up and down the stairs) and for the forward-thinking Prince Albert, her German cousin. It's both a sweet romance and a robust feminist tale, in which queenship holds out great potential for adventure, and true love needn't oppress.

The Windsors

THE QUEEN UK 2006, 103 min
Director Stephen Frears **Cast** Helen Mirren, Michael Sheen, Alex Jennings

Recounting the details of the period following the death of Princess Diana, when the Queen was widely criticized for not showing remorse or sorrow, this hugely lauded movie shows the events from the Queen's point of view. Intercut with real-life footage, it is at pains to present itself as the "real story", and Mirren certainly does a convincing imitation of Queen Elizabeth II, but it is a cold performance and a cold film, peopled with unlikeable characters, from a schoolboy-like Tony Blair (another impersonation from Michael Sheen) to a miserable Prince Charles. Overall an enervating, rather depressing experience, whose disdain for the world outside the palace is fuelled by a relentlessly pro-monarchy, anti-populist agenda.

THE KING'S SPEECH UK 2010, 118 min
Director Tom Hooper **Cast** Colin Firth, Helena Bonham-Carter, Geoffrey Rush, Guy Pearce

Scratch the stylish surface of this award-scooping heritage pic to discover a dark vision of the monarchy: a damaged institution defined by repression, abuse and infantilism. Firth, as the reluctant King George VI, manages to make an awkward, prickly character at least understandable, but it's Pearce who steals the show with his impeccable portrayal of Edward VIII, who switches between brittle arrogance and emotional disinhibition, taunting "B-b-bertie" and baby-talking to Wallis Simpson about "making drowsy". Bonham-Carter has a whale of a time as Elizabeth, the king's imperious wife, while the "speech" itself is undeniably moving – not simply a rousing personal triumph, but also an uneasy snapshot of the role of the monarch in a nation that is about to send most of its men to war.

W.E. UK 2011, 115 min
Director Madonna **Cast** Abbie Cornish, James D'Arcy, Andrea Riseborough, Oscar Isaac

Only her second feature as a director, Madonna's opulent account of the love affair between Edward VIII and Mrs Simpson was so slammed by critics that she withdrew it for re-editing. It might have made an interesting riposte to *The King's Speech*, since the key characters are presented so differently, with Wallis Simpson (Riseborough) seen as bringing glamour and pizzazz into the stuffy world of the royals. But the film's uncritical stance and over-lavish design were both seen as major flaws, as was the framing device which had Wally (Cornish), a sad New York housewife, unravelling the subsequent story of the couple via her obsession with the Duchess of Windsor (as Mrs Simpson became). If you think this is, indeed, the greatest love story of the last century, you may want to give it a second chance. Then again…

8

101 things you never knew about the British monarchy

In the thousand plus years since King Æthelstan became the first king of a (vaguely) unified Britain, a further fifty-four monarchs have ascended the throne. Here are some of the lesser known stories connected to them: the trivial and the tragic, the ludicrous and the downright unbelievable.

👑 Above the law

In UK law the monarch is considered "the Fount of Justice". This means that civil and criminal proceedings cannot be taken against the Queen. Even acts of parliament don't apply to her in a personal capacity, unless explicitly stated. The "Crown" (the government acting in the Queen's name) does not manage to get off so lightly, however, as the many instances of litigation against government departments and agencies attest.

👑 Arthur, king of legends

Heroic defender of the British against invading Saxons, King Arthur remains one of the most popular British royals of all time. Even those with a scant knowledge of British history know about his knightly court at Camelot, his wife Guinevere and his sidekick wizard Merlin. The only problem is that most modern historians think he never existed and, even if he did, there is almost nothing of substance that can be said about him. His legend blossomed in the Middle Ages, thanks to the twelfth-century historian Geoffrey of Monmouth, and such literary works as Malory's *Le Morte d'Arthur* (1485).

👑 Batwoman

Every autumn, the Queen stays at her Balmoral residence in Scotland. There she is said to enjoy a rather unusual pastime, that of unofficial bat-catcher. Assisted by a footman and a net on a long pole, she catches the bats that flit around the ceiling of Balmoral's great hall. She lets them go afterwards, of course, bats being a protected species.

👑 The bells! The bells!

After the wedding service of Prince William and Kate Middleton in 2011, the ten bells of Westminster Abbey rang for a solid three hours. The abbey's campanologists performed a total of 5000 non-repeating changes (a full peal); the first time this had happened since 2007 when they marked the sixtieth wedding anniversary of the Queen and Prince Philip.

Eight of the abbey's ten bells were cast, by the Whitechapel Bell Foundry, as recently as 1971.

👑 Biscuitgate

A "self-confessed addict" of the BBC's rural radio soap *The Archers*, the Duchess of Cornwall raised eyebrows with a much-trailed appearance on the show in February 2011. It was not her few bloodless lines of dialogue (as herself) that concerned some listeners, but the timing: her appearance occurred two weeks after a character had praised Charles's very own organic shortbread (see p.205) in what sounded suspiciously like royal product placement.

👑 The Black Prince

The son of Edward III, the Black Prince was the first English Prince of Wales never to become King of England. Military victories over the French at Crécy and Poitiers have given him an attractively forceful reputation, he even appears as a military commander in videogames such as *Bladestorm: The Hundred Years War* and *Medieval: Total War*. He died in 1376 (a year before his father) and is buried in Canterbury Cathedral with his heraldic arms suspended over his tomb.

👑 Boy Jones: royal stalker

In 1838 – a year after Victoria became queen – a fourteen-year-old boy, Edward Jones, broke into Buckingham Palace. It was the first of three illicit visits during which he sat on the throne, checked out the royal library, helped himself to food and even stole some of the queen's underwear. Known to the press as the Boy Jones, he became something of a celebrity before the exasperated authorities forced him into the navy. He was eventually transported to Australia where he died after a drunken fall from a bridge.

👑 The bride wore myrtle

British royal brides traditionally carry a sprig of myrtle in their bouquet, which is popularly believed to derive from the same myrtle used in Queen Victoria's wedding bouquet. In fact, it was Prince Albert's grandmother who gave Victoria a posy of myrtle during a visit to the German province of Gotha well after her wedding. The Queen then had the myrtle planted against a wall at her new home, Osborne House on the Isle of Wight, where it still grows today. When Queen Victoria's daughter Victoria got married in 1858, a sprig was cut from the plant for her wedding bouquet; royal bouquets have featured one ever since.

👑 Brutus of Troy, King of Britain

According to the historical chronicler Geoffrey of Monmouth, one of the pre-Roman kings of Britain was Brutus, grandson (or possibly great-grandson) of Aeneas, hero of Virgil's epic poem *The Aeneid*. Legend has it that Brutus founded London as Troia Nova ("New Troy") and named Britain after himself once he'd defeated the giants who inhabited the island – then known as Albion. Also cited by Geoffrey was one of Brutus's descendants, King Leir, part of whose story forms one of the sources for Shakespeare's play *King Lear*.

👑 By any other name

The Queen is independently and separately the head of state of fifteen Commonwealth countries in addition to the UK. She also has some lesser known, masculine-sounding titles, which include the Duke of Lancaster, the Duke of Normandy (in respect of Guernsey and Jersey) and Lord of Mann (in respect of the Isle of Man).

👑 Catch that pigeon

It's widely known that Elizabeth II loves horse racing but she is also a keen pigeon fancier. The royal connection began when King Leopold II of Belgium made a gift of some racing pigeons to Queen Victoria, and the birds were used as messengers in both world wars. The royal pigeon lofts are based at Sandringham and the Queen remains the patron of the Royal Pigeon Racing Association, which stages an annual show attracting as many as 25,000 other fanciers.

Caviar capers

One of the strangest laws to have survived into the twenty-first century is the Queen's right to any sturgeon (the fish whose eggs make caviar) found in her realm. When, in 2004, fisherman Robert Davies landed one of these large fish in Swansea Bay, he contacted Buckingham Palace only to be told that he was free to dispose of his nine-foot catch as he wished. Davies then sold it to a wholesaler who in turn planned to auction it. At this point the authorities moved in and impounded the fish on the grounds it was a protected species. According to rumour, it then headed off to London's Natural History Museum. Sturgeon are part of a small group of so-called royal fish (along with whales, porpoises and dolphins) deemed to be the personal property of the monarch.

Cedric and Miss Dimsdale

Craggy Yorkshire poet Ted Hughes was among the most enthusiastic of recent poet laureates, regarding the Queen as a kind of tribal leader. He was particularly close to the elderly Queen Mother and, according to Hughes's sister Olwyn, the two of them "became great pals with their shared love of fishing and Scotland". Hughes once gushed to a friend, "There's something about her that's kept very young ... everybody is so fond of her." Such was their friendship that they even dreamt up a pair of imaginary friends, the Rev. Cedric Potter and Miss Dimsdale, with the Queen Mum imagining their marriage announcement appearing in the *Daily Telegraph*.

Child king

The Lancastrian Henry VI (1421–71) has the distinction of being the youngest monarch to ascend the throne, at the tender age of 8 months and 25 days. Even after the regency had ended, he had a chequered reign as his benign temperament made him ill-suited for the dynastic struggles of the time. A spell of insanity led to his being deposed in 1461 by Edward, Duke of York (Edward IV), though due to the vicissitudes of the ongoing civil wars he had a further six-month spell in charge (1470–71), before being imprisoned in the Tower of London and murdered.

Christmas farter

William Camden's vast geographical and historical survey of Britain of 1586 holds the following record of an unusual form of land tenure held by one Baldwin of Suffolk: "Baldwin le Pettour (marke his name well) held certaine lands ... for which on Christmasse day, every yeere before our soveraigne Lord the King of England he should perform one Saltius, one Sufflatus, and one Bumbulus ... That hee should daunce, puff up his cheekes making therewith a sound, and besides let a cracke downeward. Such was the plaine and jolly mirth of those times."

Coronation chicken

Now better known as a rather gloopy sandwich filler, Coronation chicken was dreamt up by cook Rosemary Hume for the Buckingham Palace banquet following the coronation of Queen Elizabeth II – hence its original name, *poulet reine*

Elizabeth. Hume's aim was to create a popular recipe that commbined cheap ingredients – this was still the era of rationing – with a touch of the exotic; it had to appeal to guests from all the Commonwealth countries. The recipe calls for cold chicken pieces to be lightly dressed with a creamy mixture of, among other things, mayonnaise, curry powder and apricot pureé. It became standard fare in Britain as a result of being published in the *Constance Spry Cookery Book* (1956).

👑 Cousinly love

Following the Russian Revolution of 1917, moves were made to provide the Russian royal family with a safe haven in Britain – Tsar Nicholas II being the first cousin of George V. Initial meetings were held between the king's private secretary, Lord Stamfordham, and prime minister Lloyd George, before the rescue plans were abandoned. The king, it seems, had got cold feet after Stamfordham suggested that such a move might fuel anti-monarchist feeling in Britain. The Romanovs were left to their fate and on 17 July 1918 the Tsar, his wife and five children were executed by the Bolsheviks. Lloyd George agreed to take responsibility for the change of policy in order to protect George V's reputation; he was vilified for the death of the Russian royals until the release of state papers in 1986 revealed the truth.

👑 "Crawfie" – does nanny always know best?

Marion Crawford (known as "Crawfie") was hired by the Queen Mother, the then Duchess of York, in 1932 to help look after her two young daughters. She stayed for over sixteen years and was a loyal royal servant, even delaying her marriage so as not to inconvenience the family. But when, in 1950, her memoir of her time as a royal nanny, *The Little Princesses*, was published in America, the palace regarded it as a betrayal – even though the deal had been brokered by the Foreign Office in the interests of Anglo-US relations. Overnight Crawfie was ostracized by the royals, and although she always hoped for a reconciliation, she never saw her two charges again.

👑 David Cameron, the Queen's cousin

Conservative leader and British prime minister David Cameron is the great-great-great-grandson of Elizabeth Fitzclarence, the illegitimate daughter of William, Duke of Clarence (later William IV), and his mistress the actress Dorothea Jordan (see p.158). This makes Cameron the Queen's fifth cousin twice removed.

👑 Divine Right

In *Richard II* Shakespeare has the king utter the words: "Not all the water in the rough rude sea / Can wash the balm off from an anointed king / The breath of worldly men cannot depose / The deputy elected by the Lord." This is a spot-on summary of the Divine Right of Kings, the belief that the monarch was divinely appointed and could not be legitimately removed. Despite James I reinforcing this view in his book on kingship, *Basilikon Doron*, it was, arguably, the Stuart dynasty's highhandedness that resulted in the execution of James's son, Charles I, and the removal of his grandson, James II, from the throne. From thenceforward the monarch reigned by the will of parliament.

👑 Dorgi and Bess

Everyone has heard of the Queen's corgis – the dog breed that's now indelibly associated with the royal family. Less well-known are her "dorgis", a breed of dog that resulted when one of her corgis was mated with a dachshund named Pipkin (which belonged to Princess Margaret). There were four dorgis in the litter, named Cider, Berry, Candy and Vulcan. The last name is rather unusual: could the Queen possibly be a closet Trekkie?

👑 Edict of expulsion

Under an edict of Edward I in 1290, England became one of the first countries to expel all its resident Jews. This followed a century and a half of persecution, including the infamous massacre of 150 Jews in York in 1190 and a mass execution in 1278. Anti-Semitism had increased because of the Jews' perceived wealth – they were permitted to lend money with interest (the sin of usury, according to Christianity), which had enriched a small minority. Their expulsion enabled the cash-strapped King Edward to appropriate their property as well as their loans. Jews were only re-admitted to England in 1655, following a request from a Dutch rabbi to Oliver Cromwell.

👑 Eleanor crosses

When Edward I's wife, Eleanor of Castile, died near Lincoln in 1290, her body was transported to London for eventual burial in Westminster Abbey. The journey took twelve days, and, on the instructions of her husband, each overnight resting place was commemorated with an ornately carved stone cross. The last location at which the cortege stopped was the hamlet of Charing, near Westminster, now called Charing Cross. Only three of the original Eleanor crosses still stand (all heavily restored), while the one at Charing Cross – the most lavish – is a Victorian replacement.

The cross now standing outside Charing Cross railway station is a replacement erected in 1865.

👑 Empress of India

Princess Alexandra of Denmark, the wife of Edward VII, was the second of four female royals to receive the title Empress of India. The first was Queen Victoria in 1876. One reason for creating such an exalted title was that Victoria's daughter (also Victoria) had married Prince Frederick of Prussia and so was in line to become Empress of Germany. Such a circumstance was deemed unbecoming, since the junior Victoria would then appear to outrank her mother.

👑 "England and Saint…?"

Before the warmongering King Edward III made St George the patron saint of England in the fourteenth century, his ancestor Edward the Confessor was the most important of England's national saints. The Confessor's famed piety included taking a vow of chastity, which meant that there was no heir to succeed him (he lived with his wife Editha "as a sister"), hence the Norman invasion of 1066. Why choose St George? It was almost certainly because of his supposed warrior status, which was better-suited for rallying the troops and whipping up gung ho nationalism.

👑 ERII – no way

The red EIIR insignia of post boxes might appear to be a universal signifier of Britishness and the Crown. Not so in Scotland. When the new post boxes were first rolled out in 1952 some were attacked by nationalists because Elizabeth I had never ruled Scotland. The offending letters have never reappeared.

👑 The extraordinary adventures of Princess Beatrice's hat

With the exception of the wedding dress itself, and perhaps Pippa Middleton's figure-hugging bridesmaid's number (later rolled out by the department store Debenhams for £170), no royal attire at William and Kate's wedding received more public attention than Princess Bea's hat. Described variously as looking like a pretzel, a toilet seat and a Teletubbies head-piece, the hat became a Facebook sensation with over 130,000 "likes" before it was sold on eBay (receipts to charity) for £81,000 and a penny.

👑 Gandhi's gift

The Indian leader and pacifist Mahatma Gandhi was still embroiled in the bloody aftermath of independence and partition in November 1947 when Princess Elizabeth (later Queen Elizabeth II) and Prince Philip were married. His present to the couple, a piece of cotton cloth woven from yarn he had himself spun, was embroidered with the words "Jai Hind" ("Hail India"). This thoughtful and political gift was mistaken by Queen Mary (Elizabeth's grandmother and ex-Empress of India) for a loincloth, prompting her to remark: "Such an indelicate gift; what a horrible thing!"

Discarded wedding gift: Tangier was prone to attacks by Barbary pirates, so Charles II gave up on it. Admiral Dartmouth and Samuel Pepys supervised its evacuation.

👑 Generous dowry

One of the strangest of royal territorial acquisitions occurred in 1661 when Charles II married the Portuguese princess Catherine of Braganza, and received the ports of Tangier and Bombay as part of his dowry. Tangier in Morocco was quickly garrisoned but proved expensive to maintain and was abandoned in 1684. The Indian city of Bombay, then part of an archipelago, proved more lasting, although not for the king, who leased it to the British East India Company within a few years.

👑 George III: the odds of heirs

Despite his wife, Queen Charlotte, giving birth to no fewer than fifteen children, the long-lived monarch had no legitimate male heirs among his grandchildren. It was Victoria who ascended the throne following the death of her uncle William IV. Victoria's father, the Duke of Kent, had died of pneumonia in 1820, predeceasing his three elder brothers, his father and his daughter.

👑 Getting the sack

Beginning with Ben Jonson in 1619, one of the traditional perks of being the monarch's official poet is receiving a "butt of sack". This is a large barrel, or wooden cask, of sweet wine. John Betjeman encouraged the revival of this "payment" in modern times, which amounts to around 600 bottles of sherry. However, Andrew Motion, the last Poet Laureate, has still to receive his bottles despite having been allowed to select what he wanted from the Sherry Institute of Spain during "a very boozy weekend" in 2005.

👑 Glastonbury, home of kings

Though said, somewhat tenuously, to be the final resting place of legendary King Arthur and Queen Guinevere (see p.243), Glastonbury Abbey is, in fact, the burial site of three Anglo-Saxon monarchs: King Edmund I, his son Edgar, and Edmund II (known as Edmund "Ironside").

👑 "God Save our Gracious Queen!"

At 2012's Olympic Games, British winners will have to stand through not just one of the shortest national anthems (possibly a blessing) but also one of the most banal. Nobody has claimed responsibility for either music or words, which probably date back to the seventeenth century. Both first appeared in print in the *Gentleman's Magazine* of October 1745 following a victory against the Scottish Jacobite rebels. The Queen's official website lists the first and third of the three verses, deeming the bellicose second ("O Lord, our God, arise / Scatter her enemies / And make them fall") inappropriate.

👑 Go easy on the lampreys

Lampreys, a type of eel-like fish without a jaw, were one of the favourite delicacies of Henry I. They proved his undignified undoing after a "surfeit of lampreys" caused food poisoning and his subsequent death while visiting his grandchildren in Normandy.

👑 Gout, the "disease of kings"

The painful disease of gout, with its symptoms of swelling joints (especially in the feet) caused by an excess of uric acid, is not necessarily due to overindulgence and a rich diet, although these can be contributory factors. Queen Anne was so swollen with gout when she died that her coffin was very nearly square-shaped. The morbidly obese Henry VIII was another likely sufferer, as was George IV, while James I numbered the disease among several other chronic conditions.

👑 The great collector

Several British monarchs have been great collectors of art, none more so than Charles I, whose collecting bug bordered on the obsessive. Not only did he commission leading European artists, such as Rubens and Van Dyck a, he was also a keen buyer of other people's collections, including that of the Duke of Mantua, which supplied him with outstanding paintings by Titian and Raphael. Come the Interregnum, Oliver Cromwell saw it as a good way of paying off the king's debts. Most, but not all of it was sold off or used as payment in lieu. Then, with the restoration of the monarchy in 1660, Charles II's agents set about trying to get the lost artworks back. They partly succeeded but almost 300 works evaded their grasp.

👑 The Great House of Ease

In 1534, Henry VIII had a two-storey toilet block built at his Hampton Court palace. Known as the Great House of Ease, it had thirteen seats on each floor (thus offering relief to twenty-six people) and was constantly fed by running water from the nearby River Thames.

🜲 Happy hunting grounds

Royal hunting has a lengthy pedigree that reached its apogee under the Normans. William I and his son William II (both particularly enthusiastic) extended the areas reserved for royal use so that by one point in the twelfth century, the royal forests covered almost a third of all England.

🜲 Heirs who miss the boat

One of the strangest quirks of the British royal succession is that if Prince Charles does follow his mother on to the throne, it will be the first time a firstborn heir has succeeded a firstborn heir for several centuries. Not, in fact, since Henry VI succeeded his father, Henry V, in 1422. All successions since then have had the line broken by either usurpation, abdication, failure to produce legitimate heirs or the death of the monarch's eldest child.

🜲 Henry I: begetter of bastards

Notwithstanding a heavy military schedule, Henry holds the record for fathering the most illegitimate children of any British monarch. On top of his four legitimate children with Edith of Scotland (two of whom died in infancy), no fewer than twenty-three other children have been traced, born to several different women. Unfortunately, the death of his son and heir, William Adelin, led to a succession crisis contested between his daughter, Matilda, and his nephew Stephen (see p.116).

🜲 Holder of the royal head

Long before before the advent of Dramamine, King John employed a head-holder to counter his seasickness. Solomon Attefeld was awarded large areas of land in Kent on the basis that "as often as our lord the King crossed the sea, the said Solomon and his heir ought to go along with him, to hold his head on the sea, if it was needful".

🜲 Hypericum: a winning formula?

George VI was a particularly enthusiastic supporter of homeopathy, granting royal status to London's Homeopathic Hospital. He also named one of his racehorses Hypericum, after what is deemed by advocates to be a particularly effective remedy for nerve injuries and depression. The horse went on to win the 1000 Guineas Stakes at Newmarket in 1946.

🜲 If the footman fits...

If you want to get a job as a royal footman, you no longer have to be male, but you have a distinct advantage if you're around five feet, nine inches tall and have a 36-inch chest. That's because the footmen still wear a uniform that, in some cases, dates back to King Edward VII's reign. Because the outfit worn at state banquets costs over £2000 to manufacture, the royal household is reluctant to get out the credit card for new uniforms (and, presumably, sees corner-cutting as out of the question).

👑 Ivan the terrible letter writer

Among the many candidates for the hand of Queen Elizabeth I (see p.83), the most unlikely was probably Ivan IV of Russia (aka Ivan the Terrible). Like Henry VIII, Ivan had no qualms about changing wives on a regular basis. He courted Elizabeth through letters delivered by her ambassador, although none survive. What does is a letter dated 28 October 1578 in which he rants: "We had thought that you had been ruler over your land, and had sought honour to your self and profit to your Country, and therefore we did pretend those weighty affairs between you and us." He may well have been affronted by her refusal to marry him, but this did not stop him from later asking for asylum when things got nasty in Moscow.

👑 James I and the mulberry plot

King James was very enthusiastic about kick-starting a silk-manufacturing industry in England, and ordered 10,000 mulberry trees to be distributed about the shires – mulberry leaves being what silkworms thrive on. The site on which Buckingham Palace now stands was originally a royal mulberry garden planted by James. Unfortunately, the majority of trees planted were black mulberries (which silkworms aren't keen on) rather than white, and silk production never took off.

👑 Jimmy Carter and the Queen Mum

When US President James Carter was introduced to the Queen Mother, he flagrantly broke with royal protocol by not only kissing her, but kissing her on the lips. This was probably accidental – perhaps a peck on the cheek that went slightly askew. The Queen Mother confessed that: "he is the only man since my dear husband died to kiss me on the lips."

👑 King Edward of Estonia

Tongue-in-cheek political protest party, the Independent Royalist Party of Estonia (a country that has never had a monarchy), once included a manifesto pledge to instate – should they be elected – Prince Edward, Earl of Wessex, as king of their country. They did seek his agreement first but it seems he never responded to their letter of invitation.

👑 Last of the debutantes

The presentation at court of upper-crust young women was an annual event in British high society that had existed for over two hundred years. For the "gels" it indicated their transition into adulthood and marked the start of "The Season" – a round of social events at which they could strut their stuff and, hopefully, hook an eligible and suitably posh young man. But first they had to meet the monarch, which basically consisted of bobbing a curtsey to the Queen and then leaving her presence without turning their elegantly attired backs. By the 1950s even hidebound palace officials felt that this was an anachronism, and 1958 marked the last year that this quaint ritual took place. But not before 1400 debutantes had been presented over three days in March.

Legacies in Lancashire

It is not widely known that if you die in Lancashire intestate (without a will) and without any surviving relatives, then the proceeds will end up going to the Duchy of Lancaster, which provides the Queen with her private income. Similar quasi-feudal arrangements also pertain to the Duchy of Cornwall. The legal term for such cases is *bona vacantia* (Latin for "vacant goods").

Longest living royals

Princess Alice, Duchess of Gloucester (1901–2004), the mother of the current Duke, has the distinction of being the longest living British royal ever. She died at the age of 102 years, 10 months and 4 days. Her closest rival was her sister-in-law (their husbands were brothers), Elizabeth the Queen Mother, who was a mere 101 years, 7 months and 26 days at her death in 2002.

Marrying a commoner, medieval style

Prince William is not the first royal to marry a commoner. In 1464 Edward IV secretly married Elizabeth Woodville, the widow of Sir John Grey, much to the annoyance of his advisors, who were arranging a dynastic union with a French princess. It wasn't as romantic as it sounds. Elizabeth had resisted the over-sexed king's many attempts to sleep with her (which included an attempted rape at knifepoint) before agreeing to marry him. The ten children she bore him included the two princes murdered in the tower by their uncle, Richard III.

Master of the Musick

The English court has always employed musicians but the title of Master of the King's (or Queen's) Musick was only established in 1626, when Nicholas Lanier was appointed to serve Charles I. Nowadays, like the Poet Laureate, the composer who gets the job is under no obligation to write anything – celebratory or otherwise. When appointed in 2004, the avowedly republican Peter Maxwell Davies expressed surprise: "I initially felt disbelief as I had a reputation for being avant-garde, maverick and anti-establishment." But, like Ted Hughes (see p.246), he seems to have succumbed to royalty's allure: "I have come to realise that there is a lot to be said for the monarchy. It represents continuity, tradition and stability."

Missis Kwin

An anthropologist and ecologist's dream, Papua New Guinea has one of the most diverse populations in the world, with nearly 7 million inhabitants and a reputed 820 languages. Located north of Australia and close to Indonesia, it's a country made up of largely untouched rainforest, mountains and wilderness. It also has a Queen who lives on the other side of the world, having retained Elizabeth II as head of state when it gained its independence from Australia in 1975. As well as her proper title, the Queen is also referred to in the pidgin language of Tok Pisin as "Missis Kwin" and "Mama belong big family".

👑 Mosaic Egg

When Carl Fabergé, renowned goldsmith to the Russian royal family, set up a London retail branch in 1903, his best clients were King Edward VII and Queen Alexandra, who was the sister of the Tsarina. The absurdly extravagant "Mosaic Egg" was crafted for Tsar Nicholas II in 1914. Encrusted with tiny precious gems, when opened it displays a medallion with the Tsar's five children carved in relief. Though requisitioned by the Bolsheviks after the Russian Revolution, it was purchased by the Tsar's cousin, George V in 1933, perhaps to assuage his guilt at not providing the Romanovs with asylum in Britain (see p.247).

👑 No handicap

While Princess Anne's equestrian exploits are widely known, her brother Prince Andrew's golfing prowess tends to get less favourable coverage. His handicap of four – "a tremendous achievement", say those in the know – would be good enough to allow him to go professional and try his hand on the circuit. However, it is not his ability but the cost of his attending golfing events that has tended to catch the eye of a critical media.

👑 Opening the Innings: royal cricket or craic?

A reference to payments made to a John de Leek for expenses incurred to enable Prince Edward (the future King Edward II) to play "creag and other games" may just have been referring to an earlier form of cricket. Either that or it could have been an early spelling for the word "craic" an Irish word for fun.

👑 Oldest monarch

The oldest British monarch to accede to the throne was William IV, who was 64 years 10 months and 5 days at the death of his brother, George IV, on 26 June 1830. Sixty-three-year-old Prince Charles looks all set to beat this record (assuming he makes it to the throne), and will have passed his great-great-great-great-great-uncle's age on 19 September 2013.

👑 Pastyme with good companye

Before he turned into a bloated, wife-murdering tyrant, King Henry VIII was widely regarded as a princely ideal and a paragon of culture. The Venetian ambassador described how he "plays well on the lute and harpsichord, [and] sings from books at sight." He also composed – probably with the help of court musician William Cornysh – and there are twenty-four of his works in the so-called "Henry VIII Manuscript". These include the rollicking part song "Pastyme with Good Companye" but not, unfortunately, "Greensleeves", though the song is often attributed to him.

👑 Poetic insults

Amongst poetic barbs directed against royals, pride of place probably rests with the scurrilous courtier poet John Wilmot, Earl of Rochester, who penned the following on the death of King Charles II: "Here lies our mutton-loving king, Whose word no man relies on; Who never said a foolish thing, And never did a wise one."

👑 Poor Knights

Following the Battle of Crécy, many knights were captured by the French and, in order to raise the ransom for their release, liquidated their estates. As some form of compensation, Edward III established the Poor Knights (also known as the Alms Knights) at the same time as the Order of the Garter (see p.146). In exchange for

salary and lodging in Windsor Castle, the 26 Poor Knights had to pray daily for the Sovereign and Knights Companions of the Order of the Garter at St George's Chapel. The name was changed under William IV, after the knights objected to being termed "poor", and today the Military Knights of Windsor are made up of armed forces pensioners.

👑 Present arms

Guards at Buckingham Palace have to present arms when a royal walks past. This rule was exploited by a young Princess Anne who used to enjoy running forwards and backwards in front of them before she was forced to desist.

👑 The PM's tactics

In his dealings with Queen Victoria, the conservative prime minister Benjamin Disraeli enjoyed one of the best working relationships of any prime minister with a royal. His famous quote "Everyone likes flattery; and when you come to Royalty you should lay it on with a trowel" may explain why.

Presenting arms at Buckingham Palace.

⚜ Prince Charles – South London landlord

The single most valuable asset in the Duchy of Cornwall – the estate from which Prince Charles derives his income – is a swathe of 45 acres of Kennington in south London. It includes the famous cricket ground known as the Oval, home of Surrey County Cricket Club and the venue for the final Test match of each English cricket season. In 1845 the Duchy granted SCCC a lease of the land "to convert it into a subscription cricket ground" for 31 years at a rent of £120 per annum plus taxes.

⚜ Prince Philip and the little green men

The Duke of Edinburgh is known to have been a subscriber to the periodical *Flying Saucer Review* (and may well still be). Sir Peter Horsley, a former royal equerry who went on to have a distinguished career in the Royal Air Force, published his autobiography in 1998, claiming that he had personally investigated, on behalf of Prince Philip, many of the UFO sightings reported by Britain's service personnel. Horsley also vetted and invited a few UFO witnesses to come to Buckingham Palace and meet the prince.

⚜ Princely Whales of Scotland

Devolution in the UK (the transfer of some government powers to Scotland, Wales and Northern Ireland) has had some unusual results. For example, in the unlikely event you found yourself in possession of a whale too large to be transported to land by a "wain [wagon] pulled by six oxen", then before the year 1999 the whale would have been the property of the Queen. Since then, however, the Scottish Government Marine Directorate has stepped into the breach. A 22-page PDF complete with flow diagram has replaced the need to put in a tricky call to Buckingham Palace.

⚜ The princess and the porn

Marriage to Lord Snowdon had familiarized Princess Margaret with bohemian and outré behaviour, but when theatre critic Kenneth Tynan – a man famed for his sexual provocativeness – screened a pornographic movie after a dinner party she was attending, the response was a stunned silence. Whether or not it was the gay subject matter of Genet's *Un Chant d'Amour*, complete with erect penises, that caused the embarrassment, the day was saved by comedian Peter Cook, who provided a hilarious running commentary in the style of a voiceover for a Cadbury's Flake advert. The princess was presumably grateful that it was Cook who came to the rescue rather than Harold Pinter, who was one of the other guests.

⚜ QE1: Lottery Pioneer

Royal backing for state lotteries appears to date back to 1566 when Elizabeth I wrote to Sir John Spencer with instructions on how it was to work. The big prize was £5000 (around £850,000 in today's money) and receipts were intended for good causes. However, it took three years for the draw to take place and it was swiftly abandoned.

The Queen Mum's personal playlist

A stabilizing presence in the monarchy for the entire twentieth century, the Queen Mother proved she was still capable of taking people by surprise, even after her death, when her record collection was made public in 2011. Amid the more conventional classical albums, her eclectic collection included a large amount of Scottish folk and revealed a fondness for the music of her youth: rousing records by variety singers and music hall performers conjuring images of cheerful wartime sing-alongs. More unexpected were the calypso bands, Canadian yodelling and the only post-war pop record in her collection – Paul Simon's *Graceland*.

Queen of his heart

Despite being a habitual adulterer, George II was extremely distressed when his loyal wife Caroline, the mother of his seven children, died in 1737. When, on her deathbed, she told the distraught king that he should remarry, he was moved to respond: "No, I shall have mistresses". This would not have been news to her as he often kept her updated on his affairs.

Queenly patronage

At the time of writing the Queen is patron of 619 charities and organizations. Among the more surprising beneficiaries of this royal connection are people in the media who have fallen on hard times (the Cinema and Television Benevolent Fund and the Newspaper Press Fund). More predictable are the sporting bodies she supports, which include the Croquet Association, the Royal Caledonian Curling Club and the Royal Toxophilite Society (longbow archery to you and me). Horse racing is especially well represented, with the Seoul Racehorse Owners Association being the tip of a large equine iceberg.

The Queen's first email

Elizabeth II proved herself to be an early adopter of new technology when she visited the Royal Signals and Radar Establishment, the research hub of the Ministry of Defence, in March 1976. It was here that she sent her very first electronic mail, several decades before most other people. She was using the ARPANET network, a 1970s precursor to the Internet.

The Queen's piper

The position of Queen's piper is hardly the most dangerous army post in the world. Major Derek Potter's chief task is to play the bagpipes under the Queen's window at nine every morning for fifteen minutes when she is in staying in one of the royal residences. Highland-piping enthusiast Queen Victoria appointed the first piper in 1843.

Queen Victoria II

In 2011 the British government proposed introducing non-gender-specific primogeniture for the royal succession, meaning firstborn girls would no longer be

passed over for a younger brother. Had this measure been introduced in the reign of Queen Victoria, then her firstborn daughter would have become Queen Victoria II. Even more intriguingly, this same Victoria married the German Emperor and was the mother of Kaiser Wilhelm II. Could a great Anglo-German Empire have then been created and World War I avoided? The direct line of firstborn descendants is still going strong, and continues with the Kaiser's great-great-granddaughter, Friederike von Reiche (neé von der Osten), a 52-year-old homeopath living in the spa town of Bad Lauchstädt, near Leipzig.

Right royal Christmases

Today's royal family have a tradition of exchanging gifts at teatime on Christmas Eve, rather than on Christmas Day. This was established by the Queen, who favours a Christmas Day schedule of church in the morning, a lengthy lunch and a formal evening meal (black tie), followed by a game of charades. It is not known whether she switches on the TV at 3pm to watch the Queen's Speech (which is no longer broadcast live).

Royal bigamist

King Cnut, who ruled England from 1016 to 1035, famously had his throne placed on the beach, where he commanded the sea to stop advancing. This was to prove to his sycophantic courtiers that such a task was impossible and that his powers – compared to those of God – were limited. Despite this God-fearing humility, Cnut seems to have had no qualms about being a bigamist, marrying Emma of Normandy (widow of his kingly predecessor, Æthelred) without divorcing his first wife, Ælfgifu. Incidentally, the wireless technology Bluetooth is named after Cnut's grandfather, Harald "Bluetooth" Gormsson, King of Denmark.

The Royal Maundy

Each year on Maundy Thursday (the day in Easter Week on which the Last Supper took place), the British monarch hands out specially minted coins to a selection of elderly people as a form of symbolic alms-giving. The tradition derives from Jesus's command to his disciples "that ye love one another" (the Latin for "command" is "mandatum", hence Maundy). The practice began in the reign of Henry IV and included the monarch washing the feet of the poor, in imitation of Jesus washing the feet of his disciples. The provision of special coins was introduced by Charles II and the feet-washing ceased in the eighteenth century. Four denominations of coin are struck (from one to four pennies in value), made from sterling silver. Because of their rarity the coins are often sold on by their recipients.

The Royal Menagerie

Exotic animals were kept at the Tower of London by successive kings and queens of England for over 600 years. The first suggestion of a Royal Menagerie is a record of lions kept at the Tower in 1235, while seventeen years later Henry III was given a polar bear by the king of Norway. James I built a stone viewing platform over the animal dens so that audiences could watch the cruel "sport" of baiting:

bears, lions and dogs being made to fight each other to the death. A cheetah sent from India to George III in 1764 killed a deer in Windsor Park and lived out his days in the Tower. The menagerie was shut down in 1835, and the animals that were left re-housed at London Zoo.

The Royal Post Office

There has been a post office within Buckingham Palace since 1902. The Court Postmaster is in charge of a team that handles over 1000 items per week, with a notable increase at times of weddings, birthdays, anniversaries and bereavements. The palace fluoroscope (X-ray machine) is used to vet packages. All foodstuffs (the most commonplace being boxes of chocolates) are destroyed as a matter of course, due to the threat of poisoning.

Royal social media

In November 2010 Facebook became the latest social media outlet on which the royal family has established a presence. It had been pipped to the post by Flickr (complete with royal photostream), Twitter in 2009 and the Royal Channel that appeared on YouTube in 2007. At the time of writing 507,342 people "like" the Facebook site.

Royal tattoos

Prince Charles is rumoured to have a tattoo, though there's no evidence to support this. However, if true, it wouldn't be the first time a British prince inked his skin. Edward VII had a cross tattooed on his arm in 1862 at the tender age of 21. His son, George V, was a little older when he followed suit some thirty years later, getting a "Cross of Jerusalem" tattoo when travelling in the Middle East. He also had a dragon inked on his forearm by master tattooist Hori Chiyo during a visit to Japan.

The sadness of Queen Anne

Queen Anne, the last of the Stuarts, must count among the most unfortunate of monarchs. Such was the imperative to produce an heir (something her sister, Queen Mary, had failed to do) that Anne became pregnant seventeen times (possibly more) before coming to the throne in 1702. Sadly, the vast majority of her babies were stillborn. Only one child made it past the age of two, Prince William, Duke of Gloucester – a great favourite of his aunt and uncle, William and Mary – who died aged twelve. After Anne, the crown passed to the house of Hanover in the shape of George I.

Sandringham Time

Edward VII (1841–1910) introduced the custom of having all clocks on his Norfolk estate run half an hour fast. The idea was to ensure he and his guests would have more time for hunting. The custom prevailed after the king's death but ended in 1936.

👑 "She Didn't Flinch"

July 2003 saw the first case of a streaker at a royal garden party. The 17-year-old son of an invitee, he was stopped in his tracks by a rugby tackle from a Yeoman of the Guard. Royal decorum was never in that much jeopardy: all the young man had done was drop his trousers, shout "Wa-hey!" and stagger about with his trews around his ankles. The Queen was reported to be unperturbed.

👑 The six-fingered saint

For some Protestants, Anne Boleyn, Henry VIII's second wife, is regarded as a martyr. In the influential *Foxe's Book of Martyrs* (1563) the author states, "Godly I call her, for sundry respects." He goes on to list her piety, influence on her husband, generosity to the poor, and the fact that her daughter became a great queen, as evidence of her saintly nature. He also got in a dig against papists, suggesting they were instrumental in having her executed. In his *The Rise and Growth of the Anglican Schism* (1585), the Catholic polemicist Nicolas Sander, countered this rosy view of the queen by suggesting that she had six fingers on her right hand – a sure sign that she was evil.

👑 Sophia's spectral spinning wheel

Princess Sophia, the fifth daughter of King George III, lived at Kensington Palace in London. She never married, but was rumoured to have given birth to an illegitimate son in 1800, fathered by Thomas Garth, one of her father's equerries. Some gossip at the time suggested the father was actually her elder brother, the unpopular Duke of Cumberland. Sophia had a long but unhappy life and in old age she lost her sight. She spent hours working at her spinning wheel and many visitors to Kensington Palace have since claimed to have heard the sound of her wheel, whirring and clacking away.

👑 South Sea god

In the village of Yaohnanen on the Pacific island of Tanna in the Vanuatu archipelago, Prince Philip has been worshipped as a god for over fifty years. An ancient legend of a pale-skinned son of a mountain spirit travelling over the seas to marry a powerful woman seems, somehow, to have become connected to the prince, a link that was reinforced when he and the Queen visited Vanuatu (then called the New Hebrides) in 1974. Prince Philip is aware of the villagers' devotion and has sent them photographs of himself (now somewhat mildewed due to the humidity), one of which shows him holding the traditional pig-killing club – a gift from the islanders.

👑 Stout Yeomen

The fabulously red Yeomen of the Guard (often confused with the similarly attired Beefeater Yeoman Warders at the Tower of London) date back to 1485, when Henry VII first commissioned their services as royal bodyguards. It is claimed they are the oldest military corps in the world. Nowadays they are comprised of volunteers from the army and air force. They wear their Tudor-style stockings at around thirty ceremonial occasions every year and are usually pictured standing to attention with a halberd. The weapon consists of an axe-blade fitted at the lower end of a spike on the top of a long shaft; dating back to the 1400s, it was pioneered by the Swiss.

👑 Swan Upping

"Swan upping" is the annual census of swans that live on the Thames. It dates back to the days when the monarch's ownership of all (mute) swans was enforced: swans were regarded as a tasty delicacy and eaten at banquets. Today, the identification of swans is for their protection, rather than the culinary delectation of posh gourmands. During swan upping, the Queen's official swan marker, assisted by the royal swan uppers (and those from two livery companies), makes a five-day journey upriver. The uppers wear traditional scarlet uniforms and each of their six boats flies an appropriate flag. When a brood of cygnets is sighted, a cry of "All up!" is given. On passing Windsor Castle, the rowers stand to attention with oars raised and salute "Her Majesty The Queen, Seigneur of the Swans". After the cygnets' details have all been noted, the birds are given a health check and ringed.

👑 Sweyn's day

Christmas Day 2013 will mark the 1000th anniversary of the declaration as king of one of the least English-sounding of royals. Sweyn Forkbeard, King of Denmark, began raiding England in the early years of the eleventh century, possibly in revenge for the massacre of many "English" Danes (including his sister) ordered by

In England, wild Mute swans (Cygnus olor) are the property of the Crown, as are any privately-owned swans that escape from captivity.

the English king Æthelred. Unfortunately for him, he fell off his horse and died only a few weeks after becoming king, leaving his son Cnut (see p.259) to battle it out for the succession with Æthelred's eldest son, Edmund Ironside.

👑 Tobacco-loving witches, beware!

As well as writing about the nature of kingship (see p.247), James I produced a treatise on witchcraft, entitled *Daemonologie* (1597), in which he set out to prove "The fearefull aboundinge at this time in this countrie, of these detestable slaves of the Devill, the Witches or enchanters." As if that wasn't enough, in 1606 he launched an attack on smoking, *A Counterblaste to Tobacco*, lambasting the habit as "A custome lothsome to the eye, hatefull to the Nose, harmefull to the braine, dangerous to the Lungs, and in the blacke stinking fume thereof, neerest resembling the horrible Stigian smoke of the pit that is bottomlesse."

👑 Touched by the hand of the King

The propagation of the belief that the touch of a monarch could cure disease began with King Edward the Confessor in England. Successive English and French kings were thought to have inherited this "royal touch", which consolidated the claim that their right to rule was God-given (see p.247). In grand ceremonies, kings might touch hundreds of diseased people, who received special gold coins called "touchpieces", which they often treated as amulets. The practice died out in England after the reign of Queen Anne.

👑 Tower of London – exclusive prison

The Tower of London has variously held the nation's arsenal, the Royal Mint, the Royal Menagerie and been a royal residence. It has also served as a prison,

The earliest part of the Tower of London, the White Tower, was built by William I.

confining some distinguished figures, even though there were no dungeons as such and prisoners had to pay for their upkeep. The first recorded prisoner was Ranulf Flambard, Bishop of Durham, locked up in 1100 but escaping just a few months later. The last was Rudolf Hess, Germany's Deputy Führer, who spent a few days there in May 1941. The privilege of execution within the confines of the Tower (on Tower Green) was extended to a mere seven nobles, including two of Henry VIII's wives and Lady Jane Grey.

"Uneasy lies the head that wears the crown"

At the coronation of King Henry IV in 1399, the Archbishop of Canterbury lifted the crown to the new king's head only to discover that it was swarming with lice. This was taken to be a bad omen (Henry had usurped the previous monarch Richard II). He also suffered from a skin complaint so bad that people thought it was leprosy. He had a particularly virulent attack one week after ordering the execution of the rebellious Archbishop of York in 1405.

An unexpected guest

As you'd expect, Prince William's 21st birthday at Windsor Castle in 2003 had an exclusive guest list and supposedly tight security. That didn't stop an unknown comedian, Aaron Barshak, from gatecrashing the event dressed as Osama bin Laden (though wearing a pink dress), despite setting off alarms and being spotted on several surveillance cameras. Happily mingling with guests, he was only arrested after interrupting William's speech and kissing the prince on both cheeks. Embarrassment all round – especially for the police.

Unsteady Eddy

In 1892 the death of the future Edward VII's firstborn, Prince Albert Victor ("Eddy" to his friends), plunged the nation into mourning. However, the Prince's dissolute lifestyle and mental instability have since given rise to some very odd rumours. First up is the belief that he was serial prostitute-murderer Jack the Ripper; then there are attempts to link him to the Cleveland Street homosexual brothel scandal of 1889 – his equerry, Lord Somerset, was a client. Lastly, there is the theory that his brother George, who married Albert's fiancée Mary of Teck and became king in 1910, was somehow responsible for his death. Evidence for all three is insubstantial to say the least.

Uptown Princess

When the Friends of Covent Garden assembled at London's Royal Opera House for the fun and games of their 1985 Christmas party, they were treated to a surprise from a prestigious guest. Princess Diana took to the stage with dancer Wayne Sleep to perform a well-choreographed dance to Billy Joel's hit song "Uptown Girl". The routine was based on the original video in which the diminutive Joel dances with the willowy but statuesque model Christie Brinkley. At 5'10" Di towered over the 5'2" Sleep, allowing her to execute some moves right over her partner's head. The audience loved it, with one notable exception: Charles was said to have been less than amused.

👑 Wasted on the royals

Osbert Sitwell once organized a war-time poetry recital at Buckingham Palace. Among the readers was the renowned modernist T.S. Eliot, who monotonously declaimed a section from his long poem *The Waste Land*. Many years later, the Queen Mother recalled the event in a conversation with author A.N. Wilson: "we had this rather lugubrious man in a suit, and he read a poem ... I think it was called *The Desert*. And first the girls got the giggles, and then I did, and then even the King ... we didn't understand a word."

👑 "We are not amused"

Queen Victoria's appearance, especially after Albert's death, doesn't suggest someone who was a barrel of laughs. This seems to be confirmed by an anecdote in *Notebooks of a Spinster Lady 1878–1903* by Caroline Holland, daughter of the Queen's physician Sir Henry Holland. "Her remarks can freeze as well as crystallise," she wrote, "There is a tale of the unfortunate equerry who ventured during dinner at Windsor to tell a story with a spice of scandal or impropriety in it. 'We are not amused,' said the Queen when he had finished." However, the anecdote was contested by Victoria's granddaughter Alice, Countess of Athlone, who, in a 1976 BBC interview (when she was 93), insisted: "I asked her, and she never said it."

👑 Whitehall, before the bureaucrats

Now known for being the street in central London in which several UK government administrative buildings are situated, Whitehall was originally one of the largest palaces in Europe and the main residence for English monarchs between 1530 and 1698. King Henry VIII first established it as one of several royal homes, having ousted Cardinal Wolsey from the site. Only the Banqueting House, built by Inigo Jones in 1622 and the site of Charles I's execution, still survives.

👑 With parents like these...

Neither George II nor his wife, Caroline of Anspach, were exactly proud parents. George II said of his son Frederick, Prince of Wales: "Our first born is the greatest ass, the greatest liar ... and the greatest beast in the whole world, and we wish he was out of it." On her deathbed, Caroline consoled herself thus: "at least I shall have the comfort in having my eyes eternally closed – I shall never see that monster again."

👑 X Factor fan

Mary Byrne, a singer who came fifth in the 2010 series of the TV talent show *The X Factor*, met the Queen at a concert marking the end of Elizabeth's 2011 official visit to Ireland. "You are the lady off *The X Factor*," observed the sovereign. "Your song was fabulous." When asked if she watched the show, the Queen replied that she watches it the next day, confessing that it's often on a little too late for her.

Index

Picture credits

The publishers have made every effort to identify correctly the rights holders in respect of the images featured in this book. If, despite these efforts, any attribution is incorrect, the publishers will correct this error, once it has been brought to their attention, on a subsequent reprint.

Corbis: 12, 20 (Kieran Doherty), 22 (Pool Photographs), 28, 32, 47 (Pool Photographs), 57, 59, 64, 75, 84, 88, 99, 109, 127, 132, 161, 171, 185, 212, 215. Getty Images: 9, 40, 152, 155, 179. Library of Congress: 81 (Bain Collection), 92 (Matson Collection), 113 (Charles Knight), 137, 167, 221. Dorling Kindersley Media Library: 102, 195, 250 (Cecile Treal/Jean-Michel Ruiz), 256 (Stephen Oliver), 262 (Linda Whitwam), 263 (Stephen Oliver).

Rough Guides: 168, 206, 218, 244. Ian Blenkinsop 225; Maxwell Hamilton 150; IMW Collections 199; Moviestore Collection 234 (Rank Organisation/ Peter Rogers Productions), 240 (Samuel Goldwyn Company/Channel 4 Films/ Close Call Films); James McConnachie 70; Joe Staines 248.
Front cover pictures courtesy of Alamy, Corbis and Getty Images; inside front cover: Getty Images; inside back cover: Dorling Kindersley Media Library.